Critical Acclaim for *The Good Black*

"Like Grisham, Barrett has a knack for writing dramatically about lawyers and their world. What haunts this reader is the sadness of a man who spent his life trying to be 'a good black.' "
—*Newsweek*

"An emotional roller coaster of a book . . . Should serve as a wake-up call for those who have ignored the wide gulf between blacks and whites in the American workforce."
—Lawrence Otis Graham,
author of *Our Kind of People* and *Member of the Club*

"Paul Barrett has written a fascinating racial *Rashomon* story. With unusual empathy and evenhandedness, Barrett illuminates the complicated workings of race in a middle-class, post–civil rights society—while at the same time spinning an absorbing courtroom yarn."
—Nicholas Lemann, author of *The Promised Land*

"A morality tale with a twist . . . Has the power to unsettle us and our self-congratulatory expectations."
—*The Denver Post*

"Offers a remarkably clear portrait . . . part case comment, part biography, and part snapshot of race relations at the end of the twentieth century."
—*Harvard* magazine

"*The Good Black* tells several stories: the story of Larry Mungin; the story of how corporate lawyering operates at the end of the twentieth century; and finally, a story of race."
—*Emerge* magazine

"Powerful and poignant."
—David J. Garrow, author of *Bearing the Cross*

Paul M. Barrett is the deputy legal editor at *The Wall Street Journal,* which nominated him for the 1997 Pulitzer Prize for beat reporting. He holds a law degree from Harvard.

The
Good
Black

A True Story
of Race in
America

Paul M. Barrett

A PLUME BOOK

PLUME
Published by the Penguin Group
Penguin Putnam Inc., 375 Hudson Street, New York, New York 10014, U.S.A.
Penguin Books Ltd, 27 Wrights Lane, London W8 5TZ, England
Penguin Books Australia Ltd, Ringwood, Victoria, Australia
Penguin Books Canada Ltd, 10 Alcorn Avenue, Toronto, Ontario, Canada M4V 3B2
Penguin Books (N.Z.) Ltd, 182–190 Wairau Road, Auckland 10, New Zealand

Penguin Books Ltd, Registered Offices: Harmondsworth, Middlesex, England

Published by Plume, a member of Penguin Putnam Inc.
Previously published in a Dutton edition.

First Plume Printing, January, 2000
10 9 8 7 6 5 4 3 2 1

 REGISTERED TRADEMARK—MARCA REGISTRADA

The Library of Congress has catalogued the Dutton edition as follows:
Barrett, Paul M.
    The good black : a true story of race in America / Paul M. Barrett
        p.   cm.
    Includes index.
    ISBN 0-525-94344-7
            0-452-27859-7 (pbk.)
1. Mungin, Lawrence D. (Lawrence Dwayne)—Trials, litigation, etc. 2. Katten Muchin &
Zavis—Trials, litigation, etc. 3. Discrimination in employment—Law and legislation—
Washington (D.C.) 4. Afro-American lawyers—United States.   I. Barrett,
Paul M.   II. Title.
KF228.M86B37   1999
344.7301/6996073—dc21   99-179527
                                                                              CIP

Printed in the United States of America
Set in New Baskerville
Original hardcover design by Leonard Telesca

To my parents

Acknowledgments

Lawrence Mungin gave generous amounts of his time to make this book possible. He received neither the right to approve the manuscript, nor any monetary reward. Although he knew that I would not write his story exactly as he would, Larry trusted me to be fair, and for that I thank him.

Many other people familiar with this story from a wide range of perspectives answered my questions, sometimes at great length. Some of these people are mentioned by name in the book; others asked to remain anonymous, mostly for fear of harm to their careers. I am grateful to all of them, especially those who provided an insider's view of Katten Muchin & Zavis.

Friends and family offered encouragement and tough, thoughtful commentary. My personal editing staff included David, Paulette, and Laurence Barrett; Meredith Greene; Harry Litman; Beth Osisek; and Richard Levy. More than anyone else, Julie Cohen provided solace and wise suggestions. My agent, Julian Bach, introduced me to Dutton, where Jennifer Moore (and Arnold Dolin, before his departure) gave constructive criticism of the sort that authors supposedly don't get these days. Copy editor Navorn Johnson smoothed many bumps. This book is much better because of all of the help I received.

Contents

The
Good
Black

CHAPTER ONE

"Don't Be Afraid; I'm One of the *Good* Blacks"

MARCH 1996

Lawrence D. Mungin, a tall African-American man of imposing build, sat calmly at the plain wooden plaintiff's table in U.S. District Court in Washington, D.C. He was an attorney, and looked the part in a well-cut gray business suit. But he wasn't trying this case for a client. Mungin *was* the client. He had sued his employer, the large corporate law firm of Katten Muchin & Zavis. His claim was race discrimination.

"He's damaged goods," Abbey Hairston, Mungin's lead lawyer, was telling the jury. She was nearing the end of her closing argument. Mungin, she said, had endured "emotional pain, suffering, inconvenience, mental anguish, loss of enjoyment of life."

The jurors, seven blacks and one white, had listened to four days of testimony about Mungin's high hopes and frustration at Katten Muchin's field office in Washington. "He had to sue his employer, his dream of being a partner in a major law firm probably down the tubes," Hairston reminded the jurors. "What's he going to do? Well, he can still practice law. We're not going to deny that. He's practicing law right now at fourteen dollars an hour. He's making approximately thirty thousand dollars a year." She shook her head. He might have been making $130,000, plus a bonus. "Big difference," she said. "He was humiliated. You saw that. He was in anguish. You saw that. He didn't know what to do. He was professionally trapped.

"What do we want?" Hairston paused. "We want a million dollars."

The seven-figure demand seemed to surprise even Hairston. "Is that too much? I don't think so." The jury had heard testimony about partners at Mungin's former firm who made more than $500,000 a year. "Larry will not be on that track," Hairston said. "Larry's off the track. He deserves a million dollars.

"And the firm should be punished," she continued. "Two million dollars in punitive damages, that's what we'd like to see."

Mungin "met the qualifications. He exceeded the qualifications. He worked hard to get where he did. He came out of housing projects and got to that point. And now it may be lost. So what we want to see is justice, because justice was not served in that law firm."

Hairston, who also was African-American, believed in her client's case, but by nature, she couldn't avoid worrying. Had she convinced the jurors that, despite the absence of racist insults or overtly hostile acts, the law firm's not-so-benign neglect amounted to a violation of the federal civil rights laws?

Mungin had no such doubts. He was certain that he and his lawyers had persuaded the mostly black and working-class jury that he had been mistreated and shunted aside by his former employer—and that the reason had been the color of his skin.

Another stylish black woman lawyer, Michele Roberts, had listened to Hairston's closing from the defendant's table. She sat near her client, Vincent Sergi, a top partner from the Chicago home office of the predominantly white Katten Muchin firm. As lead defense lawyer, Roberts had told the jury that Mungin, the only black among the 50 attorneys in the firm's Washington branch, may have had a bad time at Katten

Muchin, but so did a lot of *white* lawyers. Sergi, middle-aged and unassuming, hadn't flinched as Roberts depicted the firm as a place of equal opportunity unhappiness for young attorneys. The Katten Muchin side believed that it wouldn't take the jury very long to conclude that whatever happened to Mungin, it hadn't been discrimination.

Roberts rose to answer Hairston. Her client, she told the jurors, shared their values. "It goes without saying," she said, that "it is intolerable, it is offensive, it is unacceptable, and it is unlawful to treat any man, woman, or child differently because of their race. It's conduct that has no place in this community.

"And when we see it, it is our responsibility to shout about it, to shout it out, to point it out. But as we point that finger, ladies and gentlemen, don't allow that finger, that pointed finger, to quiver. Don't allow that pointed finger to be bent. . . . When we point that finger, ladies and gentlemen, it must be straight, and it must be certain. We cannot allow those real racists the ammunition to argue that we have no credibility, that we complain whenever things don't quite go right."

Roberts reminded the jury that it was not enough that Mungin may have been "treated badly." The civil rights laws barred—barred *only*—his being "treated differently because he was black."

Something clearly went wrong with Larry Mungin's career at Katten Muchin. He arrived as an experienced associate with two Harvard degrees and an impressive personal history that began in inner-city New York. He ended up marginalized, assigned inappropriately basic work, brushed off by senior partners, told he had "fallen between the cracks."

But was he a victim of ordinary mismanagement or of race bias? While Mungin's account of what happened to him was harrowing, many of the important facts in this case could be interpreted in varying ways. This wasn't the rare, clear-cut instance of racial discrimination, such as the famous Texaco episode of 1996 in which white executives were caught on audiotape making disparaging references to blacks and contemplating destruction of documents in a pending bias lawsuit. There was no secret recording in the Katten Muchin files, no "smoking gun" memo. Mungin's case was far more typical of most discrimination suits, tinged in ambiguous shades of gray. As fervently as Mungin believed that he had been singled out for bad treatment, the law firm was convinced that his setbacks could be attributed to business problems having nothing to do with race. If anything, Katten Muchin insisted, it treated Mungin *better* because he was black.

The case captivated lawyers from Chicago to New York and made headlines in the *Wall Street Journal*, the *Washington Post*, and other publications. I followed it closely as a journalist specializing in legal affairs, but I also had a personal interest: Thirteen years earlier, Mungin and I had been first-year law school roommates at Harvard. We had talked about the role of race in his life quite a bit that year, and on and off ever since. When his suit went to trial, I began the reporting that became this book.

With striking consistency, white lawyers told me that what happened to Mungin may not have been pretty, but it was merely a function of the callous way many law firms now conduct themselves. There is considerable truth in that view. A white lawyer in Mungin's place might have had some of the same sort of difficulties.

But in a society where race permeates so much of our thinking and subtly colors so many actions, Mungin's race could not be ignored. Katten Muchin didn't ignore it. The question is what role did it play? How is it that someone with so much promise—who was raised specifically to vault over the race line, and had the skills to make it—ended up instead accusing his employer, and, by extension, "the system," of harming him because of his race?

Most black lawyers with whom I discussed the case expressed sympathy for Mungin. They said that minority associates sometimes stumble because they are excluded, consciously or unconsciously, from important relationships. Even well-intentioned white partners and their white clients typically feel more comfortable on a personal level with associates who look like them. A sense of satisfaction over the hiring of a black associate may turn sour when business goes bad or personalities don't click. Self-consciousness over race inhibits direct, honest conversation. Think what it would be like, black lawyers said to me, if you were the only white in an office with 49 blacks. Would you feel at ease? Would you trust your black employers when they told you that career reversals were simply a result of business developments, not race? These are fair questions.

When I put these questions to white lawyers, the answer I received, with jarring vehemence, was that Mungin *couldn't* have been hurt because of his race. Big law firms are dying to improve their minority numbers. Mungin was probably an affirmative action hire who just didn't work out, I was told.

The gulf separating white and black views of the Mungin case demonstrates that his story is more than a good courtroom yarn. It dramatizes the current dilemma of race in the middle and upper reaches of American society. Openly racist behavior is uncommon these days in business and professional life. But distrust and resentment are rife. Mungin was unusual in that he had the audacity and stamina to mount a serious lawsuit. But his story reflects the experiences of countless other blacks who do not sue—people who overcome obstacles, work hard, achieve some success, yet still feel thwarted. They have the graduate degree, the leather briefcase, and the right sort of suit, but they end up estranged and embittered. They ask: What more do I have to do to be treated with respect?

Katten Muchin's reaction to Mungin, on the other hand, reflects the thinking of many whites in the professional workplace. They look across the hall, the trading floor, or the corporate cafeteria, and they are mystified as to why blacks believe they are at a disadvantage or are any different from everyone else trying to get ahead in a demanding world. Many whites are persuaded that *they* are the ones held back, as corporate America gives special breaks to minorities. The question on many white minds is: Why are these people so angry?

Mungin felt doubly burned at Katten Muchin. He had

defined himself largely in terms of professional success. The law firm crushed that self-image by making him feel like a failure. Worse, he walked away feeling foolish that for his whole life, he had "gone the extra mile to show people—whites and blacks, but mostly whites—that I wasn't one of *those* blacks, one of the dangerous ones, the bad ones. Or one of the complainers, the ones demanding special treatment." Mungin had assumed that to get ahead, he needed to distinguish himself from the negative stereotypes of inner-city African-American men. By the time of his lawsuit, he was no longer proud of all the time and energy he had spent reassuring whites. "To be honest," he confessed, with a self-deprecating bite to his words, "I wanted to show that I was like white people: 'Don't be afraid. I'm one of the *good* blacks.'" But that hadn't been enough.

CHAPTER TWO

"Eat What You Kill"

APRIL 1992

On the morning of his interview with Katten Muchin & Zavis, Mungin slipped out of his soon-to-be-former office and walked toward Pennsylvania Avenue to catch a cab. He could look east and just make out the eggshell-white Capitol dome. Closer by stood the mammoth New Deal–era headquarters of the Departments of Justice and Commerce, as well as the Internal Revenue Service. Interspersed among the federal buildings were bland modern structures containing the plush suites of countless law and lobbying firms.

This part of the city gives Washington its claim to the highest attorney-per-capita rate in the world. Though one of them, Mungin saw himself as standing apart from the swarm of counselors, litigators, and strategizers. Six-foot-two, with a bodybuilder's proportions, he wore a blue-black Armani suit, high-collared white shirt, burgundy tie, and Italian loafers. He looked like he belonged in Beverly Hills, negotiating movie deals, not in Washington, where conservative Brooks Brothers was the standard. Mungin didn't see himself as standard. He was a loner: restless and unabashedly looking out for Number 1. Which explained that morning's appointment at Katten Muchin.

* * *

Mungin, 34, was jumping ship. His current firm, Powell, Goldstein, Frazer & Murphy, had temporarily frozen associates' salaries. That was a bad sign, especially when he would soon be making his move for partnership. So he had talked to some headhunting agencies that made matches between lawyers looking for new jobs and firms with openings. He had already heard from the Washington branch offices of big firms from Kansas City and Cleveland. But a headhunter in Chicago had pushed hard for Mungin to interview with Katten Muchin. The firm was confidently expanding and aiming to become a real presence in the capital. "Do *not* go anywhere else before talking to Katten Muchin," the Chicago headhunter said with all of the contrived urgency characteristic of his trade.

Was Katten Muchin really that great? Mungin wanted to know. He had never even heard of the firm.

The headhunter assured him that it was on the move, although there was a reservation: The managing partner of the Washington office, Mark Dombroff, had a reputation for being difficult. But what firm didn't have some difficult personalities?

That sounded reasonable enough to Mungin, who didn't bother to inquire further about Dombroff. Mungin would make his own judgment of Katten Muchin and its Washington big shot. He gave the headhunter permission to fax his résumé to Dombroff. But Katten Muchin would have to act fast, because he was talking seriously to the other firms.

Mark Dombroff scanned Mungin's résumé and liked what he saw. Dombroff had received a stack of responses from headhunters authorized to find candidates for the new bankruptcy-law position he intended to create. But it wasn't often that he saw a "double-Harvard"—Harvard Law School, Class of 1986, and Harvard College, Class of 1983. And there was more: Before working for Powell Goldstein of Atlanta, Mungin had spent three years in the Houston office of Weil,

Gotshal & Manges, a major New York firm with a highly respected bankruptcy practice.

In a note handwritten on the fax cover sheet that came with Mungin's résumé, the headhunter wrote:

Mark,
*   As we discussed, Larry is looking for an opportunity in the*
D.C. area. He has about ¹/₄–¹/₂ $mil in FDIC business (and he
is a minority). Please let me know if you would like to arrange
an interview with him.

Dombroff waved Mungin's résumé at Jeffrey Sherman, a junior partner who did bankruptcy work. "Listen to this," Dombroff said. "Harvard-Harvard, Weil Gotshal. His experience is bankruptcy, bankruptcy, bankruptcy. He's perfect! And," Dombroff added, "he's black."

Though he didn't say much in response, Sherman knew that Katten Muchin wanted to hire more minority lawyers. Based on Dombroff's enthusiasm, Sherman concluded that unless Mungin drooled or talked to himself, he had a lock on the bankruptcy job.

As the cabbie picked his way through the chaos of downtown Washington traffic, Mungin noticed that he didn't feel the least bit nervous. He didn't have to sell himself, he thought. He was the buyer, shopping for a new firm. The question was: What did they have to offer him?

Mungin got out of the taxi at a red-brick warehouse-style building in Georgetown. On the seventh floor, he was shown to Mark Dombroff's corner office. Stationed near Dombroff's open door were his two secretaries. Mungin took a seat. The three of them then pretended for 10 or 15 minutes not to hear Dumbroff barking and howling at the telephone.

Katten Muchin had about 400 lawyers in Chicago and five satellite offices around the country. Dombroff ran its 50-lawyer outpost in Washington, where the firm was known as Katten Muchin Zavis & Dombroff. Dombroff defended airlines on behalf of big insurance companies, particularly in connection with fatal crashes. He fought to minimize payouts to victims' families, and he was good at it. His ability to attract clients had made him a "rainmaker" and a rich man.

His phone call concluded, Dombroff summoned Mungin. Almost as tall as his guest, although thickening around the middle, Dombroff offered a strong handshake and a gleaming smile. Dombroff's suit jacket was off, and Mungin noticed that he had his initials—M.A.D.—stitched on the French cuff of his shirt. After a minimum of preliminaries, Dombroff pulled from a desk drawer an article from *The American Lawyer*, a monthly magazine that is closely read in law offices across the country. Dombroff passed the article across to Mungin.

KATTEN MUCHIN ON THE VERGE, the headline blared. "Growth to 400 lawyers from 24, the young Chicago-based firm has promising beachheads in D.C. and L.A.," the sub-headline said. "Can its acquisitive ways make it a national powerhouse?" The article singled out Dombroff as a "rainmaking dervish" who, of all the firm's recent recruits, "best embodies the Katten Muchin ideal."

Making sure Mungin didn't miss the point, Dombroff proceeded to brag that he and his 30-lawyer insurance department were bringing in $12 million a year in billings. (The *American Lawyer* article put the figure at $8 million.) Business was booming and looked to get better, Dombroff said.

"Around here," he added joyfully, "you eat what you kill!"

Crass, Mungin thought, but this was what he was looking for. He had worked hard to pull himself up from the projects. It was time to get the payoff: partnership, security, wealth. He'd had his doubts over the years about practicing big-time law, but becoming a partner was the logical next step; from there, he could decide whether to move on to another pursuit, whatever that might be. Mungin appreciated Katten Muchin's direct appeal to self-interest. "We're aware that we want to make money, and to do that we have to be honest with each other," another firm partner had commented to *The American Lawyer*.

Dombroff explained that his insurance clients frequently had to pursue premiums or other debts owed them by companies that had bought policies and then gone belly up. In the past, insurers had hired dozens of individual firms to keep track of bankruptcy cases spread out across the country. Dombroff wanted to sell his clients on the idea of Katten Muchin coordinating all of their bankruptcy cases. He allowed that he had "invented" a new legal service, and the business looked as if it could gush fees.

Bankruptcy law was Mungin's specialty. He understood the rituals and procedures of financial ruin. He hadn't dealt much with the insurance industry, but the learning curve didn't seem too steep. Most important was Dombroff's assurance that there would be plenty of work; an aspiring partner had to stay busy.

Dombroff asked about the headhunter's cryptic notation that Mungin might bring business with him from Powell Goldstein. Dombroff wanted to know whether Mungin really had $250,000 to $500,000 of annual billings from the FDIC— the Federal Deposit Insurance Corporation—a giant bank regulatory agency with the sort of bottomless pocketbook that lawyers dream about.

Mungin hedged. He *had* represented the FDIC while at Powell Goldstein; in fact, at the firm's request, he had moved from Atlanta to Washington specifically to handle FDIC work. But the headhunter had assumed a little too confidently that the FDIC would switch law firms just because he did.

Dombroff let the issue drop. There is often a certain amount of what lawyers call "puffing" in this sort of situation, especially if a headhunter is involved.

The talk turned to partnership eligibility and salary. Most big firms in major cities consider elevating salaried associates to partnership between their seventh and ninth year out of law school, although working at the same firm for all of that time isn't necessarily required. Katten Muchin was no different. Dombroff told Mungin he would have to wait until next year, at the earliest, to be eligible.

But Mungin said that wasn't what he was looking for. He was negotiating with other firms about coming in as a partner.

Dombroff wouldn't budge. Mungin would be considered

for partnership only after working at Katten Muchin for a year. That was the best he could offer, and he didn't speculate on Mungin's prospects.

Mungin wasn't happy about Dombroff's position. But he decided to continue talking, because it sounded like there was a lot of opportunity at Katten Muchin.

Mungin asked Dombroff about salary. Dombroff wanted to know what Mungin currently made. Eighty-seven thousand, Mungin answered. The older lawyer made a show of consulting a couple of sheets of paper, apparently some sort of salary roster, before looking up and offering Mungin $91,000 a year to start.

That was in the ball park for someone of his seniority in Washington, Mungin thought, although he had hoped for more. Assuming that associate salaries were set pretty rigidly according to number of years in practice, Mungin requested only an additional thousand. Dombroff said he would see what he could do.

Mungin was the one to raise the issue of race, asking how many blacks worked in the Washington office. It wasn't a huge concern of his, but he did remark that federal agencies, like the FDIC, preferred to hire outside law firms that have some ethnic diversity. It was certainly true that employing minority lawyers was a smart move for firms doing business with big corporations and arms of the government that had affirmative action goals. Mungin saw no shame in his race helping him to get the Katten Muchin job. He believed he had overcome some tough obstacles in his life, and they were made tougher by race. Getting a little credit for that didn't bother him. But like most blacks, he didn't want skin tone to be the primary reason he was hired. He deserved this job on the merits.

Race was a sensitive subject at Katten Muchin, as it was at most major law firms. Few firms were succeeding in integrating their partnership ranks. Katten Muchin's founders were mostly Jews who considered themselves liberals. They hired a fair number of black associates but had trouble holding on to them. Dombroff had participated in firm discussions about how to retain more minority attorneys. But the talk had not come to much. Dombroff admitted to Mungin that there weren't *any* black attorneys in the Washington office.

Mungin wasn't thrilled by this answer, but he didn't press the point. Dombroff seemed intensely interested in him as an individual. This was about making partner, not promoting racial solidarity.

Suddenly, Dombroff brought the conversation to a close. If Mungin wanted the job, it was his, Dombroff offered. The details would get worked out later.

Somewhat startled, the younger man asked whether Dombroff even wanted to call his references.

No need, said Dombroff. "References always say the same thing. They'll all say you're great."

The details did get worked out. Mungin accepted the idea of waiting a year before being eligible for partnership. Dombroff told him he could have the $92,000 salary he had requested. Mungin felt he was on his way.

CHAPTER THREE

"You Don't Want to Mess with This Guy"

MAY 1992

Mungin found Katten Muchin's Washington office an outwardly casual place that revolved around Dombroff's moods. Everyone, from the top partner down to the most junior secretary, was on a first-name basis. Unlike lawyers in some stuffy New York firms, men shed their suit jackets for most of the day, and women wore pants rather than dresses without risking disapproving looks. Lawyers frequently dropped by to chat with colleagues, and there was a lot of gossip. Much of the talk related to who was "in" or "out" with Dombroff. Mungin, the new man, listened closely.

Katten Muchin was one of a minority of big law firms operating in Georgetown rather than at one of the more traditional addresses on K Street or Pennsylvania Avenue. Mungin enjoyed Georgetown's distinctive ambiance, the narrow streets, some still paved with cobblestones, and the well-preserved 18th- and 19th-century architecture. He liked the whiff of money and style that came from the expensive restaurants and stores. The Kennedys had lived in Georgetown before JFK won the White House, Mungin mused. And now here he was—a long way up from the projects. Contrasting with its bulky brick exterior, the Katten Muchin office was decorated tastefully in white and beige, with lots of natural light. There were splashes of colorful, if unremarkable, modern art on the walls and vases of fresh flowers set on end tables. Individual attorneys' offices were arrayed around the perimeter of a roughly rectangular layout. Dombroff and his insurance lawyers had their offices down one hallway, to the left from the elevators and lobby; Mungin and the other bankruptcy lawyers were on the hallway to the right, along with a mix of attorneys who practiced other specialties. The arrangement had meaning: The head man surrounded himself with a loyal palace guard, and everyone else was kept at a distance.

As he settled into his own small office, Mungin carefully read several Katten Muchin documents designed to help him get oriented. He had joined the firm knowing almost nothing about it, assuming that it would be more or less like his previous employers. He was particularly eager to find descriptions of the evaluation and promotion process. Dombroff had promised that he would be eligible for partnership in 1993, and Mungin wanted to understand how the decision would be made.

The 1992 firm "Résumé" boasted of an "open, informal working atmosphere fostered by our attorneys' diverse personalities and backgrounds and the relative youth of the firm's members. We are not just lawyers; we are also artists and actors, fathers and mothers, athletes and civic leaders." Young attorneys have ready access to veterans, the résumé continued, and "initial assignments will include direct client contact." Under the heading "Associate Advancement," it stated, "We believe in advancing attorneys based solely on merit. An associate's progress is evaluated periodically on both a formal and informal basis. Each associate receives regular semiannual reviews based on evaluations from those attorneys with whom he or she has recently worked." The "Firm Reference Manual," which was stamped HIGHLY CONFIDENTIAL INFORMATION, stated: "Associates receive performance evaluations twice annually, during the second calendar quarter and in October."

* * *

Around the same time, Bruce Shortt also had been reading up on Katten Muchin. Shortt was a corporate lawyer with Weil, Gotshal & Manges in New York, and a friend of Mungin's from the days when they worked together in Houston. He had recruited Mungin out of Harvard Law School to work for a firm in the oil patch capital. Mungin had sent Shortt a copy of the *American Lawyer* article Dombroff had used as a prop in the job interview. The firm "sounds like the place that will get me what I want," a cheerful Mungin told Shortt in a subsequent phone conversation.

Shortt wasn't so sure. Reading between the lines of the trade magazine piece, he saw hints of peril. Katten Muchin had grown quickly, not by the old-fashioned method of developing talent from within, but by gobbling up smaller firms and bringing in outside rainmakers like Dombroff. Katten Muchin's leaders portrayed themselves primarily as savvy entrepreneurs, not professional service providers. That could mean that expansion and profits were valued over legal craft, Shortt told Mungin. He didn't like the fact that Mungin was joining a relatively new field office, started only in 1989. You could get lost working in an outpost, far from headquarters, Shortt said. "Think real hard about this," he advised.

But Mungin had already taken the job and wasn't turning back. He told his friend he would be working with Dombroff— "a real player" at the firm. "I'll have some real access to power."

Mungin's faith in Dombroff—a man who himself had been with Katten Muchin for all of three years, and whose ties to the firm were based on money, not personal loyalty—made Shortt even more worried. He thought Mungin was being naive and was making an important career decision without much research.

Don't worry, Mungin said. There would be lots of work at Katten Muchin. He would be fine.

That's what Jeff Sherman had told Mungin at their first lunch: "There's a lot going on, complex work, varied work."

Sherman had been Dombroff's first recruit for the hybrid insurance-bankruptcy practice. Smart and talkative, Sherman had more experience than Mungin, and he admired Dombroff's scheme for the new practice. Years earlier, Sherman had seen Dombroff conduct a professional seminar on deposing witnesses and had been struck by his unapologetic aggressiveness. You don't want to mess with this guy, Sherman thought to himself.

Dombroff had lured Sherman from another Washington firm, using the same sort of gung-ho spirit that had enticed Mungin. Like Mungin, Sherman was something of a journeyman, having made stops at several other firms before arriving at Katten Muchin. Dombroff had given him a hero's welcome. Immediately after Sherman's job interview, Dombroff had taken him—physically, by the arm—to the office of Patricia Gilmore, Dombroff's second-in-command. "This is Jeff Sherman," he told Gilmore. "Do you know what he's been doing for the last six years? Bankruptcy! Bankruptcy for AIG!" AIG, short for American International Group, was one of Dombroff's major insurance clients. By coincidence, Sherman had been doing some bankruptcy work at his last firm for some AIG subsidiaries.

Sherman was given the title "income partner," a job category used by Katten Muchin and some other firms to give associates a promotion without actually letting them into the partnership. Sherman could vote on certain firm management questions, but he was paid a salary—about $120,000—rather than a share of the firm's profits, which could be $400,000 or more for a typical "equity partner."

Sherman explained to Mungin that the majority of their work concerned AIG, a huge multinational holding company based in New York whose subsidiary insurance firms sold policies covering everything from aviation disasters to supermarket slip-and-fall claims. At any given time, more than 100 AIG corporate policyholders, including truck-rental agencies, hospitals, road-builders, and high-tech manufacturers, were in bankruptcy courts around the country, keeping their creditors at bay while they tried to reorganize, or, in dire cases, liquidate. AIG frequently had an interest in these proceedings—for example, if it were seeking back premiums owed by bankrupt companies.

Amid the general money-grab occasioned by corporate bankruptcies, disagreements often arise among creditors and between creditors and debtors. Dombroff believed AIG wasn't pursuing its claims systematically enough. His idea was that Katten Muchin would step in and supervise AIG's bankruptcy work nationwide, litigating some cases and overseeing smaller local firms in others. AIG would have one central bankruptcy clearinghouse. This service, Dombroff hoped, would become an adjunct to the existing trial and counseling work he offered AIG and other clients.

The thought crossed Mungin's mind once he had been on the job for a few weeks that it probably wasn't ideal for the new insurance-bankruptcy practice to be built almost entirely on the needs of one client. If AIG had a change of heart about law firms, what would happen to Katten Muchin's Washington bankruptcy group? But that, he decided, was Dombroff's problem. Mungin wasn't the sort to challenge the office's top partner. He might have plenty of opinions, but he didn't voice them. He was circumspect, wary.

In the spring of 1992, Sherman was jetting around the country, coordinating AIG activities in dozens of cases. "This is a truly national practice," he exulted during one of his early conversations with Mungin. "We're really goin' and blowin'!"

Mungin wasn't familiar with the term "goin' and blowin'," but it fit somehow with Sherman's persona. Usually clad in a baggy, inexpensive suit, Sherman loved to gab about bankruptcy law or office personalities. He zealously collected valuable old hockey and baseball trading cards and frequently could be found on the phone with other collectors. Like Mungin, he had grown up in Queens, New York, although in a nicer area. They talked about their shared hometown and generally got along pretty well.

Mungin's role was to supervise the researching and drafting of memoranda and court pleadings that Sherman needed to represent AIG in bankruptcy court. Stuart Soberman, a younger associate, assisted Mungin. They were Sherman's team, as Sherman imagined it. In some instances, Mungin stepped into the lead role, as he did, for example, with the Leeds matter. Leeds Building Products Inc. sought bankruptcy court protection under Chapter 11 of the U.S. Bankruptcy Code in 1991, after the building market had collapsed. The debt-ridden Marietta, Georgia, manufacturer and operator of building supplies stores couldn't get any more loans from its bank. Among the bills Leeds couldn't pay were several hefty ones from AIG; the insurance company wanted some $5 million in premiums. Leeds argued that its AIG insurance policies were contracts of the sort that a debtor in Chapter 11 proceedings could slough off in the name of getting a fresh start.

Mungin jumped on the issue, working for weeks on a detailed brief on this intersection of the law of insurance, contracts, and bankruptcy. Mungin represented AIG officials who were deposed by Leeds's attorneys, and he was preparing for a hearing set for May in the U.S. Bankruptcy Court in Atlanta, when a compromise was worked out. Leeds agreed to pay AIG about $1 million, the policies were canceled, and both sides avoided the risk of losing in court.

Mungin came back to Washington with a modest victory: His legal work had forced a brisk resolution, and AIG was glad to get anything on policies that had looked as if they would have to be written off. Leeds eventually pulled itself together, emerged from Chapter 11 protection, and went about its usual business. Sherman was more than satisfied with Mungin's effort.

Not everyone at Katten Muchin was as enthusiastic about Mungin's arrival. Before he interviewed Mungin in April, Dombroff had faxed a copy of his résumé to Vincent Sergi in the firm's Chicago office. Dombroff then placed a follow-up phone call to Sergi. "On paper, he looks good," Dombroff told his colleague, suggesting he bring Mungin in for an interview.

Sergi, the senior partner who supervised all Katten Muchin bankruptcy lawyers and therefore, in theory, would be

Mungin's boss, had serious reservations. First, he doubted there was enough bankruptcy work in Washington to justify an additional lawyer. Second, while Mungin's résumé had obvious strengths, he had worked for three law firms in six years since leaving law school. Why had he moved around?

Sergi and Dombroff had some history of disagreement. Two years earlier, Sergi had opposed Dombroff's whole idea of setting up a new insurance-bankruptcy practice in Washington. In his Finance and Reorganization Department in Chicago, Sergi supervised experienced bankruptcy attorneys who could fly to Washington any time Dombroff needed their help. The nation's capital wasn't a commercial center in its own right, so there wasn't a lot of local bankruptcy work of any size. Sergi doubted that Katten Muchin had a long-term interest in setting up a bankruptcy group there.

Despite Sergi's hesitation, Dombroff had demanded his own bankruptcy people based in Washington. Each partner had his strength: Sergi was a Katten Muchin lifer, with a strong practice in Chicago and secure ties to the men who founded and still dominated the firm. Dombroff was a profitable newcomer, who didn't want to be second-guessed by the home office. The clash had to be taken to the managing partners, Allan Muchin and Michael Zavis. Their ruling was that Dombroff would have his way. The managing partners made no secret of the fact that they viewed Dombroff as a gold mine, and they wanted to keep him happy.

Sergi saw adding Mungin as compounding an earlier bad decision. Dombroff brushed off this concern. He informed Sergi that Mungin had initiated each of his previous departures and that there was plenty of bankruptcy work in Washington. Since Dombroff still had the support of the top partners in Chicago, Sergi knew there wasn't anything he could do to stop the lord of the Washington fiefdom.

Within Mungin's first few weeks on the job, he got a phone call from Sergi, whom he still hadn't met. They agreed Mungin should visit headquarters to "get to know the lawyers in Chicago so that they could help support him and get him involved in their matters in Washington or on the East Coast," as Sergi later put it in a deposition.

In early June, about a month after he had started work, Mungin arrived at Katten Muchin's offices in a dark, shiny tower near the Loop, Chicago's famous business district. The 16th-floor reception area had the same sort of off-white, modern decor as the D.C. office. Mungin got a friendly greeting from the receptionist, but then a confused look when he asked for Vincent Sergi. After several phone calls among secretaries, there was bad news: Mr. Sergi wasn't available just now, and actually, no one knew where he was, or whether he would become available later.

This puzzled Mungin. Sergi was the head of a department and an important member of the firm. They had made a scheduled appointment. No one knew where he was? It didn't seem plausible. In any event, it was rude and unprofessional. But there wasn't much to do about it, so Mungin contained his annoyance over having flown from Washington only to be stood up by his own boss.

Sergi had arranged for Mungin to meet a series of other lawyers in the Finance and Reorganization Department, including Laurie Goldstein, the nominal co-head of the department, but not as weighty a figure as Sergi. Mungin moved from office to office, exchanging credentials and pleasantries. But the other attorneys didn't seem to have a clear idea of why he was there or what he was going to do in the Washington office. Mungin's references to Dombroff and his sidekick, Patricia Gilmore, caused awkward silences among his hosts. Mungin flew home to Washington that night without having met Sergi—the man who had invited him—and feeling more than a little befuddled by the experience.

CHAPTER FOUR

"Play by the Rules and the System Will Treat You Right"

1966–1975

In the early 1970s, the student body of Bryant High School in Queens boasted a United Nations–like array of African-Americans, Puerto Ricans, Jews, Asians, and Greeks. The white kids of northern European extraction were more and more the minority. Archie Bunker, the embattled middle-aged bigot of the brilliant 1970s sitcom *All in the Family*, was supposed to have lived not far from Bryant. A central theme of the show was his dismay at what had become of the old neighborhood. At the real Bryant High, the Class of 1975 belonged to Larry Mungin, just the sort of confident, accomplished African-American who fed Archie Bunker's feelings of insecurity.

Larry's first years were spent in Brooklyn, before the Mungins moved to Queens. His family called him by his middle name, Dwayne, to distinguish him from his father, Lawrence Lucas Mungin, Jr. The father, known as "Junior," drove a cab from time to time, repossessed cars, and even did some private-eye work, or so he said. What he didn't do was pay the rent steadily. "He was what black people call 'no good,' meaning not that he was evil or malicious; he just wasn't responsible for his family," Larry told me. "He was a ladies' man, a good-times man."

Born November 19, 1957, Lawrence Dwayne Mungin was raised by his mother, Helen, to be the antithesis of his father. He would study, succeed, go to college, get a job, wear a jacket and tie, and make a good living in the white world. Helen had a fierce, at times harsh, love for her three children. It was studded with rules, rewards, and penalties. She warned them that she always knew what they were doing, and they believed her. After she kicked Junior out for the last time, she told Larry, then still a grade-schooler, "He will ask for your forgiveness some day. Don't give it to him. If you do, I will haunt you for the rest of your days." It was an impressive threat to a child still scared of the dark.

The family lived in a fourth-floor walk-up flat in the poor, all-black, Bedford-Stuyvesant section of Brooklyn. Well aware that Bed-Stuy was deteriorating into a pernicious slum, Helen volunteered her children to be bused to a predominantly white school in a better-off neighborhood in nearby Queens. She knew that classrooms where most of the students were white offered newer books and fewer students per teacher. She wanted her kids to see middle-class life and to learn that they could keep up with whites. Questions of convenience or racial solidarity never came up in the Mungin family. "We saw it like going into a different land, an opportunity," Larry recalled later. "Pretty soon, we took white kids for granted, no big deal."

His brother and sister had much the same recollection, but theirs was accented with hints of racial tension that Larry somehow overlooked. Deborah, the oldest, remembered being followed around in stores in Queens by nervous white clerks. "They thought all black kids shoplifted, which we didn't," she said. "My mother would have *killed* us." Deborah remembered at least a few occasions when a passing car filled with whites would erupt with yells of "Niggers! Get out of here, niggers!" But Deborah said she and her brothers just ignored them. Larry told me he didn't even remember these incidents, which he acknowledged might strike some as strange or implausible. "It just shows I wasn't fixated on [race], I guess, even when it was shoved in my face."

After they had moved to Queens, Kenneth, the younger brother, recalled, there were periodic rumbles between all-black gangs from the projects and all-white gangs from surrounding neighborhoods. The semi-ritualized fights weren't particularly threatening to anyone smart enough to stay out of the way. But Larry appeared to be oblivious to the violence, his brother said. Years later, Larry attributed his youthful inattention to race to his mother. "You are a human being first," Helen liked to say, "an American second, a black third." The Mungins had an individualistic sense of themselves as destined to make a mark, regardless of the racial boundaries of their inner-city world.

Her own mixed parentage surely contributed to Helen's view of race. She was the natural daughter of Lilian Kemp, a white woman from Germantown, Pennsylvania, who left her family and ran off to New York with a black man whose name had slipped from the Mungins' memory. Soon after the lovers conceived Helen, the father died, leaving Lilian, a poor factory employee, alone and pregnant in the big city. When Helen was born in 1936, Lilian pleaded with a black co-worker to adopt the mixed-race girl. Louise Dicks, a plucky Harlem widow who had come north from South Carolina, agreed.

Louise took great pride in Helen's light complexion. In Harlem at that time, "high yellow" skin tone was an emblem of sophistication and beauty. Helen grew into a statuesque beauty, with large chestnut-brown eyes. "Everyone thought my mother was the prettiest; I saw her as the prettiest," Larry told me. "When she came walking home from work and I saw her, and she waved, I was so proud."

Social station couldn't have been the source of Helen's or Louise's considerable pride. After working for many years in a New York pocketbook factory, Louise retired and hired herself out as a domestic. She refused to wash windows, though, because she considered it too strenuous and beneath her. She also boasted that she worked for well-to-do Jews, not for Italians or Irish.

Louise didn't talk much about politics, but on top of the wood television cabinet in her living room was a large framed photograph of the Rev. Martin Luther King. "We were for Martin Luther King, not Malcolm X," Larry recalled. Deborah added: "Our mother and grandmother just didn't make a big thing of race—it was there, but get past it." Late in her life, Louise had a white boyfriend named Fred, who attended family gatherings. Deborah married a white co-worker from the post office; Kenneth wed a woman of Puerto Rican descent. Larry was single but had dated white women. None of these instances of race-crossing occasioned much discussion among the Mungins.

As a boy, and later as an adult, Larry saw his grandmother as a success. She made her own clothes and saved enough to go on out-of-town trips. She rooted for the Yankees because they were the "high-class" New York ball team. At her church, Greater Central Baptist in Harlem, Louise headed the Willing Workers, a women's good-works organization. Never was her dignity more striking than during the portion of certain Sunday services when she led the Willing Workers down the center aisle toward the pulpit, stepping in syncopated time and clapping her white-gloved hands, as the organist pounded a rousing rhythm and the voices of the choir soared. "She didn't have money or education, but in that church, she belonged; she was part of something bigger," Larry said.

Louise discouraged her daughter from applying to college, urging Helen instead to look for a secretary's job and a husband who owned a house—into which Louise could move in her old age. Junior Mungin didn't have a house. A slim, ebony-skinned charmer from coastal South Carolina, Junior behaved like a gentleman to woo Helen, but once they were wed, he fell back on dissolute ways. Helen eventually ran out of patience with him and ordered Junior to leave. But he remained in New York for a while and showed up on holidays with gifts and candy for the children. In time, he moved back to South Carolina.

Helen persevered, finding work as a secretary at the New York City Housing Authority, where one of the perks was special access to a subsidized apartment. She chose a decent project in Woodside, Queens, close to Astoria, a white neighborhood of small single-family houses. Self-sufficiency preoccupied Helen. She lectured her children that only "shiftless" people took welfare if they actually could work. " 'If you get your education and play by the rules, the system will treat you right.' That's what she always said, and we believed it," Deborah recalled. Report cards got microscopic attention. Talking street talk, rather than "proper" English, earned a grounding. "You couldn't hide from her," said Kenneth. "If you were supposed to be studying but weren't, she'd find out, even though she was at work. She was always pushing—'Do better, do better.' "

Helen, who considered herself to be black and had mostly black friends, wasn't ashamed of her racial identity and didn't cut her children off from theirs. The kids sang gospel songs when they accompanied their grandmother to her all-black church. They went on church-sponsored outings to an upstate resort run by "Peg Leg" Bates, a black vaudeville entertainer. They also heard stories about the South. When Helen and Junior were driving to South Carolina in their early days together, they would stop around Baltimore. Light-skinned Helen, who had been sitting in the front passenger's seat, would move to the back, so that they appeared to be chauffeur and employer. It was the mid-1950s, and they didn't want to test the tolerance of southern police for what would appear to be a black man riding alongside a white woman.

Helen's concern was that her children not get bogged down in race. She feared that as blacks in the inner city, Larry and his siblings would be associated with drugs, street crime, radical politics, and poverty—especially poverty. The Mungins weren't destitute. They always had enough to eat. But Helen wanted her children to do better than that. She wanted to launch them up and out of the projects. Her middle child took her ambition further than she ever dared hope.

When the Mungins moved to Woodside Houses on Halloween Day, 1966, the Queens project was still integrated, although working-class whites were leaving as more blacks came in. To Larry, Woodside was a step up. There were playgrounds, trees, even squirrels that ran among the red-brick buildings. He went to the racially mixed neighborhood schools and immediately was put in "advanced" classes, where he was often the only black in the room, or maybe one of two. He recalled taking this entirely in stride. It seemed natural to be the exception and to be among whites. It was what his mother expected.

By the time he could read, Larry could keep himself occupied without playmates. He collected baseball cards and sports magazines and memorized lists of national capitals, exotic animal species, and the dates of famous movies and names of their stars. He later mastered Scrabble, which he played by himself when there wasn't an opponent around. He pestered adults with trivia quizzes. He was a bit of a show-off.

Helen took the children to the library every week, and she bought them a *Funk & Wagnall's* encyclopedia sold at the A&P supermarket for $1 per volume. Larry read it from end to end. His brother and sister remembered years later that at age 11 or 12, he never looked happier than on a Friday night, sitting in front of the television, watching an adventure program called *Wild, Wild West* while simultaneously fiddling with a solo Scrabble game, leafing through an encyclopedia volume, and organizing his baseball cards. "He didn't need other kids," Deborah said. "He did his own thing."

As a teenager, Larry added to his reading list motivational books by Norman Vincent Peale, vocabulary-builders, and get-rich-quick guides. In the summer, when he wasn't working, he took his brother to the integrated Astoria public swimming pool, where Kenneth splashed in the shallow end. Larry taught himself to swim with a book he borrowed from the library.

In the face of occasional light teasing for being a book-worm, he developed a preternatural sense of certainty about what he was doing. "He had a purpose, and nothing—*nothing*—was going to get in the way," recalled Deborah, who was less focused and sometimes resented her brother's self-confidence. His aim wasn't a particular career or material goal. He wanted to get "out of the projects."

Larry's best friends growing up were the sons of working-class Jewish families like the Nathans, who also lived at Wood-side Houses until they saved enough money to move farther out in Queens, to a predominantly white neighborhood. Ira Nathan owned a minority interest in a hardware store, and it was expected that his son, Randy, would go to college. Larry adopted that assumption for himself. Despite some obvious cultural differences, Larry felt a strong tie to the Nathan family, and they in turn embraced him as something like an honorary nephew. He hung around their apartment and enjoyed their frequent verbal skirmishing—something Helen Mungin would never tolerate. Larry attended Randy's bar mitzvah and sat at the main table, the only black face on the dais.

Although the Nathans were far from rich and the Mungins weren't on welfare, his family's more severe money worries caused Larry emotional pain. Helen compulsively stocked canned food, not just in the kitchen cabinets, but in closets and cabinets throughout the apartment. Peas, string beans and corn nibblets, peaches, pineapple slices, and glazed carrots—the cans were stacked everywhere. Though by the time he was a teenager he understood that the bomb shelter–style preparations were one of the ways Helen kept anxiety at bay, Larry was still embarrassed by the habit. He ran on the track team for a while, but his mother said she couldn't afford to buy him real track shoes; he wore his tattered all-purpose canvas basketball sneakers. He sometimes couldn't afford the $1 ticket at the local movie house but was too proud to let Randy Nathan lay out the money.

* * *

In Horace Greeley Junior High School, down the block from Woodside Houses, Larry spent most of the school day with the white kids in advanced classes. But at lunch time, there were two lines in the cafeteria: the regular line, where white students paid for their lunch, and the poor kids' line, where black students like Larry, who qualified for the free-lunch program, got their food. Larry was supposed to walk with his white classmates to the cafeteria, and then, while they got on their line, he was expected to get on the free-lunch line—the black line.

Larry could overlook many sources of racial friction that distracted other kids, but being publicly typecast in the cafeteria was more than he could bear. The humiliation and apprehension gave him a stomachache. Mungins were supposed to be at the top, the elite. He couldn't stand being thrown in with the other poor black kids. The situation pained him so badly that he began hanging back, waiting until his advanced classmates had gone through their line and were sitting in the eating area. Then, when the lunch period was almost over, he would try to mix into the free-lunch line so that he wouldn't be seen there by the whites. In ninth grade, when his big sister Deborah had graduated from junior high, diminishing the chances of his actions being reported at home, Larry tried a new plan. He skipped lunch altogether. He hid in the library, reading or doing homework, until his next class started. Hungry was better than ashamed. His mother never found out, breaking the spell of her omniscience.

Larry never rebelled against Helen's regime of hard work and achievement. From grammar school on, he earned top grades. He took up French in junior high, and won citywide awards for his proficiency. He worked standard teenage jobs— bagging groceries, pulling weeds, standing behind a department store counter—and gave his mother one quarter of what he earned. In a tumultuous time of riots, protest, and Black Panther militancy, Larry's exemplary behavior evoked effusive praise, even gratitude, from whites. In eighth grade, he found and turned in a lost wallet containing $15. Principal Max Scher wrote him a letter of commendation: "Too many are looking to find fault with your generation. If only these same people would look a little beyond the noisy few, they would see the conscientious, honest, dedicated many. May I again congratulate you on your honesty. I know that this is just one sign of the good that you will continue to do throughout your life."

By his middle teens, Larry had made Helen's command his own: Get your education, play by the rules, and the system will treat you right. The system held up its end of the bargain at Bryant High School, a massive tan brick structure not far from Woodside Houses. In his junior year, Larry decided that he needed to burnish his résumé for college. Guidance counselors suggested that he shoot for local New York schools like Adelphi and St. John's, but Larry aimed higher. He signed up for the speech and debate team and in only his second competition, won a citywide prize. Already six feet tall, slim, and handsome with a medium-length afro, Larry took naturally to public speaking and debate. He enjoyed the highly structured research, the rehearsal, the scripted drama and competition. His smooth bass voice—some people told him he should have tried opera—added gravity to his presentation.

Larry's immediate success qualified him for the national high school debate tournament in New Orleans. Bryant paid his way to the Crescent City—his first airplane trip—and put him up in a proper downtown hotel. Larry accompanied Michael Reiner, Bryant's debate ace, star athlete, and senior class president. What impressed Larry the most about Mike was that the following fall, he was headed for Cornell, one of the Ivy League schools. Larry didn't know much about the Ivy League, but he knew it meant class and it could take someone far away from Queens.

In New Orleans, Larry delivered a talk he called "The Prying Eyes," about the dangers of official incursions on personal privacy. He felt oddly calm in front of the large crowd, as if he had been giving speeches for years. To the shock of everyone except Larry himself, he finished his first national tournament in 13th place, one spot *ahead* of Michael Reiner. He felt like Hank Aaron, taking away Babe Ruth's home run title. If he could keep up with the legendary Michael Reiner in one area, why not others? Larry decided to run for senior class president and to apply to the Ivy League—not just to Cornell, but Princeton, Yale, and Harvard, too.

In student politics, he was at a disadvantage: Because he didn't socialize much, he wasn't particularly popular. Luckily, Deborah, who had just graduated and was working in the area, was much more of a socialite. She came back to the school to do some behind-the-scenes politicking, and that did the trick. Larry became Bryant's first-ever black senior class president. Old walls were breaking down. Outside of school, government agencies, universities, and some private employers were reaching out to racial minorities. "It was a good time to be young and black," Larry told me.

There was promise even in a seemingly ordinary summer clerk's job he landed in the record department of Alexander's department store in midtown Manhattan. Larry loved the $2-an-hour job. Young people lingered in the record department. Dressed in the required jacket and tie, he answered questions and took their money. Each morning, he rode the subway in from Queens, getting out a couple of stops early to walk a few blocks down Fifth Avenue. He surveyed the mostly white, well-to-do shoppers and businesspeople. How could they be so much better off than he was? he wondered. What did they have that he didn't?

He was determined to get it, whatever "it" was. One day, he would walk down Fifth Avenue in a fine suit, and people would wonder what *his* secret was.

In a prom photograph from June 1975, Bryant High's senior class president appeared self-assured and eager to take the next step in his life. Larry was dressed in a disco-era powder blue tuxedo, with a floppy black bow tie. His aviator-style glasses reflected the late afternoon sun as he and his date, a pretty African-American girl in a white summer dress, posed in front of the clay-red brick of Woodside Houses.

* * *

There was, however, a bleaker side to Mungin's life as a teenager, and it was reflected in the profound melancholy that often gripped his mother. Although capable of showing great exuberance when it came to her children's accomplishments, Helen grew deeply frustrated with her own life. She worked hard but didn't get ahead. Her adoptive mother was an exacting and intrusive critic, second-guessing everything from dinner recipes to child-rearing. Helen never stopped resenting her husband's having abandoned the family. Her children saw her as a fortress, both restricting and protecting them. But Helen wasn't impervious; she had her weaknesses. She dulled her disappointment and yearning with alcohol. By Larry's teenage years, her drinking had become excessive, a problem that strained their relationship.

Helen's alcoholism prolonged her dark moods and made her older son wary of her. He felt guilty—was it his fault she drank?—and wanted to get away from her. He gradually lost a friend, making him even more of a loner. He was ashamed of this aspect of his mother but didn't dare talk about it with anyone. Mungins had nothing in common with the winos who loitered near liquor stores. Larry felt that he alone in the family acknowledged Helen's problems, and it angered him. In a semi-autobiographical novel he began writing in his early 30s, he lashed out at his siblings in an imagined conversation about Helen's drinking: "How could you have missed it? You mean you never heard the click when the vodka bottle hit the floor in the bedroom closet? And you never saw the gin bottles in the hamper? Where the hell were you two?

"I've got to escape from this chaos," said Larry's alter ego in the novel.

One evening when he was 15, Larry heard his mother sobbing in the kitchen. He found her standing at the sink, with her head back, drinking from a white plastic bottle of Clorox. He yelled for Helen to stop and ripped the bottle away from her. She was choking and weeping at the same time. He forced her to drink some milk in the hope that it would coat her stomach. Helen eventually calmed down, and survived without lasting physical damage. Humiliated, she refused to let her son call an ambulance or doctor. But it was still a terrifying experience for Larry. How could she do this to the family? What would they do without her? He worried that she would try something like this again, but was too embarrassed to tell anyone that his mother had attempted suicide. So far as Larry knew, no one ever mentioned the incident after that night.

Larry maintained a highly disciplined, achievement-oriented public persona while struggling privately to understand and endure his mother's difficulties. His success in the world brought him a sense of order and calm. It also pleased Helen, of course, and sometimes would forestall her descent into gloom. As for making sense of the less happy aspects of his family life, Larry never sought complex psychological explanations. Even as an adult, he simply associated a generalized depressive quality with the physical circumstances and social status of inner-city life. Fear of that dark cloud helped propel him away from Woodside. Shame over that fear—and over his resentment of his mother—made it difficult for Larry to reveal himself to others. "In the projects, you don't count," he told me. "We were invisible. My mother was very unhappy. I wanted to escape that unhappiness. I wanted out of there. I wanted not to be like my mother."

Harvard and Princeton made no secret of their ardor for Larry; he hadn't been shy about seeking recognition for the challenges he had faced. "I believe it takes courage to become the 'man of the house' when there is no father," he wrote in his application to Harvard. "I believe it takes discipline to work twenty-plus hours a week, have many responsibilities, and still do well in school. Most importantly, I believe these are the qualities Harvard is looking for." Larry knew he got an extra boost because the Ivies were striving to integrate. He also knew he didn't need much, if any, affirmative action to get into college. He was within Harvard's range on his college boards—670 verbal, 600 math—and had an A average at Bryant High, where he made the honor society and graduated near the top of his class. His portfolio included not only honors for debate and student government, but also the award as Bryant's best French language student.

Helen wanted Larry to go to Princeton because it was closer to home. Mother and son visited Princeton's woodsy New Jersey campus, where Larry was shown around by a black undergraduate guide. Trying to make Larry feel at home, the guide took him to an all-black dorm, and then showed him a radio station that seemed to be run by black students. The guide "was very proud to show me the black students at Princeton," Larry said. But "I didn't want that at all. I wanted to get out of this. I wanted to get out of the ghetto."

Harvard presented itself differently. The campus tour wasn't racially oriented (although Larry would later discover plenty of self-segregation there). But more important was the pitch delivered by a Harvard alumnus-recruiter. "You know, Larry," this businessman told him in a telephone conversation, "if you go to Harvard, you will never have to worry about money again for your whole life."

"He was speaking my language," Larry later said.

On the April day that he was accepted by all four of the Ivies to which he applied, Bryant High School celebrated his victory. People clapped him on the back as word spread through the halls. His social studies class gave him a raucous ovation. Helen Mungin wasn't any less thrilled. She taped a hand-written poster to their apartment door that evening. It said: "Winner takes all!!! That's my son! Harvard, Princeton, Yale, or Cornell—the choice is up to him." She signed it, "Mom, your major rooter."

CHAPTER FIVE

"You'll Get Screwed the Way I Got Screwed"

SUMMER & FALL 1992

One day in late August 1992, Mungin and Jeff Sherman received a memo from Dombroff. "Confirming our discussion," it stated, "nothing"—and *nothing* was underlined—"is to be sent to AIG without first being reviewed by Pat Gilmore or me."

"Can you believe this bullshit?" Sherman demanded. Routine bankruptcy paperwork flowed between the firm and AIG constantly. Dombroff and Gilmore didn't trust attorneys who had been in practice six or eight years to handle this correspondence independently?

"This is bullshit," Sherman repeated.

Mungin mumbled only muted agreement. On the merits, Sherman was correct. Practicing law this way was wasteful. It also flatly contradicted the firm's own documents on how younger lawyers would have direct client contact. But Mungin refrained from saying or doing anything that could be construed as insubordination. He understood that Dombroff and Gilmore were trying to assure that all client loyalty flowed to them, not their underlings. Mungin would have to win their trust gradually. He saw his future at Katten Muchin as depending on Dombroff, and, by extension, Gilmore. It didn't depend on Jeff Sherman.

A diagram of a large law firm looks like a pyramid. At the top are the equity partners, who own the firm and share in its profits. Below them are a larger number of salaried associates (and sometimes income partners). The equity partners supervise legal work, whether trying cases in court or cutting corporate deals in the conference room, and they maintain ties to clients. The associates do the heavy lifting in the law library, produce drafts of briefs, and piece together the inches-thick documents that memorialize mergers and stock offerings. If each partner can keep enough associates billing enough hours, a corporate law partnership can be a very profitable institution.

Understanding the nature of the law business in the late 1980s and 1990s is vital to understanding Larry Mungin's experience. In the old days, associates with top credentials would choose a firm and stay there until death or retirement. In exchange for their early years of toil, they would receive vital practical training (which American law schools largely eschew). At the most prestigious law firms, not everyone was promoted to partner, but diligent workers who missed the cut were placed with lesser firms or with the staffs of client corporations.

No more. To maximize revenue, firms have expanded and radically increased the ratio of associates to partners. This is called "leveraging," and it means that even Harvard and Yale lawyers routinely fail to make partner, and bounce from one firm to another. There has been a simultaneous consolidation in the industry overall, with a few dozen firms becoming behemoths—some with more than 1,000 attorneys—and dozens of slower-moving partnerships collapsing. Partners, meanwhile, behave like free agents, willing to take their clients to the highest bidder. Corporate clients have played a major role in stirring competition: They make greater demands on their outside lawyers, with the threat always hovering that a displeased in-house counsel will switch law firms the way marketing VPs switch advertising firms. At bar association conferences, it is now fashionable to speak of law as a business. Call it a profession, and rivals wonder whether you're one of those soft antiquarians.

The change in big-firm law practice happened to coincide with the arrival, in serious numbers, of women and non-whites. Previously, members of these groups hadn't been welcome in the relatively stable old boys' club. By the time social attitudes changed and law firms began accepting attorneys who weren't white men, economic attitudes and circumstances had also changed. For many promising law school grads of the mid-1980s or later—whatever their demographic characteristics—grabbing the low rung of the corporate law firm ladder proved much less attractive than they imagined it would when, as college students, they decided to apply to law school.

Mark Dombroff personified the new businesslike approach to law practice. He had to think in terms of dollars and cents, because his specialty was representing insurance companies. The major insurance carriers formed the vanguard among corporate clients that were demanding more competitive prices and services from their outside lawyers. The insurers could do this because of sheer market muscle: They had huge amounts of legal work, which they could, and did, shop among various law firms.

Sensitive to the changing times, Dombroff was prepared to bargain, for example, by offering his clients discounts, something that would be abhorrent to a big-firm traditionalist. He leveraged heavily, employing many associates per partner, and made no pretense of providing his underlings with the sort of formal training and collegial atmosphere that they would have found at the better old-line firms.

Dombroff believed that without his lucrative insurance practice, Katten Muchin's Washington office was nothing. He was resented in Chicago because of his arrogance. Just before he was admitted to the partnership in 1989, he visited Katten Muchin's home office and gave a self-congratulatory presentation on how he could cut costs and hike profits. "A lot of us listening were interested in talking money," said one former Katten Muchin partner, "but this guy was so crass and so full of himself that it was a little embarrassing."

The firm's plan was to use Dombroff's revenue flow to attract other lawyers with steady clients to join the Washington office. But Katten Muchin wasn't a brand name in the capital, and it proved harder than expected to lure attorneys with reliable profit streams. In 1992, three years after opening, the Washington outpost was still a rickety scaffolding built around the Dombroff money geyser. The top partners in Chicago understood that they couldn't afford to push Dombroff around. Katten Muchin partners in Washington were even less able to resist him, as was reflected by the fact that his annual take-home share of firm profits was close to a million dollars—more than twice as large as theirs.

Dombroff attended law school at American University in Washington and went to work for the federal government, rising quickly in the Federal Aviation Administration and then the Department of Justice. He defended the government when its air traffic controllers or airport authorities were sued after air crashes. Dombroff distinguished himself in this obscure area, making contacts throughout the aviation and insurance industries. Then, after 15 years on the federal payroll, he decided to make some real money.

In earlier times, a departing civil servant in Dombroff's position would have had to hang out his own shingle, or maybe join a small firm of trial lawyers. But in the mid-1980s, the old taboo against firms bringing in "lateral" partners, who hadn't been reared in the firm culture, was vanishing. Dombroff was snapped up by a prestigious New York firm trying to expand its wobbly Washington office. When that shop soon suffered a wave of defections—more evidence of the new hurly-burly in corporate law—Dombroff began talking to Katten Muchin. The managing partners in Chicago saw Dombroff as a natural fit. He was talented, imaginative, and good at pleasing clients. As a younger man, he had made pocket money as a magician, and he still livened up legal conferences by performing illusions.

In insurance circles, Dombroff attracted attention by urging his clients to fight more aggressively in court to cut jury awards to the families of plane crash victims. This was a switch from the approach that prevailed in the 1970s and most of the 1980s, when insurers and airlines tried to settle quietly and not make a spectacle of battling the relatives of blameless casualties. But Dombroff insisted that he could save his clients big money in court. Once he moved to Katten Muchin, he fulfilled this hard-nosed promise, shaving millions of dollars off of judgments against one major insurer in a series of trials involving three fatal crashes of USAir flights. Dombroff made his purpose plain. The simple but harsh truth, he told juries, was that this sort of legal proceeding wasn't so much about justice as it was about putting a price tag on death.

He was fiercely devoted to his big insurance clients. They were the ones who made it possible for him to buy a striking home in the Virginia countryside, which he and his wife made available as a featured stop on an exclusive garden tour. But when he was off trying air crash cases, Dombroff couldn't very well keep track of what was going on back at the office. Over the years, he had turned to a trusted deputy, Patricia Gilmore, to supervise the non-courtroom aspects of his burgeoning practice.

A former secretary who earned business and law degrees from the University of Santa Clara in California, Gilmore had worked as a junior attorney for Dombroff at the Justice Department and then followed him to Katten Muchin. She offered unwavering loyalty in exchange for a secure job serving Dombroff's clients. Much of what Gilmore oversaw at Katten Muchin had to do with coverage disputes: Did a particular policy require an insurance company to reimburse a corporate policy holder for some sort of loss—from a spill of toxic waste, for example, or from asbestos contamination? Not surprisingly, insurers tended to want legal arguments maintaining that they *didn't* have to pay claims. Gilmore lacked Dombroff's trial skills, but she carried out his dictate that the insurance clients were to be kept happy and constantly aware that it was Dombroff and Gilmore who deserved their appreciation.

Dombroff's other insurance lawyers, who assisted him with trials or wrote memos for Gilmore on coverage questions, either accepted that they wouldn't have much to do with clients, or they left the firm. "You had to understand Mark; there wasn't any question but that everything was done for him— not the firm, for *him*," explained a former Dombroff associate who had known him for more than a dozen years. "Mark got the credit, Mark got the big pay, and everyone else, except maybe for Pat, was expendable."

Jeff Sherman had never accepted this reality. From earlier work at his previous firm, he had his own ties to a couple of officials at the big insurer AIG. It annoyed him that Gilmore wanted to be present for every meeting with AIG executives. She didn't know as much as he did about bankruptcy law, in Sherman's opinion, and he didn't think she should get credit for work he was doing. As Mungin's early months at the firm went by, he observed this tension growing.

More through dutiful silence than through words, Mungin tried hard to distinguish himself from Sherman, who also complained that Dombroff was reneging on his promise to allow Sherman to develop his local bankruptcy practice. From his first meeting with Dombroff, Mungin had sensed that the managing partner had no great affection for Sherman, and now the rift was obviously widening.

Never sentimental when it came to office politics, Mungin expected that Sherman would eventually leave or be forced out and that another bankruptcy lawyer, Stuart Soberman, would go with him. That would leave Mungin as the sole bankruptcy lawyer. Dombroff and Gilmore would be dependent on him for the entire insurance-bankruptcy practice. He expected that they would hire a new junior associate to do the low-level work, and that he would step up and do the more complex coordination of bankruptcy cases around the country. When the time came in late 1993, surely the main attorney responsible for AIG's bankruptcy concerns would be elevated to income partner.

None of this was explicitly confirmed by Dombroff or Gilmore. But when Mungin pressed Dombroff for guidance on how to allocate his time between AIG assignments and other matters, Dombroff responded, "Just do the work I hired you to do, and you'll be fine." That seemed like reassurance, if not exactly stirring encouragement.

Black professionals bear extra burdens in the workplace, and lawyers at big law firms are no exception. Whatever their backgrounds, blacks who have succeeded are seen by other blacks and many whites as pioneers and role models. Even though the black middle class has grown impressively in the last 30 years, black professionals are still treated as exceptions to the rule, the rule being black membership in the working class or underclass. As distorted as this perception may be, it is keenly felt by those labeled as trailblazers.

Mungin had long sensed the weight of being among what the black intellectual W. E. B. DuBois called the "talented tenth"—those responsible for leading the race to equality. In work settings, Mungin spoke with a precision that guaranteed his being described as "very articulate," a euphemism used by many whites to describe a black person who doesn't use street vernacular. He never used profanity, even in jest. He stressed his Harvard pedigree, both because he was proud of it and because he knew it sent another reassuring signal to whites. He didn't crave white approval for its own sake, but as a means to get ahead. He played the game according to the rules he found in place. That game, he felt, dictated that he distinguish himself from the place and people of his youth. He dutifully visited his sister, Deborah, and her family, who still lived at Woodside Houses, but his ambivalence over returning to the projects was palpable. In her small apartment, he praised his sister's dexterity as a mother; giving me a tour outside, he consciously tried to steer away from old acquaintances. "I don't want to talk to these people," he said. "I don't have anything in common with these people." The comment, surprising in its bluntness, lacked hostility or condescension. Rather, Mungin sounded lonely, as if he was describing true strangers. His mother had died, and his brother had moved away. Childhood friends like Randy Nathan were long gone. Other than his sister's family, he had no remaining ties to Woodside.

Despite his alienation from his past and membership in the contemporary version of DuBois' talented tenth, Mungin wasn't immune to infuriating stereotypes in middle-class white circles. When he returned from work dressed in a suit, he got friendly nods from neighbors in his apartment complex in Alexandria, Virginia. Later the same evening, however, wearing sweat clothes on his way to the gym, he found that the same neighbors would visibly tense up. On the elevator, some women would punch the control panel and get off at the next floor, or clutch their handbag to their chest, as if Mungin were about to rip it away from them.

"I understand what's going through their minds, but how do you think that makes me feel?" Mungin asked angrily. "I'm black, so they think I'm going to rob or rape them. But I'm the same person who walks in with the Armani suit. Don't they see me? The answer is no. They see a black man. *I* am the one who is robbed. I am robbed of my reputation because of the color of my skin."

Race had crept up on Mungin and forced its way into his life. In his youth, he had avoided the issue—amazingly—and had few *visible* racial scars from that period. But he encountered isolated examples of hostility as soon as he arrived at Harvard. As a rule, he didn't react outwardly; he walked away. But by the time he reached his mid-30s, he had accumulated enough unhappy experiences that it was becoming difficult to contain his building anger. The effort made him weary. It left him confused about his black identity. He couldn't ignore it anymore, as was illustrated by his asking the question at his job interview about the number of blacks in Katten Muchin's Washington office. Being the sole black attorney worried him, but he didn't want to make a stink about it. When some of the black secretaries at Katten Muchin went out of their way to strike up conversations with him, and he learned that they had various grievances tied to race, he did nothing to investigate or come to their aid. Indeed, he speculated in conversation with his brother, Kenneth, that the secretaries were using race as an excuse, that they might be cooking up an unjustified lawsuit. Larry sounded to Kenneth as if "he was the big company man—just work hard, everything will be fine, no complaining," Kenneth told me later. In retrospect, Larry felt chagrined that he had dismissed the secretaries' complaints so quickly. "I didn't go into the place looking for discrimination," he said.

The Washington office of Katten Muchin had its own committee for hiring new associates, and in August 1992, some members came to Mungin and asked him to join. He agreed, but with misgivings. He had been there only three months. How much did he know about the firm? He assumed he had been picked because he was black. But he didn't want to become the expert on black hiring. He worried he would be expected to work miracles.

At his last law firm, Powell Goldstein, Mungin had felt pressured to take under his wing a younger black associate, Anthony Boswell. Boswell admiringly recalled Mungin as his "own private drill sergeant," demanding and scrupulous. "He always told me, 'You have to be better [than the white associates] or you won't survive.' . . . He also warned me, 'Don't use race as an excuse; just get it right.' " Mungin sometimes was so tough when reviewing Boswell's work that white associates at Powell Goldstein approached a partner to complain that Mungin was abusing Boswell. The younger black lawyer had to reassure everyone that he welcomed Mungin's gruff attention. "I admired him; he cared," said Boswell, who also left Powell Goldstein for another job.

Still, Mungin didn't want to be typecast as an African-American big brother at Katten Muchin. He wanted to devote his energy to doing work that could be billed to clients. The hiring committee meetings were every bit as fatuous as he feared, especially when the topic was why this or that potential black recruit had gone elsewhere. The group did take one specific action on minority hiring: It signed up for a program at

George Washington University Law School, under which law firms agreed to hire black students to work as part-time clerks during the school year. Janice Jamison, the GWU minority clerkship candidate sent to Katten Muchin, was a bright, energetic young black woman. The committee asked Mungin to play a dual role as Jamison's work-assignment coordinator, funneling research tasks to her from other attorneys, *and* as her mentor, making sure she received any personal or professional guidance she required. The committee didn't explain why Mungin should be entirely responsible for Jamison, but the reason was obvious. And for that reason, Mungin refused. Wasn't the whole point of this program and minority recruitment in general to *integrate* the firm?

The committee relented. A white, first-year female associate was appointed Jamison's work-assignment coordinator. Mungin would serve only as her mentor. But he remained suspicious about his colleagues' sincerity regarding the minority clerkship experiment. Since he didn't give voice to his uneasiness—as always, he was outwardly polite—his fellow committee members in all likelihood hadn't a clue that for Mungin, this minor episode was a source of exasperation.

That fall, the tumult of the 1990s legal marketplace jarred the embryonic insurance-bankruptcy group at Katten Muchin. The shift began when AIG underwent an internal bureaucratic reshuffling. The authority to assign bankruptcy work to outside counsel moved to a different division of the company. Executives in that division thought some of the bankruptcy assignments going to Katten Muchin could be handled more efficiently by in-house lawyers. These executives also had strong personal ties to a New York firm specializing in bankruptcy law. This was all very bad news for Dombroff's insurance-bankruptcy dream. At first, AIG merely required the Katten Muchin lawyers to coordinate their work with the New York law firm. But gradually, in late 1992, it became clear that AIG intended to send the vast majority of its more complex bankruptcy assignments to the New York firm—not cutting off Katten Muchin entirely, but leaving it with more routine, less challenging work. For all of his big talk about creating a hybrid insurance-bankruptcy practice at Katten Muchin, Dombroff hadn't persuaded other insurance clients to funnel sizable amounts of bankruptcy work to the firm. AIG, it turned out, was practically the whole ball game, and now AIG was bringing in a new team.

Once these developments became clear, a dejected Sherman composed an obituary for his brief career at Katten Muchin: "The whole reason we're here has disappeared," he said to Mungin. With a push from Dombroff, Sherman began looking for a new job. He apologetically told Mungin that he planned to try to take Soberman with him, but that it would be too hard to find a firm that would be willing to take Mungin as well.

Mungin tried to stifle his amusement. He had no intention of becoming part of a trio led by Jeff Sherman. Sure, Mungin was worried by the AIG situation. But not *all* of the AIG work was disappearing. And Dombroff hadn't sent Mungin any signals that *he* needed to look for another job. On the contrary, in November, only seven months after starting with Katten Muchin, Mungin received an $8,000 raise—a healthy 9 percent increase—that boosted his base salary to an even $100,000. He also received a $4,200 bonus for his performance in his first five months; on an annual basis, the bonus would have come to $10,000. How else could he read that, except as an indication that the firm valued him? In any event, Katten Muchin had promised that there would be plenty of work for Mungin to do. If it didn't come from AIG, it would come from Chicago, Mungin thought.

"You'll get screwed the way I got screwed," Sherman warned.

But Mungin just smiled and said he would be fine, thanks.

Dombroff later remembered that Mungin came to his office in December 1992 to ask what Sherman's departure meant for him. "My reaction," Dombroff said in a deposition, "was that it was a great opportunity" for Mungin, who, as "the only bankruptcy lawyer within the office," would be much in demand.

CHAPTER SIX

"A Balls-Out Firm"

In the early months of 1993, Mungin began to worry that Sherman's warning was coming true. Maybe they *were* going to screw him.

One day, Pat Gilmore appeared at the open door of his cubbyhole of an office. Despite her proximity to power in the person of Mark Dombroff, Gilmore tended to plead when she wanted something done. To the same degree that Dombroff was blunt, Gilmore was circuitous. She wondered if, possibly— yes, she knew it was the last minute—could Mungin accompany her and Dombroff—yes, that very morning, *now*—to a seminar they were scheduled to present at a Washington hotel. In the audience would be insurance and aviation executives. Lawyers like Dombroff and Gilmore provided the entertainment, free of charge, in hopes of lining up new clients.

As he grabbed his overcoat, Mungin mused that, on balance, he was glad to be included, but it seemed odd that he hadn't been given any time to prepare. He had no idea what his role was supposed to be. Then Gilmore told him about the overhead projector. For some reason, the hotel wasn't supplying a projector, and the Katten Muchin lawyers had to bring their own.

Would he mind terribly carrying it down to the cab? Gilmore implored. Now Mungin thought he understood the reason he had been invited.

If he were a first- or second-year associate, doing this sort of errand *might* be appropriate. But Mungin had been out of law school for almost seven years. That was supposed to mean something. Big law firms identify associates by "classes," meaning year of law school graduation. Salaries are ordinarily set by class, as is eligibility for partnership. Doing work suited for a younger class would be insulting to any associate. Mungin felt the sting more keenly because he didn't have personal relationships at Katten Muchin that served to secure his place at the firm. No partner had stepped forward to be Mungin's mentor, or, as some would have put it in Katten Muchin's home office, his "rabbi." He didn't have ties to a client that made him valuable; Gilmore and Dombroff made that impossible. His credentials and his skills were all Mungin felt he could rely on. That's why being asked to lug an overhead projector—an imposition another attorney might have shrugged off—struck Mungin as insulting, even alarming. Was this how Dombroff and Gilmore thought of him?

At the hotel, Dombroff rattled the chandeliers with a tirade against plaintiffs' lawyers. Gilmore followed with a more sedate dissertation on policy-coverage and bankruptcy issues. Mungin operated the projector during Gilmore's talk. He wondered whether the insurance executives assumed that he was a paralegal, or lower. Near the end, Dombroff asked Mungin to step forward and say a few additional words about what insurance companies need to know about bankruptcy law. Mungin kept it simple, and the session ended unremarkably.

When it was over, Dombroff stalked out of the hotel to hail a cab. Mungin followed with the projector, Gilmore trailing somewhere behind. To kill a few seconds while they waited at the curb, Mungin tried awkwardly to make conversation with Dombroff.

"Well, that was pretty good," he said.

No, it wasn't, Dombroff snarled in response. The session was "a total waste of time."

If it was a waste of time, Mungin wondered, why did they drag him along? Just then, a cab pulled up. Mungin lifted the projector into the trunk, and then he remembered why.

Mungin began getting e-mails in early 1993 about Jeff Sherman's "receivables." Receivables are the money owed to a firm by its clients, but not yet paid. Sherman had left without collecting at least $300,000. Now he was at a new firm and had little incentive to go after past fees, which, if collected, would flow into Katten Muchin's bank account. Since Mungin was the sole remaining bankruptcy lawyer in Washington, and had worked closely with Sherman, Chicago wanted him to dun Sherman's ex-clients. Mungin feared that he wouldn't get any credit for this mop-up operation and worried that many of Sherman's clients would turn out to be defunct companies or broke individuals. But he began negotiating an agreement under which Sherman promised to try to collect some of the fees, in exchange for Katten Muchin's allowing him to keep a small portion of what he brought in. Sherman seemed to enjoy dickering over the arrangement, wasting hours of Mungin's time. Mungin, meanwhile, was sorting through dozens of Sherman's old files, trying to figure out which contained evidence of living, breathing clients. It was arduous work.

In the office, Mungin contained his growing irritation. At home, though, he began to keep a bare-bones diary—just jottings in a stenographer's pad—and it was there that he expressed his frustration. He wrote of having "nagged, begged and basically [done] collection work in my *partnership* year," adding, "[N]ever in all my years have I heard of associates being forced to do this stuff." Mungin's efforts netted $11,000 for Katten Muchin.

As the last of the more challenging AIG assignments evaporated, Mungin found his time consumed with what amounted to highly specialized paper-shuffling—something that a paralegal could do with the supervision of a second-year associate. The pattern went like this: AIG would alert Gilmore that a corporate policyholder had gone into bankruptcy. Gilmore would pass the relevant documents along to Mungin, who would review them to see whether it was possible for AIG to file with the relevant bankruptcy court a "proof of claim," the formal document seeking to collect on a debt—usually back premiums or other payments owed by the insolvent company. Gilmore, eager to please AIG, almost always pressed for at least going through the motions of seeking money for the client. Mungin was sometimes forced into the position of pointing out that they didn't have a legal leg to stand on, because, for example, the deadline for filing proofs of claim had passed. Then Mungin would file the documents—or not file them, if Gilmore relented—and the process would start over again with a new case.

Gilmore did sometimes defer to him. In one early 1993 exchange of internal e-mail, she suggested that they file a proof of claim in the bankruptcy of a company called Blaze Trucking. Although the filing deadline had passed, Gilmore urged pressing ahead, making the technical argument that "we did not receive notice of the bankruptcy."

Mungin countered that AIG and Katten Muchin had to observe all of the niceties of the Bankruptcy Code. "I am not comfortable filing a proof of claim after the bar date has passed even if we did not receive notice," he wrote back. "Before filing claims after the bar date (and to protect the client and the firm) we need for the client to represent, preferably in writing, that it did not have timely notice of the bankruptcy (although even that will probably not be enough)."

Gilmore retreated, following Mungin's advice. But this sort of petty victory was hardly the foundation on which to build a bid for partnership.

Mungin returned to Dombroff's office in the winter of 1993 for another talk about where the bankruptcy practice was headed. Dombroff, this time clearly annoyed by the question, got up from behind his desk and paced. He said that with Sherman gone, he was counting on Mungin to do the AIG work.

Mungin didn't want to be so confrontational as to say that the AIG work was increasingly simple and not appropriate for someone with his experience. Instead, he inquired as to who would be looking after his interest in becoming a partner. Would it be Dombroff and Gilmore in Washington? Or Sergi in Chicago?

Dombroff replied that it would be Sergi. He was the head of the Finance and Reorganization Department, and Mungin was a member of that department. Sergi was responsible for Mungin.

But he had almost nothing to do with Sergi, Mungin pointed out. In nearly a year at the firm, he had only participated in one FAR department meeting by speakerphone. He hadn't received any substantial work assignments from Sergi.

Mungin said that as far as he could tell, he was excluded from Sergi's department and was doing only insurance work.

Dombroff sympathized. He promised to tell Sergi to include Mungin in meetings.

What about assuring that he started getting assignments from his department? Mungin wanted to know.

Dombroff had grown impatient. As he sometimes did to conclude a conversation, he simply walked out of the room. "Just do my work," he said, as he disappeared into the hall.

So Mungin did the work, assuming that he could not be faulted for performing as instructed by the top lawyer in the office. At the same time, he decided he had to try to build a relationship with the bankruptcy attorneys in Chicago. He had met Sergi just one time after the senior lawyer failed to show during Mungin's only visit to Chicago. In December 1992, Sergi, unannounced, had stuck his head in Mungin's office in Washington. Mungin had been in the middle of a business phone call. They shook hands, and Sergi hustled off. By the time Mungin got off the phone, Sergi had disappeared. Mungin was puzzled by what seemed to him to be Sergi's indifference toward integrating him into the bankruptcy practice in Chicago.

Dombroff, for his part, called Sergi to convey Mungin's

disappointment at being excluded from finance department activities. Sergi agreed to invite Mungin to Chicago again, to "reintroduce" him to lawyers there who might be able to send him work. But Sergi had many priorities higher than looking after Mungin. There still weren't the makings of a significant bankruptcy practice in Washington, Sergi believed, and it was Dombroff who had to worry about keeping his senior bankruptcy associate occupied.

In 1993, Vincent A. F. Sergi was coming into his own as a leader at Katten Muchin & Zavis. As firm veterans loved to recount, there were only two dozen lawyers when they began in the mid-1970s. The partners were just in their mid-30s. A handful of associates, including Sergi, fresh from Northwestern University Law School, were in their late 20s. Two decades later, the firm grossed $125 million, according to *The American Lawyer*.

Katten Muchin specialized from the start in tax, real estate, and commercial lending transactions. Its clients were wealthy individuals and small privately held companies and partnerships. Katten Muchin attorneys were known for being gutsy. They pushed tax shelters right up to the line. They took risks, and they invested their own money in their clients' deals—something that "white shoe" law firms frowned on because of the danger of conflicts of interest.

The firm cultivated an image of *not* being part of the mostly WASP Chicago legal elite. The name partners were Jews who didn't mind being thought of as outsiders. They didn't play by country club rules. "Many people said, 'You guys will never survive together. You're all too aggressive, you'll be trying to kill each other,' " founding partner Michael Zavis told *The National Law Journal*. Other Chicago lawyers described Katten Muchin as a "balls-out firm." Zavis and his colleagues relished this reputation.

Katten Muchin lawyers identified personally with their clients, storied Chicago financiers like William Farley and Jerry Reinsdorf. Farley built an empire in apparel and textiles. A leading midwestern real estate baron, Reinsdorf became a national figure in the sports business by acquiring control of Chicago's Major League Baseball White Sox and National Basketball Association Bulls. Katten Muchin grew, too, facilitating its clients' ambitions and ingesting smaller law firms. By the late 1980s, the firm had attracted a slew of major corporations and banks as clients.

"We don't have the seventy-five-year-old partner sitting in the corner someplace who founded the University of Chicago in 1803," Zavis said to *The National Law Journal*. "We're more flexible. We can move quicker." Zavis led the firm's geographic expansion, insisting that Katten Muchin ought to become a national institution, like some other regional firms were doing in the 1980s. Many of his partners were skeptical, wondering why they needed the headaches and high overhead of offices in Los Angeles, New York, and Washington. There was a particularly intense internal struggle in late 1990 and 1991 over whether to absorb the remains of a smaller firm in L.A. But Zavis rammed the deal home. Another partner, who heard the remark, told me that on the way out of the meeting at which the move was ratified, one of Zavis's partners commented with characteristic Katten Muchin imagery: "You know why we're doing this merger, don't you? Because Zavis has a stiff prick and has to ejaculate."

Sergi wasn't an obvious fit in this fast-paced atmosphere. In his early years, he struggled with the intense pressure and long hours that were expected at the firm. Some of the older lawyers wondered if he would wash out, but he didn't. He worked around the clock to smooth out the kinks in real estate loan documents, and then he pulled himself together to join the clients for the ritual celebratory dinner. He won the attorney's equivalent of a battlefield commission into the partnership: He had proved his loyalty under duress. And even though he wasn't a great legal scholar and was anything but dashing, Sergi became an expert nurturer of client relationships. Law schools don't teach this skill, but it is a vital part of law firm life. Sergi entertained tirelessly at high-priced restaurants and Bulls games. By the 1990s, he was one of the firm's heaviest billers. "I'd have to say that Vince came to swing one of the big dicks around the place," said one former partner. At Katten Muchin, there wasn't a compliment more grand.

The 30 or so lawyers Sergi supervised in the Finance and Reorganization Department focused primarily on representing banks and commercial lending companies that extended credit to companies and real estate developers. Since borrowers of this sort frequently run into trouble repaying loans, the Katten Muchin lawyers stood ready to "restructure" financing deals—by, for example, stretching out a loan's repayment period or having the lender give the borrower a new cash infusion to help it through a rough patch. Then, if things really fell apart, Katten Muchin lawyers would get involved in "reorganizing" an insolvent borrower, or seeing that its assets were sold off. "We made money in both directions," chuckled a former Katten Muchin bankruptcy lawyer in Chicago.

By 1993, Sergi was no longer a detail man. Younger lawyers did the drafting; he focused on the big picture and on keeping clients happy. Presiding over a series of conference rooms awash in paper, he worked on several projects simultaneously and was easily distracted. He disliked formal meetings, preferring to pull people aside in the hall. "Hey, do you have time for a deal this afternoon?" he would ask. "It's really quick."

In Chicago, other partners and most associates saw Sergi as one of the "nice guys" in a firm filled with sharp elbows. He could get more temperamental partners—the "screamers"—to calm down and compromise. Although he had an annoying tendency of not returning phone calls, he would stop in the hallway to chat about weekend plans or inquire about an ailing spouse. The native New Yorker prided himself on being a compassionate liberal. He enjoyed mentioning his days as a Peace Corps volunteer in Malaysia. The firm as a whole, in fact, leaned toward liberal, Democratic causes. With encouragement from the top partners, some lawyers worked on "pro bono" cases for the poor; others tutored minority schoolchildren. A number of partners were major contributors to Jewish charities.

Aspects of the firm's culture, however, contradicted its

socially progressive self-image. As was the case at too many law firms, some women lawyers and staff members complained of what they saw as unwelcome sexual attention. A former member of the firm's professional staff conceded that in the late 1980s and early 1990s, there were at least several women who said they had been harassed in the office. The firm resolved all of these complaints privately, without litigation. A veteran Chicago lawyer basically sympathetic to Katten Muchin said the firm "always had a reputation for being a little worse than most [on gender relations], but that reputation was that there was a lot of consensual sex, with officers screwing enlisted women, rather than a place where harassment was tolerated." The situation had eased by the early 1990s, according to some. "Let's just say we had a problem with women, and I'm not proud of it, and I think it's over—I hope it is," one former Katten Muchin partner, male, told me.

On the question of race, there was much talk at the firm about the need to hire and promote minorities. Sergi often took the lead on the topic, bringing it up at partner meetings and in informal conversation. All lawyers had to attend "diversity training" seminars. But despite the talk, Katten Muchin didn't retain many of the black lawyers it had hired over the years. Few stayed more than three or four years. In 1993, the 400-attorney firm had only one black partner and six black associates, including Mungin. Small as that number sounds—it works out to 1.8 percent black attorneys—Katten Muchin was only a little bit below average. A *National Law Journal* survey in 1996 found that only 2.4 percent of the lawyers at the 250 largest law firms were black.

The reasons why black lawyers left Katten Muchin—and big law firms in general—varied, of course. Like many others, some blacks found jobs they liked better. Law firm life wasn't for everyone, after all. Talented African-Americans were in demand in business as well as law, and white Katten Muchin partners noted that some of their best-qualified lawyers left for other fields. A few black associates were fired for inferior performance; it was suggested to others that, while they were

competent, they weren't on track for partnership and therefore ought to look elsewhere. The same happened to numerous white attorneys. But proportionally, something went
wrong with black lawyers much more often. No one would say
it out loud, but there was a sense on both sides of the race line
that black lawyers didn't fit in at Katten Muchin. The same
problem existed at most other major law firms, causing blacks
great frustration.

By the 1990s, Edward Shealy, a black administrative super-
visor, had become Katten Muchin's institutional memory on
the experiences of black lawyers. Black associates regularly
confided in him, sharing their anxieties. In a deposition in
the Mungin case, Shealy recalled that in the fall of 1994, litigation partner Frank Grossi asked him about "the reasons why
the firm was having a problem with minority associates."
Shealy said he told Grossi that minorities "had the feeling that
they were being treated differently and pressured to perform
in exceptional matters, and they were having problems with
just all kinds of areas relating to their work."

In an unusually candid summary of the attitude among many
white lawyers toward black associates, one ex–Katten Muchin
partner told me, "Anyone who spends any time in the profession
would know there are lots of minorities, African-Americans especially, who are running around with Harvard and Yale degrees
who are not qualified in any sense. They have been solicited and
tutored and polished up and sent out to the profession and
they're not up to grade, for whatever reason." This is not an unusual opinion among white lawyers at Katten Muchin and other
elite firms, merely one that is rarely articulated.

The same white partner said with certainty that Mungin fit
the pattern: "The word is he wasn't very competent; that's
what I heard from people he worked with." This partner was
at the firm during all of Mungin's tenure but never worked
with him, or even met him. Once Mungin filed his suit, it became conventional wisdom that he didn't work hard, wasn't
diligent. "There were questions about his competence that
should have been explored," another veteran white lawyer
close to Katten Muchin management told me.

In fact, the lawyers in Washington who worked most closely with Mungin never questioned the quality of his work. Katten Muchin never raised the issue at trial. The notion that he was a Harvard affirmative action phony, a spoiled and lazy African-American, was an example of raw stereotyping.

Fearful of offending a powerful hometown law firm, most black alumni of Katten Muchin—not to mention African-Americans still at the firm—hesitated to complain publicly. But the case of Elaine Williams provided a rare window on race relations in Katten Muchin's home office.

A graduate of prestigious Amherst College and the top-rated University of Chicago Law School, Williams worked for another Chicago firm and the city government before she was recruited in 1988 by Sergi. Bright and vivacious, she was soon promoted to income partner. After working for a time in the Corporate Department, she moved to the Finance and Reorganization Department, where she reported to Sergi. But rather than benefiting from her relationship with him, she found that her career stalled. Williams blamed her boss, saying he didn't involve her in client relationships. "Like some of the other African-Americans, I found I was just forgotten, left out, which was very strange because I had been told I was doing so well," Williams told me later.

It is beyond debate that blacks at Katten Muchin, and other major law firms, have experiences unimaginable to whites. Shortly after she joined the firm, a female income partner "ordered me to clean a conference room," Williams recounted in a deposition in the Mungin case. "And when I attempted to introduce myself to her and let her know that I was a new attorney in the office, she said, 'I don't care who you are. I want you to go in there and clean this conference room.' "

Williams refused. " 'You can call the kitchen [or] you can clean it yourself,' " she recalled telling the partner. "And I was very upset about the comment, so I went to talk to the head of my department. . . . And his only response was he laughed and said he wasn't surprised that she confused me with the help."

When she was promoted to income partnership, Williams was entitled to choose a new secretary. But she was told that she had to select from a limited pool. " 'Some of the secretaries at the firm will not work for blacks or women,' " Williams said a woman administrator told her. " 'So when a black attorney, and sometimes the women, need a new secretary, we have to screen very carefully the pool of secretaries that will be made available to them.'

" 'You're telling me that there are secretaries who will not work for blacks or women and they continue to be employed by the firm?' " Williams said she responded. "And she said, 'Yes.' "

Black lawyers were sometimes addressed with the insulting label "you people," Williams recalled. One senior male partner confronted her in front of several secretaries, saying, " 'I don't know why you people think you are entitled to black holidays like Martin Luther King Day. Mail isn't delivered on those days. But mail is delivered on Jewish holidays. I don't think that's fair. Do you?' "

Williams suggested that the partner "get over it," and pointed out that she worked on King Day and the Jewish holidays, whereas the partner, a Jew, stayed away from the office on the Jewish holidays.

She left the firm on a paid medical leave on May 1, 1992—by coincidence, the same day that Mungin started work in Washington. Williams suffered from depression, which she and her psychiatrist attributed partly to her alleged mistreatment at work. Shortly after she filed a complaint against the firm in August 1992 with the Equal Employment Opportunity Commission, Katten Muchin cut off her disability benefits. She then filed suit in federal court in Chicago, charging the firm with race discrimination and retaliation. The suit claimed that Williams had been excluded from client activities and given menial work assignments. The firm systematically judged blacks by tougher standards, the suit further alleged. "If there was a tiny flaw in a document, you can be sure that it would be made into a huge deal that a black had made a mistake," Williams told me. "Whites could make a mistake or two because the assumption was that they were competent, whereas the assumption with a black was that you weren't competent—and any mistake was proof of the stereotype."

The suit also alleged that women at the firm were barraged with "unwelcome sexual remarks, jokes, and suggestions from the male capital partners." On one occasion, the Williams suit asserted, a "white, male, Jewish capital partner walked up to Ms. Williams in the hall and, apropos of nothing whatever, announced that he wanted to 'fuck' her."

Williams (somewhat surprisingly) later approached the same partner to inquire about sex harassment accusations against yet another partner. The only difference between the accused partner and himself, said the lawyer Williams approached, was that "when I ask the girls, they say yes."

The firm and Sergi vehemently denied all of these allegations. Partners felt personally wounded by the charges, because they thought they had gone out of their way to help Williams. The general consensus among the partners was that she was temperamental and mistakenly expected client relationships to be handed to her, rather than having to earn them. Williams pointed out to me that in earlier years, lawyers of Sergi's vintage themselves had been introduced to real estate and banking clients by older colleagues like Michael Zavis.

Sergi and his partners fully expected that Williams's suit would evaporate, but in the meantime, they were indignant that her accusations attracted even a modest amount of attention within the legal community. How could people think that Katten Muchin—*Katten Muchin!*—would discriminate? *The Insider's Guide*, a thick employment reference book popular among law students nationwide, qualified its otherwise positive assessment of Katten Muchin in 1993 by observing that the firm "employs very few minority attorneys. Although the firm has made an effort to recruit more minority law students in recent years, it has had difficulty retaining them. One contact disclosed that 'all five black people who worked there have left recently.' "

This was not the way Katten Muchin, with its aspiration to being a national firm, wanted to be seen by would-be attorneys at Harvard, Yale, and the University of Chicago. Interestingly, among veteran black attorneys in Chicago, Katten Muchin was viewed as "no better or worse than anyone else," according to Victor Henderson, an African-American with the firm of Shefsky & Froelich. "This is a tough business for everybody these days, and blacks face extra problems because they don't look like and don't sound like the white partners," said Henderson, who headed a Chicago organization for minority lawyers. "Clients sometimes don't have faith in black associates. Katten Muchin isn't the only place where that is true."

Mungin learned of the Williams suit through office gossip in the late summer of 1992. But he was careful not to express any reaction in front of colleagues. He didn't know Williams and couldn't judge her credibility. Whatever the merits of her suit, he thought, she had no chance against a big, powerful law firm.

Just one month before Williams left Katten Muchin and Mungin arrived, *Chicago Lawyer* magazine had warned its readers that "employers are facing more employment discrimination charges, and law firms are no exception." The local trade publication quoted Joel Henning, a management consultant, as saying, "Law firms are very vulnerable because they've generally been run with a minimum of management attention to [employment] issues." Law firms "have been lucky, damn lucky," but that luck is running out, Henning added.

George Galland, a Chicago plaintiffs' attorney who had pressed several high-profile cases against law firms, also predicted more suits, but with secretaries or paralegals as the plaintiffs, not attorneys. "[Attorneys] have much more to lose," Galland told *Chicago Lawyer*. "A mid- or high-level attorney who decided to sue in connection with a cutback or firing may never eat lunch in town again."

Elsewhere in the same issue was a more technical article on a major reason for the likely uptick in discrimination suits against employers of all sorts. On November 21, 1991,

President George Bush signed the Civil Rights Act of 1991. After a long legislative battle, and the coinciding Clarence Thomas–Anita Hill affair, Republicans dropped their opposition to the act in hopes of softening their image on the race issue. The act undid several earlier Supreme Court decisions that had made it harder for workers to file discrimination suits. And it went further, creating additional remedies for employees, including the right to seek compensatory and punitive damages, in addition to the traditional remedy of back pay and attorney's fees. Most important, the 1991 act allowed employees to present their cases to juries, rather than judges. Juries are thought to be less punctilious in requiring plaintiffs to satisfy the fine print of complicated statutes. The amendments "will cause a substantial increase in the number of discrimination charges and lawsuits filed against employers," predicted the article's main author, Michael Warner, a partner with the big Chicago firm of Seyfarth, Shaw, Fairweather & Geraldson.

Mungin arrived for his "reintroduction" to the Chicago office on a chilly morning in February 1993, determined to "meet the important players . . . who were going to be directly voting on my partnership chances," as he later testified. He reported first to Sergi's office, where papers and books were spilling off every surface. At least Sergi didn't stand him up this time. They spoke for four or five minutes, the phone ringing almost the entire time. Mungin said he wanted to do more than just Dombroff's insurance-related work. He wanted to participate in projects coming out of the Chicago office and to develop his own practice in Washington.

Sergi didn't object to any of that, in theory. He said he would ask other partners to keep Mungin in mind when they had bankruptcy work on the East Coast. Developing one's own practice is a fine idea, Sergi continued, although they didn't discuss how Mungin might actually accomplish that from an office in Washington, where he was the only lawyer left doing bankruptcy work.

Sergi politely reminded Mungin that he—like Jeff Sherman and Stuart Soberman before him—had been hired specifically to work with Dombroff's insurance group. If the Chicago office could find Mungin other work, "we want to do it," Sergi later testified that he said. But he made no hard promises. Sergi, who had other things to do, then ushered Mungin to the office of Jeff Marwil, an associate specializing in bankruptcy, who was to take Mungin to lunch.

Mungin was miffed. He had come to Chicago to talk to partners who could steer him work, he told Marwil. Mungin realized he sounded rude, but he didn't want to waste another trip to Chicago. Eventually, he recruited partner Mark Thomas to join Marwil and him for lunch at a bar-and-grill. For some reason, perhaps the informal atmosphere or his sense that Sergi wasn't taking his concerns seriously, Mungin for the first time told someone from Chicago that he was worried about working for the Dombroff-Gilmore team. He described how only Dombroff or Gilmore could communicate with clients and how basic his AIG assignments had become.

Thomas said he understood. Over the past several years, he had been asked by Dombroff and Gilmore to do work on the bankruptcies of companies insured by a Dombroff client. A sensible, unpretentious young partner, Thomas hadn't enjoyed working with Gilmore. She treated him as if he were her associate, barring him from contacting the client insurance company. Thomas wasn't alone; others in Chicago didn't like Dombroff and Gilmore on a personal level and resented their jealous attitude toward the insurance practice.

This was, in a sense, reassuring to Mungin. At least it wasn't just in his head: Gilmore really was hard to work for. But in another sense, Thomas's comments couldn't be seen as encouraging. The people to whom Mungin's fortunes were tied were unpopular in the home office—despite Dombroff's revenue flow.

Lunch adjourned and the three lawyers returned to the office. Overcoming his dislike of formal meetings, Sergi had assembled a dozen lawyers in a conference room. Mungin worked his way through the group, smiling and shaking hands. He had never met most of these people and felt very much the outsider. But he intended to show them that he was willing to make an effort, if they were. Sergi signaled for quiet. He introduced Mungin as a visiting colleague, "working for Patty Gilmore, our bankruptcy specialist in Washington."

Mungin leaned over to ask his lunchmate, Marwil, whether Sergi was being serious or sarcastic about Gilmore's bankruptcy prowess.

"He's kidding," Marwil said.

Mungin didn't take any pleasure in the joke.

The rest of the meeting proceeded swiftly and predictably, with promises that Mungin would be kept in mind whenever Katten Muchin clients had bankruptcy matters in Washington or elsewhere on the East Coast. Mungin left for the airport without a single specific assignment, however.

He was sitting in his office back in Washington the next day, wondering whether the trip accomplished anything, when he got a phone call from Mark Thomas. "Forget what I said" about Gilmore, Thomas told him. "I don't want it repeated."

Great, Mungin thought. They knew he was stuck in a bad situation, but they were afraid to do anything about it. They were even afraid to joke about it.

CHAPTER SEVEN

"What Are You Doing with That Nigger Friend?"

1975–1977

Larry Mungin arrived at Harvard in the fall of 1975, eager to make good on his break from Woodside. He was mature enough to know that most white students—middle class or wealthier, bred in suburbs, small towns, or fancy urban enclaves—wouldn't be sure what to make of a black from the inner city. But he was willing to persuade them that he wasn't what they imagined. He was the star of Bryant High School. He was the ace debater, the senior class president, the French-language prize winner. He worked hard and wanted the same things they wanted. He had left behind the undisciplined and the unruly, the drug dealers and the down-and-outers. He was there to get the magical Harvard education that would open up the white world.

Mungin was the first of his four-man freshman rooming group to arrive. He hadn't slept much the night before because he was so excited. Here he was in Harvard Yard, the hub of an academic kingdom whose preeminence and quiet self-confidence were reflected by magnificent Widener Library, fronted by its grand pile of stairs and pillars. Widener's neighbors, sturdy red-brick Georgian-style buildings, bespoke

Harvard's roots as a colonial-era seminary. Within the Yard's black wrought-iron gates, the noise and bustle of Cambridge seemed distant. Students tossed Frisbees on the well-kept lawns. Tweedy professors strolled in pairs. To Mungin, it seemed like a dream.

He was assigned to live in Wigglesworth Hall—what a name! His roommates, all relatively well-to-do, had gone to famous prep schools. Mungin might have been a little intimidated, but this was Harvard, he thought. It would be "All for one, one for all!" These guys were going to be his *connections*.

A few weeks later, Mungin was recalling the excitement of move-in day with Fred Haber, his bookish roommate from Manhattan. They were joking about parents and their worries. Mungin recalled how unhappy his mother had been about his moving "so far away" to Cambridge.

Fred laughed about his own mother's discovery on that first day that her son had a black roommate. As Fred recalled the conversation years later, he reported to his roommate that Mrs. Haber first noted that Larry had decorated his bedroom with photographs of his favorite old-time movie performers. A short time later, she was "surprised" to meet Larry for the first time, because she didn't expect "a black kid from New York" to be a fan of 1940s Hollywood. "Her jaw dropped," Fred remembered.

Larry recalled a slightly different conversation with Fred, one without reference to movie stars. In Larry's version, Fred simply conveyed his mother's reaction to the news of Larry's race by saying, with alarm, "Don't tell me, you have a black roommate!"

At the least, Mrs. Haber had revealed some ordinary middle-class stereotyping, the sort of thing normally kept under wraps in polite white society. It had been exposed by the tumult of her son's arrival at Harvard. By laughing at it in that early freshman-year chat with Larry, Fred doubtless meant to show scorn for his mother's reaction.

Caught off guard, Mungin laughed, too. But it was a forced laugh. He didn't really see what was so funny about Fred's story. Imagine: The woman was dismayed over her son's having a black roommate. Ha, ha, ha!

Mungin began shifting gradually to a more wary attitude toward his roommates. It wasn't that they excluded him or weren't friendly. It was more that he realized that, because of their close quarters, they inevitably would be able to learn a lot about him, and he about them—more than he might want to know. He didn't want to learn about his roommates' racial faux pas, or those of their parents. Why was it his job to absolve Mrs. Haber by chortling along with her son?

It is said that Harvard students aren't more intelligent than those at other top schools, just more ambitious. Harvard has more money, more distinguished professors, more exotic courses, more Rhodes Scholars—more of almost everything. And Harvard students tend to harbor the illusion that they can do just about anything.

Mungin wanted to be treated like any other promising Harvard student. But in little ways, some having nothing to do with race, he felt out of place. In the well-stocked newspaper and periodical room in Widener Library, he looked fruitlessly for his favorite New York paper, the *Daily News*, a blue-collar tabloid specializing in crime, gossip, and sports. A librarian politely informed him that Harvard did *not* subscribe to tabloids. Mungin wasn't crushed, but he began to realize that escaping from home had its costs. He missed collard greens, which his mother had prepared. One day, he heated some on a hot plate in the Wigglesworth room, but his roommates complained about the pungent aroma. He didn't do it again. He still wore bell-bottom pants and polyester shirts, which were fine in Woodside but stood out amid the khaki slacks and button-down Oxfords in Cambridge. He couldn't afford to throw away usable clothes.

Mungin didn't react to not fitting in by rebelling or pitying himself. He felt intensely proud of having been invited to Harvard. The university represented quality and achievement, and he saw himself as "a quality person." He had been accepted by an exclusive society, even if he didn't feel all that comfortable within it. Both the pride of the insider and the discomfort of the outsider would stay with him.

As in grammar and high school, Mungin's friends in college and law school were white. He didn't avoid blacks as individuals. But he steered away from black campus groups, and he avoided the dormitories that were unofficially known as black havens. In the Freshman Union, he kept his distance from the "soul tables."

A huge dining hall with a three-story vaulted ceiling, the Union was both cafeteria and social center for the freshman class, a place where students from different dormitories were supposed to mix and meet. At almost all times, however, one or more of the Union's long wooden tables were occupied exclusively by black students. No one suggested, let alone mandated, that the blacks segregate themselves. It was a phenomenon that began early in the first semester, year in and year out, and was hardly unique to Harvard. It reflected blacks' desire to establish an identity and to overcome insecurity in what for many of them was a strange new environment. It also reflected whites' timidity about approaching blacks outside of lecture halls or gymnasiums. There was much whispering about the soul tables, but no serious effort to pierce the invisible barrier surrounding them.

Some black students didn't sit at the soul tables, of course, and Mungin was one of them. He couldn't understand the point of coming all the way to Harvard, the springboard into the mainstream, only to separate himself from the mainstream. For the same reason, he didn't sign up with campus organizations based on race. He didn't dislike the blacks who joined these groups and sat together for meals. He just thought he knew better than they did what was good for Larry Mungin.

On the other hand, he never overcame his uneasiness within the majority white student culture. He felt nervous and exposed, for example, on the day that the instructor of his freshman expository writing class read aloud an essay he had written, entitled, "Nana," which was what he and his siblings called their grandmother, Louise Dicks. The unsentimental account told of his grandmother's migration from South Carolina to Harlem and the hard times that followed. "She found a job in a handbag factory where she had to work all kinds of hours at very low pay for almost 40 years," 18-year-old Mungin wrote. "She was poor, black, single, a mother, and she didn't have more than a sixth-grade education." After her daughter had married and started her own family, Nana married a truck driver known as Daddy-o. He "frightened me because he used to sleep with his eyes open," Mungin wrote, "and later on in his life when he started to drink heavily, he would get drunk and yell with his terrifying husky voice." Despite Daddy-o's raging, Nana cared for him until he died in 1969, leaving her alone again.

"When I told her that I was going away to college in Cambridge," the essay continued, "she asked me why I had to go so far away, but she said that if that was what I wanted, then I should go. She didn't know where or what Harvard was, but she asked me to write to her sometime."

The vitality and honesty of the piece elicited praise from the instructor. But Mungin felt troubled. He wondered if he had told too much—about Nana's ignorance, for example, or, in another passage, about her ritualized shouts of grief at Daddy-o's funeral. Such displays were normal in Nana's Baptist church, but probably alien to the average Harvard student. Had he betrayed her, or himself? Had he put himself back on the black kids' lunch line at Horace Greeley Junior High?

His two closest friends freshman year were Steve Toope, of Montreal, and John Boris, of Meriden, Connecticut. Toope was active in the arts and went on to become the dean of the law school at prestigious McGill University in Montreal. Boris was a language maven like Mungin, and joined the U.S. Foreign Service, serving in embassies around the world. Serious and intellectual, they won his trust and he opened up to them, to a degree. Mungin invited them to visit his family's apartment in Woodside and showed them the neighborhood. Toope warmly recalled the visit in a letter: "We sat up very late one night talking about all sorts of things—ourselves, our plans, our ideals, our futures. What did we really know?"

One evening during freshman year, Toope, Boris, and Mungin dropped by Toope's room after taking in a movie. They found Toope's roommate there, along with a visiting friend from Yale. The guest from New Haven seemed strangely uneasy over Mungin's presence. When Mungin excused himself to use the bathroom, the Yalie, now clearly agitated, got up to leave. Mungin soon discovered why. On the bathroom mirror, there was a message written in toothpaste. It said: "Hey, Steve, what are you doing with that nigger friend?"

Stunned, Mungin came back out into the living room. He wanted to say something, but couldn't. Toope, confused, went to look in the bathroom. He came back out, obviously upset, and began apologizing, while the roommate played dumb. There were more apologies, and then there didn't seem to be anything more to say, so Mungin left.

Mungin and his friends didn't dwell on the incident while they were at Harvard. Mungin couldn't believe something like that could happen at the great school. How often did whites refer to him as a "nigger" behind his back? What precisely did they mean by it—that he was dumb, uncivilized? Mungin never saw the Yalie again, and he tried to put the whole thing out of his mind. Years later, Toope, by then a prominent legal academic, brought up the toothpaste occurrence during a telephone conversation. "I don't know how you handled that so well," he marveled.

"Well, what else was I going to do?" Mungin asked. "What choice did I have?"

The summer after his freshman year, Mungin accepted an invitation to visit a female classmate who lived on the New Jersey shore. Mungin asked whether his being black would cause a problem.

No, of course not, the young woman said. Her parents were liberals.

At first, the visit appeared to go smoothly enough. For a couple of days, the two students wandered the boardwalk and the beach, killing time and eating ice cream cones. Their friendship was warm but platonic.

On the morning of the third day, however, Mungin's friend came to him, looking devastated. He had to leave, she said. Her father didn't want them walking around together. The suddenly unwanted houseguest didn't need anyone to explain that this was about race. The young woman's parents feared that people would think their daughter had a black boyfriend.

That night, back in Queens, Helen Mungin prodded her son into recounting the story. Enraged, she wanted to call up the family and cuss them out. Larry talked her out of it. "Just forget it," he said.

Furious, she turned on *him*. "Why did you go down there anyway, looking for trouble? You go to Harvard. You're educated. What did you expect?"

He didn't have a good answer. Maybe he expected that after proving that he wasn't one of *those* blacks from the ghetto, he would be treated with some respect. But he swallowed that bitter thought and said nothing. Back at school in September, the young woman never mentioned the visit. They rarely seemed to cross paths anymore.

Although Mungin didn't become close to his freshman roommates, he did befriend a blond Californian named Scott Karlan, who lived on the ground floor of Wigglesworth. The son of a wealthy Beverly Hills doctor, Karlan was a straight-A pre-med student who nevertheless was enough out-of-step with the crowd for Mungin to feel a kinship with him. Karlan flagrantly disdained New England and its formality. He wore loud Hawaiian shirts, baggy shorts, and flip-flops, as much as the Cambridge weather allowed. Uninterested in competing for honors or prizes, he wanted to get through Harvard as fast as possible and get back to southern California. They shared lunch frequently and agreed to room together for their sophomore year.

As much as he enjoyed Karlan's company, rooming with him exacerbated a feeling Mungin had that he was falling behind, even though it was only his second year. He hadn't traveled to Europe and Mexico the way Scott had. Karlan got As in his tough science and math classes and was on track for medical school. Mungin took a less-demanding group of courses in the Government and Anthropology departments but had managed only Bs. He didn't know what to major in, or where he was heading. Academic advisers told him that many students who were standouts in high school had the same experience at Harvard. It was a school filled with top achievers, but everyone couldn't stay at the top.

Mungin knew one thing: He couldn't graduate from Harvard with Bs and nothing else to show for the time. He had to distinguish himself. But how could he do it, going up against the likes of Scott Karlan? He had tried out for crew, on the theory that he was the right shape for the sport: tall, lean, and strong. But 5:30 a.m. practice on the misty Charles River hadn't unlocked a passion for rowing, and Mungin quit.

His other extracurricular activity was working, which kept his student loans at a manageable level and gave him some pocket change. The school had at first assigned him to swab toilets and sweep floors in student dorms. But Mungin hated doing what he considered poor people's work. Even though plenty of white kids on scholarship pushed mops, Mungin insisted on finding something else. He landed a cushy sit-down job, operating the slide projector for art history lectures. But that still didn't put him in Scott Karlan's league.

Then a plan presented itself. While working at a summer office job after his sophomore year, Mungin heard some colleagues talking about someone who had joined the Navy and become a code breaker. It was top secret, and the Navy would teach you a foreign language.

There it was: clear as the peal of a ship's bell. Mungin decided to become a Navy cryptographer. *There* was something the Scott Karlans couldn't say they had done. Harvard didn't have any objection to his taking time off, as long as he promised to come back and get his degree. Without telling anyone in his family, he enlisted. After taking some aptitude tests, he was told he could choose any assignment he wanted. But why not finish college first, a recruiter suggested, and come in as an officer candidate?

Mungin brushed off the idea. He wasn't going into the Navy as a *career*. Once he had his college degree, he could do better than that, he thought. Right now, he was restless and dissatisfied with being an also-ran at Harvard. The Navy was a way to give him back the sheen he had at Bryant High. He'd go in as an enlisted man. He picked Russian as his language, over Chinese or Arabic, and soon was off to the Great Lakes Naval Training Center near Chicago.

Helen Mungin was so shocked and angry when Larry told her of his Navy plans that she began weeping in frustration, and then hit him soundly on the shoulders and head. She thought he was quitting Harvard for good. When she calmed down and heard him out, she still didn't approve. Helen was hurt that he hadn't consulted her. He couldn't tell her that part of the reason he wanted to go away was that he had grown tired of coming home to her un-air-conditioned apartment on school breaks. He had less and less to talk about with his mother, for whom Harvard was so foreign as to be incomprehensible. He still had a few old friends in Woodside, but he had less and less in common with them also. The Navy seemed to solve a whole collection of problems.

The strategy couldn't have worked better. He received favorable treatment in boot camp from commanders impressed by his background and skills. Unlike at Harvard, where he didn't stand out academically, in the Navy Mungin was once again a star. He even won the Navy League Award as the top seaman in his basic training group of 300, an accomplishment that gave his worried mother some relief. Deborah, who had thought that maybe, for once, her show-off brother had slipped at college, was exasperated at his turning the Navy into a new venue for accomplishment. She had worked at boring clerk's jobs since graduating from high school.

The family traveled to Chicago for Mungin's basic training

graduation ceremony, where he received several prizes. It was like the glory days of his late teens all over again. When the applause had faded, and the audience was beginning to leave, Deborah turned to her mother and asked in a jealous voice, "Does he *always* win?"

CHAPTER EIGHT

"A Cocky Guy in for a Fall"

THE EARLY 1980s

Professor Alan Dershowitz, Harvard's celebrity criminal defense lawyer and author, teased students about their overdeveloped competitive urges. Mungin, who took a class from Dershowitz, enjoyed his irreverence and remembered one of his jokes:

Two men are camping in a tent. They realize a huge bear is circling hungrily outside. One man begins to lace up his running shoes.

"Don't be silly," the other man says. "You can't outrun a bear."

"I don't have to outrun the bear," came the reply. "I just have to outrun you."

When he returned to finish college and then went on to law school, Mungin ratcheted down his assumption about achievement. He decided that he didn't have to outrun all of his classmates, just half of them.

The Larry Mungin who came back to Cambridge for his junior year in September 1981 was a strikingly different person from the gawky teenager who heated collard greens in his Wigglesworth room. He had taken up weight-lifting during his four years in the Navy and added 30 pounds of muscle to what had been a slender 165-pound physique. He wore tightly fitting T-shirts, including one popular in Naval intelligence that bore the motto IN GOD WE TRUST. ALL OTHERS WE MONITOR.

Mungin no longer felt driven to fit in at Harvard. He was now more mature than his classmates. In the Navy, he had helped task forces carrying thousands of sailors keep track of potential enemies. He had additional money from the GI Bill to supplement his scholarships, making him feel like less of a charity case. To his new neighbors in Lowell House, one of the college's "Oxbridge"-style upper-class dormitories, he was aloof and a little mysterious. He had a chance to start over at Harvard as a new man.

On those occasions when he sat serenely in the high-ceilinged Lowell House dining hall, he might entertain a small group of listeners with elliptical talk about monitoring Russian transmissions in the Persian Gulf during the Iranian hostage crisis. Mungin had worked with other intelligence personnel in a special top-secret compartment, deciphering the rattle of Russian military conversation. He had seen extraordinary sights: the luxuriant jungles of Sri Lanka, the glittery wealth of Hong Kong, the eerie orderliness of Singapore. He had stayed a night at the Ritz Hotel in Paris and had strolled the streets of London. Scott Karlan had graduated by the time Mungin returned, but other Scott Karlan types at Harvard no longer had anything on Larry Mungin when it came to worldly adventure.

This was the Larry Mungin I met in 1982, when I, too, was a Harvard undergraduate and lived in Lowell House. He was one of only a few African-Americans in the large dormitory, and that, combined with his military experience and imposing physical presence, set him apart. I knew him well enough only to nod hello, but in the spring of 1983, Mungin sought me out because he had discovered that we had a common interest: gaining admission to Harvard Law School.

He struck me as earnest, proud, and a bit obsessed; he had applied to no fewer than 17 law schools.

He had decided on a law career while in the Navy. He wasn't a math-and-science person, so medical school was out of the question. But he wanted a secure, prestigious profession, in which the path to advancement was well marked. In the early 1980s, law still appeared to offer those qualities. Graduate respectably from a top law school, join an established firm, and follow the rules. Success seemed assured.

One graduate-student couple who lived in Lowell House suggested to Mungin that he might want to try something "more creative than law." Mungin was amused. As he saw it, he didn't have the luxury of being "creative" the way middle-class whites did. He had to lock in a career that would guarantee that he wouldn't ever slide back toward poverty. It might be nice to try being a writer; his essays always won praise. But he couldn't afford the risk of failure.

When it turned out that Mungin and I got the nod from Harvard Law School, our dining hall conversations led to an almost offhand agreement to split a dorm room. Mungin explained later that he was impressed that I was the editor of the college newspaper and therefore "a quality person," as he was. For my part, I thought it would be a good idea to have a roommate who was quiet and serious. The small guilty thrill I got from crossing the race line was a bonus.

For nine months, beginning in September 1983, we shared a three-room suite in Hastings Hall, a dignified old brownstone building on the law school grounds. I immediately became something of a race burden to Mungin. Members of the Black Law Students Association approached him to ask, first, why he had failed to join the association, and, second, why he was rooming with a white. What was he trying to prove?

As he recounted the conversation to me, Mungin politely told his inquisitors that it wasn't any of their business whom he lived with or which organizations he joined. He added that they shouldn't assume that he thought the way they did just because his skin was dark.

"I don't have to measure up to the expectations of comfort-able kids from the suburbs, who don't have the loans that I have," Mungin said to me. He thought they wasted a lot of time feeling sorry for themselves and haranguing the law school dean over issues he considered marginal, like how many minority professors had gotten tenure. This was law school, after all, a place to get a credential, not play militant. In any event, he said, "I define what it means to be black. What I do is, by definition, black."

His defiance impressed me. It was also a relief. Mungin never tried to make me feel guilty with talk of "systemic racism." It wasn't that we avoided the topic of race. He chided me for subscribing to *The New Republic*, a centrist political opinion magazine that at the time had a neurotic fixation on the foibles of the Rev. Jesse Jackson. We also surveyed the building debate over affirmative action, fueled by the Reagan administration's efforts to roll back preferences based on race. He scorned the notion that the U.S. would operate as a "color-blind" society were it not for such programs. But he didn't deny that preferences for blacks in admissions and hiring in some cases hurt individual whites. That was the cost of re-pairing a history of racism, he said. And he bluntly acknowl-edged his own stake in the debate. In gaining admission to Harvard Law School, he said later, "I was definitely affirma-tive action, and they liked the Navy." His college transcript—dominated by Bs and B+s, with a smattering of As, and a solid but unremarkable LSAT score of 39 (out of a possible 49)—wouldn't have done the trick on its own. He felt his journey from Woodside deserved some recognition. "I don't think I was the dumbest person at Harvard Law School," he added.

He got no argument from me on his being a suitable candi-date for Harvard Law. For one thing, I was the beneficiary of an older form of affirmative action, that for well-connected white boys. In the spring of 1983, I had languished on the law school's "waiting list," neither accepted nor rejected. I made plans to attend Columbia. When I casually mentioned this situation to a campus newspaper source of mine, who hap-pened to be an official at the college, he promptly contacted the law school admissions director, an old friend of his. A week later, I received word that Harvard Law School would have me after all. The admissions game is not a pristine art, let alone a science.

My thinking on affirmative action for blacks was pragmatic. As a society, if we wanted to achieve more thoroughgoing integration, we needed to give qualified blacks an extra nudge into professions from which they had been excluded. In the early 1980s, only about one out of 100 attorneys at the nation's 250 largest law firms was black. Mungin intended to become a partner at a corporate law firm and make a lot of money. I believed that he would reach his goal, and his achievement would provide a model for others like him. Mungin, interestingly, didn't invoke such justifications. He said he deserved to be there for his own sake. "Once you have been poor, you never want to go back," he told me. Other blacks would have to find their own paths.

He could be jarring on the subject of individual responsibility. Once, when we were walking along Massachusetts Avenue toward Harvard Square, we passed a group of rambunctious black teenagers, shouting in street talk, seemingly oblivious to the white pedestrians who were anxiously stepping out of their way.

Mungin scowled at the kids. "Maybe if they would go to school and spend their time studying, they would make something of themselves," he said sharply.

"Nice guy," I responded.

"Well, they're just confirming every stereotype," he snapped. Mungin was always thinking about showing whites that they were wrong to assume that blacks tended to be disruptive or troublesome. He didn't relish the task; in fact, he grew to resent it more and more.

Mungin never complained in law school about his brushes with racial embarrassment or hostility. We killed a lot of time comparing our respective upbringings—a favorite topic of his. But I heard only the heroic, uplifting side of the story. Not until after he joined Katten Muchin & Zavis would I hear about the all-black lunch line, the "nigger friend" message written in toothpaste, and the strange summer visit to Atlantic City. In law school, Mungin kept those experiences entirely to himself. "To be honest," he said later, "I bottled it up and moved on."

Knowing little about military life, I questioned him about the Navy. He had remained in the Naval Reserves while in law school and read Russian-language newspapers to keep his skills sharp. He described the service as mostly a benign floating bureaucracy, with intense periods of action, as when he served in the Persian Gulf. As I later learned, though, he'd had to navigate with great care to avoid racial confrontations while on active duty.

There were white seamen on one submarine who simply wouldn't talk to blacks. Mungin, an elite specialist who served for relatively short periods of time on different warships, ignored the bigots and minded his own business. Why provoke ignorant kids?

Mungin was seen as a loner, recalled Carson Wiley, a white fellow intelligence specialist who served with him on the frigate USS *Kirk*. "But he didn't flaunt Harvard. He didn't even mention it for a couple of months. I guess I wasn't surprised when he finally did tell me. You could tell there was something special about the guy, the way he talked and carried himself. It made sense that he had come from Harvard. . . . The thing that didn't make sense was why was he an enlisted man, not an officer." Wiley, who attended a junior college in Maryland, wrote home to his parents, "This guy, Larry Mungin, keep an eye out for his name in the papers, or in politics. He's going to make a difference some day."

Carson Wiley was grateful when Mungin tried to help him improve his vocabulary and passed along some of his Norman Vincent Peale inspirational tracts. Others in the Navy took a dimmer view of the unusually motivated black seaman. While stationed in Japan, Mungin had a superior, a second-class petty officer, who seemed incessantly irritated by him, without there being any obvious reason. This bothered Mungin, because the non-commissioned officer, or non-com, was otherwise smart and competent. Mungin made quiet inquiries as to what was going on. He heard back that the non-com indeed had a gripe. "It's not that he's a nigger," he explained to a peer, out of Mungin's presence. "It's that he's an arrogant nigger."

The Navy at that time was sponsoring racial-tolerance seminars and demanding an end to old ways. The incident in Japan was a lesson to Mungin that no matter what an institution's leaders might promise, race could jump out and hit him in the face at any time. It had happened at Harvard; why not in the Navy? In the end, he didn't confront the non-com or bring the situation to anyone else's attention. No point in that. Mungin wouldn't get anything from the effort, except possibly a demerit.

At times, Mungin insulated himself with sheer lack of awareness. While he was training at the Defense Language Institute in Monterey, his mother and Kenneth came to visit, and the three of them took a driving excursion to Lake Tahoe and Reno. One evening, they pulled into a motel parking lot, looking for a room. Larry went in to inquire.

"Sorry, no vacancy," he was told.

He came back out, confused because a neon VACANCY sign was blinking in the desert dusk. To the consternation of both her sons, Helen stormed out of the rental car and into the office. As Kenneth later recalled it: "A minute later, she came back out, mad, real mad. She had asked for a room, and the clerk had said, 'Sure, we have a room.' The clerk thought she was white. My mother had very light skin. Well, she told him we didn't want that damn room, and she came back out and told us, 'Those sons of guns didn't want us because we're black. Let's go!'"

Helen's glower signaled that she didn't want to discuss the encounter, and it was never mentioned again within the family.

On November 19, 1978, Mungin's 21st birthday, he was stationed in San Angelo, Texas, for training. He was surprised when he didn't receive a card or gift from his mother to mark the day. Helen was big on birthdays, and the year before, she had sent a homemade cake, timing it so it arrived exactly on the 19th. But she had been depressed lately, Mungin knew from visits home. Maybe the cake would come the following week.

The next day, the company commander called Mungin to his office. "Your mother died yesterday," he was told.

Mungin was unprepared for the news, but not surprised by it. The alcohol, the low moods—these were the warnings. Had Helen run out of purpose when her older son left home and became someone increasingly hard for her to understand? The hospital listed the cause of death as a heart attack. Larry wondered whether it wouldn't have been more accurate to ascribe it to terminal frustration. Helen Mungin was only 42 years old.

In the self-deprecating, semi-autobiographical novel Larry wrote some years later, his alter ego reflected on his mother: "Ma was in many ways the perfect mom for a Harvard graduate, a double-Harvard graduate, that is. Her complexion was very light, almost too light to qualify as high yellow." The memoir brought to the surface Larry's ambivalence about Helen. She was beautiful, determined, and proud, but not trained to be anything more than a clerical secretary. Her pride led to disappointment and drink. Did she waste her life? Or was it a triumph, in that she raised three good children who survived the perils of the inner city? "There is more to life than being an effective breeder," the memoir noted. Still, and above all, Helen provided the inspiration that shaped Larry's dreams. "She was unique," the memoir said. "I am heir to this uniqueness. Her uniqueness was born out of love and death and racism and hope."

After Helen's funeral, the Mungin family loaded itself into a roomy black limousine. Just as the car was pulling away, the rear curbside door flew open—and in jumped Junior Mungin.

"Whew!" he declared. "I almost missed the funeral. I had to

sit all the way in the back!" Junior had come by bus from South Carolina.

Lucky you sat in the back, Larry thought, looking away from his father. You wouldn't have been welcome in the front pew.

At the reception, Junior, lean and dapper, was the life of the party—telling stories, drinking, and acting perfectly at home. When the day was over, he got back on the bus for South Carolina, leaving Kenneth, then 15 years old, without a parent to look after him. Deborah had to step in to take care of her younger brother. When Larry arrived back at his post in San Angelo, he found a letter from his mother, perhaps the last she ever wrote. "Dear Dwayne," it said, "Happy 21st Birthday. I hope you have a wonderful life. Love, Mom."

Harvard Law School can be a daunting place. Mungin was undaunted.

The sheer volume of assigned work approaches the absurd: thousands of pages of cases and articles to read, mock-briefs to write, classroom questioning to prepare for. Many students approach the task page by page, book by book, dutifully slogging through the material in the fashion that got them the grades and test scores needed to gain admission in the first place. While a certain amount of slogging is mandatory, some students discover early on that the fundamental purpose of law school isn't to absorb entire bodies of substantive law, but to learn the trade's strange vocabulary and way of thinking. Mungin made this discovery and suffered less as a result.

"Thinking like a lawyer" means being able to drain any proposition of emotion and values, and construct arguments for and against it. A talented attorney, it is taught at Harvard, can take either side of a dispute; it all depends on circumstance and who is paying the bill. Mungin figured out the underlying purpose of law school and didn't panic as the assignments in Torts, Contracts, and Property piled up. Answers on exams didn't have to include every conceivable point, just enough to show the professor that the student could manipulate the material in lawyerly fashion: weighing competing interests, balancing factors, underscoring tensions between judicial precedent and wise public policy. "You just have to know how to play the game," Mungin told me.

Some Harvard professors and deans preach about dedicating oneself to the poor, minorities, battered wives, and so forth. But the true purpose of the school manifests itself in a massive recruiting drive each fall, entirely dominated by the powerful law firms that represent the rich and the well entrenched. Most students find the generous starting salaries offered by the firms too sweet to turn down, especially when they have loans to repay. The money speaks. "This is the real world," it says. For many of those graduating in the mid- and late 1980s, however, a shock lay ahead. Only after working for four or five years would these success-crazed attorneys learn that a Harvard degree and honest labor no longer guaranteed partnership at the better-known firms. The profession had become a business, and business-getting was now the only way to assure partnership.

Mungin did not fall in love with the law. He liked the idea of being a *Harvard lawyer*, which retained some panache, even as the profession changed. By Harvard standards, his initial goal was relatively modest: a job with a solid, not necessarily dazzling, law firm that would pay well, not be all-consuming, and lead to a secure partnership. In fact, thriving in the still nearly all-white law firm world wouldn't be easy for Mungin, as it wasn't for many other blacks. But he didn't worry much along those lines while we were in Cambridge. By talking to upperclassmen, he learned that grades in the B range, together with an impressive résumé, were enough to get the sort of job he wanted. "I had a strategy," he told me later. "Keep a low profile, do what was necessary to get the good job." He thought the late-night library rats were wasting a lot of time, trying to make the top 5 percent of the class.

Mungin drew a lesson from the Dershowitz bear joke. He outran half of the class, graduating roughly in the middle. He skipped extracurricular activities, didn't do research for a professor, or help poor people fight their landlords. Instead, he filled his plentiful spare time by reading and working out. His literary tastes ran from *People* magazine to Viginia

Woolf. A connoisseur since youth of trivia about movie stars and athletes, he jokingly kept me up to date on the doings of Michael Jackson, Jack Nicholson, and Magic Johnson. Every evening, seven nights a week, he put himself through an elaborate 90-minute regimen of weight-lifting and other exercises. It cleared his mind, he said, adding without embarrassment that he liked to look good.

He occasionally dated a woman who had been a friend from college. Lizzie was attractive, smart, and quirky, the daughter of a prominent family of California lawyers. She was also white, a fact on which Mungin never commented. In truth, he almost never said anything at all about his intimate relationships, if there were any others. Mungin later surprised me by calling Lizzie, from whom he had drifted apart, the "one true love of my life." He said on several occasions that her family had treated him with respect and courtesy when he met them.

Having been accepted by Harvard College, Mungin didn't feel he needed to prove himself at law school the way he had by winning his many honors in high school, or by joining the Navy during college. He saw law school as something of a resting place, where he could build reserves for the challenges that lay ahead. He didn't worry about an honorific judicial clerkship or a job with one of the ritziest Wall Street firms. In fact, while New York remained the undisputed headquarters of corporate law, Mungin saw the city as too expensive and the Wall Street firms as places where associates toiled with only minuscule hope of partnership.

After his second year of law school, he went to Houston for the summer to work with Porter & Clements, a new and highly regarded firm eager to hire Harvard graduates. Mungin, by then well traveled, was curious about the South. He chose Houston because it was a regional business capital and was close to beaches on the Gulf of Mexico. The corporate legal community there was sophisticated but relatively small. Harvard lawyers could make a mark. The summer experience was pleasant, and without seriously considering any other possibilities, Mungin accepted the firm's offer of full-time employment. "I saw Houston as a new horizon, a challenge," he explained.

Porter & Clements associate Bruce Shortt, a fellow Harvard Law alumnus, had helped recruit Mungin and continued to look out for him once he arrived in south Texas. "He was very articulate, with a striking resonant voice," Shortt recalled. "He has the sort of personality, intelligence, and ability to present himself well that you're looking for. The Navy was very impressive; his language studies caught my attention. He presented a complete package that I thought was pretty interesting." Less than a year after Mungin arrived, Shortt was lured to a new job with the Houston office of Weil, Gotshal & Manges, a 500-lawyer firm based in New York and well known for its bankruptcy practice. Shortt told Mungin that if he wanted to come along, an offer could be arranged. Mungin, who had developed an interest in bankruptcy law, would get a $20,000-a-year salary increase to $65,000, and a big step up in status. He accepted. The Harvard degrees were paying off.

Bankruptcy law was booming in Texas as a result of the early-1980s oil industry crash and the first rumblings of coming disaster in savings and loans and real estate. It seemed natural for Mungin to make bankruptcy his specialty. Traditionally viewed as an ethically suspect backwater associated with Jewish lawyers who were locked out of other specialties, bankruptcy law was becoming an entirely respectable practice area in the late 1980s. That was especially true at Weil Gotshal, which, not coincidentally, had begun 60 years earlier as a Jewish firm.

Mungin enjoyed the aura of a sophisticated New York firm without having to live in New York. Unlike the sweatshop atmosphere for which New York law firms were famous, Houston's less frenzied culture dictated saner work days and a friendlier office environment. The cases for which he did research and drafted memos were some of the biggest in the country, including the Texaco and Eastern Airlines bankruptcies. Weil Gotshal moved lawyers back and forth freely between New York and Houston, depending on where they were

needed. But these trips of a week or two to New York were anything but a hardship for Mungin. He didn't have a family to
worry about, and his only daily personal commitment was
spending time each evening in the gym.

When Weil Gotshal asked him to come north to help with an
overload of research and document-drafting, Mungin stayed
in first-class hotels on Central Park South, not far from the
firm's offices in the General Motors Building. At lunch time,
he sometimes strolled along Fifth Avenue, dressed in an im-
ported gray suit, fulfilling the dream of the bony teenager
who took the subway in from Queens to work a cash register
at Alexander's. It was a shame that his mother didn't live to
see that all her worrying and prodding had paid off. Her son
had scaled the walls of poverty and race. He was on the other
side now.

Outwardly, Mungin's life appeared to be clicking along
nicely. He had a high-paying job in a city with a relatively low
cost of living. His colleagues at Weil Gotshal couldn't have
been more friendly. Many of the white lawyers went out of
their way to demonstrate their acceptance of minorities. But
as comfortable as he was made to feel, Mungin found himself
less than enthusiastic about trying to move up the ladder at
Weil Gotshal. He didn't gobble up assignments with the insa-
tiable appetite expected of associates competing to make
partner. This was the time to ignite the booster rockets if he
wanted to distinguish himself. He had conserved energy in
law school for this very effort. But the rockets never fired.
Oddly, given how driven he had been earlier in his life,
Mungin glided, as if on auto-pilot. Perhaps he had permanently burned off some of the adrenaline that fueled his ascent to Harvard.

He justified his performance by telling himself that the
odds of making partner at Weil Gotshal were extremely long.
The firm was attracting the most ambitious bankruptcy jocks
in the country, and it was common knowledge that to stay on
track for partnership, an associate had to work at a six-and-a-
half-days-a-week New York pace. Mungin decided he simply

didn't want to work at that frantic rate. He was grateful for the top-quality training he received from Weil Gotshal, but he didn't intend to sacrifice his body to a firm that in all likelihood wouldn't make him a partner in the end anyway. By effectively taking himself out of the running, he never tested his chances.

Some of his seniors at Weil Gotshal noticed that Mungin wasn't pushing himself. He also had one small blemish on his record: failing one part of the Texas bar examination the first time he took it in the summer of 1986. It had been a difficult season. His grandmother died that summer, causing Mungin great pain and distraction. He had to organize her funeral and get her affairs in order. He simply didn't study as much as he should have, especially given that Texas has some idiosyncratic laws in such areas as the regulation of oil and gas production. Mungin wasn't alone; he knew at least a couple of white associates in Houston who had attended top northern schools but failed part or all of the exam. And when he took the test again six months later, he passed easily. Neither Porter & Clements nor Weil Gotshal ever made an issue out of the embarrassing episode.

In his third year at Weil Gotshal, Mungin received a performance review embedded with an important message. As he recalled it, the review stated, "We are happy with your work. You are fully meeting expectations." But then it continued, "It looks like you are coasting."

That kind of tepid comment from a big law firm is a polite way of saying that an associate ought to start thinking about a new job. Mungin didn't even consider objecting. "They were right," he told me later. "I was coasting." Rather than try to change the firm's perception, Mungin decided it was time to leave Houston.

He had noted other signals that his future wasn't in south Texas. As other young lawyers got married and shopped for houses in the suburbs, he remained single and continued to rent a small condo. "I wasn't ready to settle down; I wasn't a Texas person," he said later. For the first time in his life, he felt adrift, uncertain of what his mission was. He had in many ways stripped himself of personal attachments. He grew up in the projects, but never wanted to go back. Harvard had allowed him to escape, but he hadn't ever felt he fully belonged in Cambridge. Now, he was in a city that still seemed strange after nearly four years' time. He liked barbecue and the Gulf Coast, but that wasn't enough to make a life.

He had left his childhood and teenage friendships behind when he went off to college. As an adult, he felt friends were a luxury that he often couldn't afford. He didn't have time to nurture others, or tend to their problems. He had enough on his mind. He became accustomed to flying solo, focusing on his target. Eventually, he found he couldn't break the habit. Even when it would have been profitable, and possibly fun, to become active in various Harvard alumni activities, he didn't do it. He didn't want to take part in the endless résumé comparisons, or listen to charming vignettes about precocious infants. He kept his few college and law school friends at a distance, preferring only occasional contact. "They're only a phone call away," he liked to say.

In Houston, he tried a series of new hobbies: playing guitar, windsurfing, scuba diving, even flying lessons. Nothing stuck. As his 30th birthday neared, his unsettled feeling prompted him to start writing a fictionalized memoir, an exercise in self-examination. Never completed, it was harsh: the story of a self-caricature, "Lawrence Dwayne Monroe," a "really cocky guy who is in for a fall." (Mungin consented to read extensive excerpts aloud to me, but refused to part with a copy of what looked like a 150-page manuscript.)

In one passage, the protagonist meditates on his origins:

Unlike a lot of people born in Harlem, I survived the drugs and alcohol and violent crime. I survived the daily heart-wrenching degradation of a future of inferior education, the cycle of grinding poverty, the relentless despair. Yes, I survived Harlem chiefly because my family moved to Brooklyn when I was two days old. For most of my life, in fact until I was 25, I never knew that Harlem was my birthplace. I believed that I was born in a hospital in Brooklyn called Sydenham. But one day, when I heard that the city planned to demolish Sydenham in 1982, my sorrow turned to bafflement when the evening news described it as a 75-year-old hospital located on 127th Street in Harlem. Yes, Harlem. Lawrence Monroe was born in Harlem.

Therefore instead of mourning the loss of a hospital in Brooklyn that day, I ended up mourning the loss of my respectable birthplace, a borough called Brooklyn. . . . I shouldn't be embarrassed since countless outstanding individuals were born in Harlem hospitals. But for me, this revelation caused a fundamental identity crisis because it clashed with my exalted self-image. The revelation forced me to reexamine my self-image, to reshape myself and then to accept my new self. I found the process uncomfortable and threatening.

"This was true," Mungin said, interrupting his reading. "For all those years I was at Harvard, I hadn't known I was born in Harlem."

Lawrence Monroe comes across his birth certificate, prompting an extended consideration of his father, "Junior Monroe":

My general impression of him both as a child and as an adult was that he was unemployable. Funny thing, although from time to time as I grew up, he dropped by for a meal, full of booze and broken promises, it never occurred to me to ask him what he did for a living. Perhaps I feared that he would be uncharacteristically honest and answer, "Son, your daddy is a professional leech. He sucks the blood of even his closest family members and would never consider holding an honest-to-God job. That's your daddy, son." But that's silly. He must have had a job somewhere.

Mungin's introspection about his family was heightened by the death in 1986 of his grandmother. Her passing left him without any older relatives with whom he felt a close bond. "She lived with incredible dignity: a person who worked in a factory and cleaned floors, but had pride and self-respect until the end," he said. Members of Greater Central Baptist, his grandmother's church, told Mungin that the Willing Workers would miss her leadership. She'd had a good life, they said. Mungin wondered who would say such things about him at his funeral.

Almost against his better judgment, Mungin in this period allowed the icy estrangement from his father to melt a bit. Junior Mungin periodically called Deborah and would ask that his greetings be passed along to Larry. Through the mid-1980s, Larry rejected these overtures. But after his grandmother's death, his attitude changed. As he felt increasingly unmoored in Houston, a yearning for personal connections began to grow. What was his father like after all these years?

Lawrence Lucas Mungin, Jr., had returned more or less permanently to South Carolina in 1975. But his son didn't know much about his life there, beyond that Junior lived on the coastal island of Edisto, his birthplace, and that there were a lot of Mungin relatives in the area. Larry hadn't been to the Sea Islands since early childhood. He couldn't remember clearly what they looked like. He imagined southern rural poverty: shotgun shacks and hungry children.

In mid-1987, Junior alerted Deborah that he had "come into some money" and wanted all three of his children to visit, with Junior picking up the tab. Larry was suspicious, given Junior's history of financial irresponsibility. He wasn't sure he wanted to spend any time with his father, anyway. After Larry sent word through Deborah that he would pass, Junior made a rare phone call to his son in Houston. "Come down, Dwayne, and see how I live," the father said.

"No. I'm not interested in you," Larry said, conscious of how cruel that sounded.

"But I'm your father."

"No, you're not a father. You left. You haven't been a father to me." Larry recalled his mother's warning that if he ever absolved Junior, she would haunt him like a ghost.

But his resolve softened over time. In 1988, plans were made for a Mungin family summer reunion on Hilton Head Island, south of Edisto. Larry reluctantly agreed to attend; curiosity about his father overcame trepidation. Junior didn't show up at the reunion events, so Larry drove his rental car up the coast to Edisto to have a look at his father. As he crossed the drawbridge on the road to the main part of the island, he still half-hoped that he wouldn't find Junior or see anyone else he knew. Expecting scenery of heat-baked deprivation, he was relieved to discover that Edisto was basically a less-developed Hilton Head. He drove by pungent marshes and magnificent live oaks draped with Spanish moss. He stopped at a gas station, where the woman behind the counter said, sure, she knew his father, and gave him directions.

"You don't look like Junior," the clerk said to Larry. That was true; he favored his mother.

Junior came slowly to the door of his small cinder-block house.

"It's me, Daddy. Dwayne, your son."

The dark-skinned older man hesitated for a minute. "Oh, it's you!" he said, hugging his son. "And you're so tall! I wouldn't have recognized you. What are you doing here?" He spoke in the local manner, putting the accent on "Head" in Hilton Head, and on the final syllable of "Edisto." He pronounced Dwayne, "Dwen."

Junior affectionately demanded information from his son. Larry answered haltingly. They hadn't talked seriously for 20 years.

Was Larry married?

No, still single at 31. "Maybe I'm not the marrying kind," Larry added. Like father, like son, he thought to himself.

They got into Larry's rental, and Junior gave a tour of the island, from the beach, where white people's expensive vacation homes stood on spindly stilts, to the secluded inland creeks and shaded side roads, where Mungin cousins lived in more humble dwellings. The canopy of moss-festooned oaks was so thick in places that only a few slivers of light could cut through at midday.

They stopped at the home of Chick Morrison, Junior's friend and a deacon at their church, First Baptist. Larry was surprised to learn that his father, the good-times man, was a trustee of the church. Age had worked some changes on Ju-

nior. Still, as glad as he was that they had had their own reunion, Larry couldn't see himself living anywhere near his father. Junior hadn't lost his hustler's instinct. Larry didn't want
to worry about having his pocket picked by his own dad.

Junior asked to be dropped off at his "club," which turned
out to be a tumble-down shack in an area called Steamboat
Landing. The club was a place men gathered to relax, play
cards, and drink beer. It wasn't Fifth Avenue, but Larry found
that he liked the humble spot. It reminded him of a movie clip
he had seen of an African village, which had a dwelling where
the men gathered, apart from the women.

"Will you come back?" Junior asked.

Larry smiled, but didn't answer.

Despite his ambivalence about Junior, Mungin concluded
that he wanted to be closer to his family—though not so close
that he would have to deal with relatives on a daily basis. As a
geographic compromise, he gave his name to some headhunters in Atlanta, which was east of Houston, while still a
healthy distance from the Sea Islands and Queens. After
his desultory time with Weil Gotshal, he was determined to
get back on track with his next job. Atlanta was known as
the "black Mecca" because of its popularity with African-
American professionals. Mungin had never fraternized according to skin color, but he thought he might feel more "at
home"—whatever that meant to him at this point—in a place
where he would be typical, not exceptional.

He had no difficulty securing interviews with several
prestigious Atlanta firms. Weil Gotshal provided positive references, emphasizing his ample skills rather than the less-
than-overwhelming motivation he had demonstrated. As an
associate four years out of Harvard, he knew enough about
bankruptcy law to be of great use to a new employer. Third-
and fourth-year associates are highly marketable because they
don't have to be trained from scratch. They also don't have to
be paid a lot, relative to the rates at which their time is billed
to clients. An associate paid $80,000 to $100,000 in 1990

could be expected to work billable hours worth $200,000 to $300,000 a year. Therein lies the beauty of "leveraging" a lot of associates.

Mungin accepted an offer from Powell, Goldstein, Frazer & Murphy, one of the few Atlanta firms that had a genuinely national practice, focusing heavily on litigation and representing banks. Housed in modern, glass-and-chrome offices, Powell Goldstein had a friendly tone that Mungin appreciated. With its many banking clients, and a growing real estate department, 300-lawyer Powell Goldstein needed more bankruptcy attorneys. Eager to recruit additional minorities, the firm was impressed by Mungin's Harvard–Weil Gotshal pedigree. He, in turn, saw advantages in the fact that Powell Goldstein's bankruptcy department wasn't as busy or dominant as Weil Gotshal's. The competition at Powell Goldstein wasn't as grueling; the billing expectations were more reasonable. Powell Goldstein told Mungin there was room there for him to grow, and he believed it.

CHAPTER NINE

"Saving Mungin"

SPRING 1993

Mungin enjoyed Atlanta, but soon Powell Goldstein persuaded him to transfer to the firm's Washington office to serve an important government client, the Federal Deposit Insurance Corp. One assignment involved tracking the assets of Washington real estate magnate Dominic Antonelli, Jr., whose empire had collapsed in the late 1980s. Antonelli's alleged misdeeds contributed to the ruin of a local bank, according to the FDIC. Mungin and other lawyers sought with mixed success to recover the taxpayer millions lost in the bank's downfall.

Jane Saunders, a more junior Powell Goldstein associate, accompanied Mungin to court appearances on behalf of the FDIC and other clients. She later told me that he worked efficiently and without flair. "He didn't file a lot of extra motions" or keep the meter running unnecessarily. Saunders, who is white and now works in Washington for another employer, considered Mungin a model for how to practice law sensibly. "He would get on the phone and juggle a lot of issues quickly," she said, telling adversaries: "This is what I'm looking for. What can you do?"

But Mungin didn't feel settled in Powell Goldstein's

Washington branch. Like a lot of firms at that time, Powell Goldstein was tightening up after having expanded too quickly in the late 1980s. Some associates were being laid off—something that elite firms rarely did—and associate salaries were frozen. "It was ridiculous to stay there," Mungin later said. With the rest of the Powell Goldstein bankruptcy department back in Atlanta, he "had no support, no mentor, no one to look to. Once the FDIC work dried up, they would have fired me." He imagined his Atlanta superiors demanding, " 'Where's your client base?' It was going to be, 'What have you done for me lately, Larry?' "

Nine months after arriving in Washington, he left Powell Goldstein for the Katten Muchin D.C. office dominated by Mark Dombroff and Patricia Gilmore.

One day in the early spring of 1993, Gilmore asked Mungin to join her for lunch at a restaurant with a view of the Potomac. She wanted to persuade him to file a claim on behalf of AIG in one of the more than 100 bankruptcy cases he was following. He thought the claim couldn't be brought for procedural reasons. But Gilmore didn't give up.

When they were seated, she told him that he had done a good job on all his work for her. The flattery put Mungin on his guard. Gilmore said that she knew that the AIG work wasn't as challenging as he would like. But the client really needed this claim filed.

The bankruptcy in question was almost wrapped up, Mungin pointed out. It was too late. Around the office, Gilmore frequently complimented Mungin's bankruptcy knowledge, going out of her way to refer to him as "the expert" in front of other people. But he found this routine patronizing. Everyone knew that his assignments had become pathetically elementary.

Mungin tried to steer the conversation to the topic of his future. He told Gilmore that he had been "marketing" himself, trying to develop client contacts and improve his stature at the firm.

Gilmore seemed uninterested. She said that it sounded to her like things were going all right.

"Do I look to you and Mark for support?" Mungin asked, referring to his hopes of being promoted to partner.

That wasn't her responsibility, Gilmore said, adding that Mungin reported to Vince Sergi in Chicago.

But he did practically all his work for her and Dombroff, Mungin pointed out.

Gilmore had had enough. "You have a job, a paycheck, no wife and kids," she snapped. "What's the problem?"

Stung, Mungin could not think of an answer.

Later, as it echoed in his mind, Gilmore's harsh remark struck Mungin as deeply demeaning. He had merely asked whom he should look to for support in his effort to advance in the firm. What was wrong with that? Gilmore had said, essentially, that he ought to be grateful for having any job at all. But he had every right to his ambitions, Mungin thought. Then this question came to mind: Would Gilmore have said that to anyone else in the Washington office?

Mungin answered himself: Only if the someone else sorted mail or answered phones. Only if the someone else were black.

The marketing trips to which Mungin referred during his lunch with Gilmore had been another source of friction, as illustrated by a misadventure in Milan.

A generation earlier, elite law firms would never admit to selling themselves the way that a State Farm agent distributed business cards at a Rotary Club dinner. Of course, fancy lawyers back then relied on college and law school ties, not to mention polite persuasion on the golf course. But by the early 1990s, marketing was no longer shameful. It was actively encouraged at Katten Muchin. When Mungin detected that the quality of the AIG work was falling off, he decided he should do some client development for himself. The problem was, he didn't really know what he was doing.

Over the years, he had taken pleasure trips to Italy and had even made friends there. A gifted linguist, he'd learned enough Italian to carry on a basic conversation. Katten Muchin purported to have an office in Milan. In fact, the office was a single Katten Muchin partner of Italian descent, Joseph Tomasetti. Nevertheless, Mungin decided in early 1993 that he would fly to Milan, meet Tomasetti, and try to make contacts among Italian lawyers who might have clients with bankruptcy problems in the U.S.

This was a wobbly notion. Katten Muchin lacked a reputation in international law. Mungin, though a competent bankruptcy lawyer, had no specific experience with the concerns of multinational companies. When he told Dombroff about his planned trip, the managing partner dismissed the idea.

Despite Dombroff's discouragement, Mungin flew to Milan. He was gone for only four days. He met Tomasetti, who introduced him to several Milan lawyers. Business cards were exchanged, Mungin had a couple of dinners with his new acquaintances, and then he flew home. He stayed in touch with Tomasetti and consulted by telephone on a couple of occasions with contacts in Milan, but the trip produced no business.

Mungin, who had laid out more than $2,000 of his own money, asked Dombroff if he could be reimbursed.

Dombroff refused.

Mungin wanted to know who would support his client-development efforts.

Dombroff said he didn't know, but it wasn't going to be him. He suggested that Mungin try Chicago.

Assuming that Vince Sergi wouldn't be any more accommodating than Dombroff, Mungin ultimately put in for only $100, which barely covered his business dinner expenses in Milan. The firm reimbursed him for that amount, and he ate the $1,900 difference. Mungin's judgment could be questioned for taking the expedition, but he believed he had been mistreated, again. As he saw it, Katten Muchin urged young lawyers to develop their own clients, yet the firm didn't back him when he tried, however inexpertly, to do precisely that.

Vince Sergi called one day in April to convey ominous news: Michael Zavis was concerned about Mungin's hours.

Mungin was dazed. Michael Zavis—the co-managing partner in Chicago, one of the firm founders? *Michael Zavis* was reviewing his hours? That was normally the sort of thing a department head did, not one of the top two figures at the firm.

Sergi said they needed to keep Mungin busier. The managing partners were getting more vigilant in trying to weed out weak performers.

Mungin admittedly hadn't paid close attention to his monthly quotient of billable hours. He protested to Sergi that he had been doing things like chasing Jeff Sherman's receivables and taking marketing trips, which ate up time but couldn't be billed. Also, Gilmore had taken away some of the AIG work he had been doing and given it to younger associates who could be billed at lower rates.

"But if you want me to maintain higher hours, I'll do it," Mungin said. "I'm on it."

Katten Muchin expected associates to bill an average of 167 hours a month, or roughly 2,000 a year. Mungin had billed an average of 142 hours a month in 1992 and 136 a month for the first three months of 1993.

Was there a problem with his work? Mungin asked Sergi.

No, he was told. Chicago just wanted to see his hours go up.

Mungin was shaken by this warning from the highest reaches of the firm. But there was more. A few days later, Gilmore dropped by his office, unannounced. She had talked with Sergi. They had agreed that the firm would cut the hourly rate at which AIG was billed for Mungin's doing basic bankruptcy work. That way, Gilmore could shift more of that work back to Mungin. All right?

"All right, I guess," was all Mungin could muster. He felt like he had been punched hard in the gut. He was nauseated, dizzy. What were they doing to him? First the quality of his assignments had sunk, now the tangible measure of his worth. They were cutting him down in every important way.

A memo from Gilmore arrived shortly, saying that Mungin's hourly rate for most of his AIG work would drop to $125 from $185. For AIG, this was a bargain: The insurer would get the services of an experienced associate at a discount. For

Mungin, it was a serious blow. At a big law firm, the upward march of a lawyer's hourly billing rate indicates his rising value and stature. A rate slash usually indicates the opposite. Katten Muchin was now making official what previously had been tacit: Mungin was being treated as if he were a second-year associate.

The question naturally occurred to him: Should he quit? Walk away before things got even worse? Is that what Sergi and Gilmore were trying to tell him?

No. He wasn't a quitter. Leaving Katten Muchin after less than a year would prompt other firms to ask questions, Mungin thought. And if he were measured by the nature of the AIG work he had been doing the last few months, he would be ruined. More generally, other firms might hesitate to hire him now that he was almost seven years out of law school. He was becoming long in the tooth for an associate who didn't have any business to bring with him.

In any event, Sergi didn't actually *say* that the firm wanted to get rid of him, Mungin thought, and Gilmore always seemed satisfied with his work. He would follow orders: get the hours up, keep Gilmore happy, and see what happened in the fall, when partnership and compensation decisions would be made.

Sergi saw the related issues of Mungin's billing rate and his low hours as confirming that there just wasn't enough bankruptcy work to justify his employment in Washington. But no one wanted to fire Mungin, either. Dombroff and Gilmore found him useful. Someone had to do the routine bankruptcy work. A more junior lawyer could have done it, but Mungin was highly competent, and now, he could be billed out at a lower rate.

Sergi had a separate concern: He didn't want to fire a Harvard-trained black lawyer, especially with the Elaine Williams suit pending. The firm had enough problems on the race front. Sergi didn't know what sort of future Mungin had at the firm. But for now, he wanted to hang on to Mungin.

Sergi saw himself as "saving" Mungin. It was he who persuaded Gilmore to shift the basic AIG work back to Mungin. She had wanted to slash Mungin's rate to $100 an hour; he had nudged it up to $125. "The idea was to try to . . . keep him occupied so as to keep him employed," Sergi later said in a deposition. "I had no interest in seeing anything other than trying to find more work for Larry."

The Mungin rescue mission, then, amounted to shoveling yet more low-quality assignments in his direction. This busy-work affirmative action, though aimed at retaining a black associate, had a corrosive side effect: It typecast Mungin as someone who did primarily simpler tasks, at a lower rate, than were done by white attorneys at his level of seniority. "Help" of this variety can kill a career. It doubtless contributed to the unfounded perception in Chicago after Mungin filed suit that he was an affirmative action problem case.

In the spring of 1993, Katten Muchin updated a seven-page brochure for clients describing the Finance and Reorganization Department. The pamphlet stressed that the firm had expanded to seven offices and that the department's 30 attorneys "handle matters involving all aspects of federal bankruptcy law," among other areas. Eleven of these lawyers were listed as contact "partners," along with their direct telephone numbers. Vincent A. F. Sergi was listed as a Chicago contact. In Washington, Lawrence D. Mungin appeared as the department's "partner."

When a copy of the brochure reached his desk, Mungin felt a new surge of frustration. Despite his visits to Chicago, he had received no substantial work from Vince Sergi or others in his department. Yet when it came to boasting about the firm's capabilities, Mungin was used as a symbol of the department's presence in Washington. He wanted to be a partner for real; the firm made him a fake partner in a pamphlet.

During the same period in spring 1993, Mungin received a couple of errant telephone messages and a piece of misaddressed correspondence that raised new concerns. The communications were meant for two of the bankruptcy lawyers in Chicago: Mark Thomas, the partner who had gone to lunch with Mungin in February, and Charles Thomson, an industrious associate of roughly Mungin's seniority who worked closely with Thomas. Ordinarily, Mungin would have made little of the mistaken messages. But his anxiety about his status prompted him to speculate that Thomas and Thomson might have been doing bankruptcy work for the Washington office. He asked around, and, sure enough, his suspicion was accurate.

At various times during 1993, Thomas and Thomson were recruited by Gilmore to handle bankruptcy research and consulting for another Dombroff insurance client, Associated Aviation Underwriters, known as AAU. Some of the work concerned AAU's involvement in the bankruptcy of the small-plane manufacturer Fairchild Aircraft in San Antonio, Texas. Some of it concerned the far larger Eastern Airlines bankruptcy in New York. In addition, Thomson pursued a claim for AIG in bankruptcy proceedings in Chicago concerning a company called Moreco Oil.

Mungin didn't know why Gilmore had used the Chicago lawyers for these assignments. In fact, she had relied on Thomas and Thomson to do insurance-related bankruptcy work before Mungin had joined the firm. It was as a result of that experience and Gilmore's condescension and jealousy over her clients that Thomas had developed a low opinion of her—an opinion that Thomson shared. Nevertheless the pair of Chicago lawyers had been successful in their earlier work for AAU and had impressed officials at the insurance company. So it wasn't surprising that Gilmore would ask them to do additional work for AAU. Mungin was unaware of this history. But whatever the reason for the Chicago lawyers' involvement, he didn't understand why, if there were worries about his hours and billing rate, he hadn't been included in these assignments. This was work being assigned out of the Washington office, where he was listed as the bankruptcy "partner." Further, the AAU assignments related to Fairchild and Eastern were more complex than the AIG claims-processing he normally did at a $125 hourly rate.

Later in the summer, Mungin received a copy of promotional material for another project that he had been left out of: a legal seminar in Orlando for airport operators. Dombroff had called on lawyers from Chicago, Washington, and the firm's small Miami office to give presentations on topics like litigation, pollution liability, and the impact of bankruptcy law on the airlines and airports. The speaker on bankruptcy: Charlie Thomson from the Chicago office. In a deposition, Thomson later described his talk as "your basic Bankruptcy 101"—certainly a topic Mungin could have handled. Mungin wasn't even invited to attend. He said later that he felt so "humiliated" over the episode that he didn't complain to Dombroff or Gilmore.

By the summer of 1993, Mungin concluded that Katten Muchin was taking advantage of him. He suspected, moreover, that it was happening at least partly because of his race.

This was a critical turn in his thinking. It didn't happen overnight, and it wasn't straightforward. For most of his life, following his mother's preaching, Mungin had tried to look away from race. Yet now, at Katten Muchin, he began seeing race everywhere. As Mungin explained it later, he felt for the first time that the old formula—follow the rules, and the system will treat you right—had misfired. He had followed the rules, but his job was falling apart. He was failing. "I didn't go in [to the firm] looking for it," Mungin told me. "But when I began to suspect that they might be screwing me, I looked more closely." He didn't find epithets scrawled in the men's room, or anything so obvious. His evidence was all based on inference and built on the foundation of his being the sole black lawyer in the Washington office.

So far as Mungin knew, only one associate in the Finance and Reorganization Department had had his billing rate cut, and that was him. He felt as if Sergi's department had hired him out at a discount to the Dombroff-Gilmore insurance operation.

Sergi had come down on him for low hours, but Mungin was aware of at least one other Washington office associate of comparable seniority, John Enerson, an energy lawyer, who had even lower hours. Yet Mungin learned that Enerson had a higher base salary. In fact, Mungin discovered that of the six associates in Washington who were seven years out of law school, he was paid the lowest base salary.

Mungin believed that Gilmore favored the Chicago bankruptcy lawyers, Thomas and Thomson, who were white. Why was Thomson asked to give the Orlando bankruptcy speech? That was the sort of exposure to potential clients that Mungin needed.

Mungin didn't have the benefit of knowing a more experienced lawyer with whom he felt comfortable enough to discuss his fears. This is a common problem for first-generation professionals, who can't turn to a father or an uncle, and especially for many blacks, who don't find natural mentors where they work. Mungin certainly didn't think he could air his suspicions with any colleagues at Katten Muchin. He assumed—realistically—that this would result in his being branded a whining minority employee. He decided to try to gut it out. But his antennae were up, and he was taking notes in his steno-pad diary. There weren't many cheerful entries.

Back in February, he had recommended to Dombroff that the Washington office hire a second- or third-year associate to handle the low-level AIG claims so that Mungin could be freed to do more complex work (although Mungin hadn't specified what that complex work might be). Dombroff agreed. Mungin then recruited Anthony Boswell, the young associate who had worked under him at the Powell Goldstein firm. Dombroff interviewed Boswell, liked him, and recommended to Chicago that he be hired. Mungin was relieved. In his diary, he recorded that he himself called Sergi to recommend Boswell. "I . . . spoke highly of Tony and added that, like me, Tony was black."

But Sergi never interviewed Boswell, rejecting the hire for the simple reason that if there wasn't sufficient bankruptcy work to keep Mungin busy, Katten Muchin didn't need another Washington associate in that area. Dombroff decided not to quarrel. Mungin, however, seethed over what he considered a direct affront. "I was shocked and so was Tony," he wrote in his diary.

Mungin felt that he had tried to take a constructive step to remedy his problem, only to be thwarted by Sergi, whom he considered distant and uncaring. Mungin went over and over the experience in his mind and eventually concluded that if Boswell were white, he might have been hired, or at least interviewed in Chicago. Mungin had no proof of this, but still believed it strongly—and all the more so after two other incidents involving Janice Jamison and Antonio Barros.

In June of 1993, Mungin had lunch with Jamison, the black law student clerk from George Washington University. Although he had been designated her mentor, he had refused to coordinate her work assignments out of concern that that would allow the rest of the office to ignore Jamison. Mungin had chatted with the intelligent, pleasant young woman many times, but he had never encouraged her to speak about her general impressions of the firm. Now, at the end of her time with Katten Muchin, he invited her to assess the experience. He asked her to say what was really on her mind.

Jamison thanked him for his concern. But unfortunately, she said, her nine months of part-time work at Katten Muchin hadn't gone well. She had been given few challenging assignments. The white woman associate named as her work coordinator had been absent from the office most of the time because she was helping draft legislation on Capitol Hill. Jamison said she would never come back to work full time for Katten Muchin.

Mungin felt guilty that he hadn't urged Jamison to reveal her troubles to him earlier. He should have stepped in and done something to help her. But his lapse was overshadowed, Mungin thought, by the firm's failure to take the minority clerkship seriously. He apologized to Jamison and said he wished he had asked sooner. When he returned to the office,

Mungin wrote a memo announcing that he was quitting the hiring committee, but without saying why. He felt he didn't have the energy to spare for a confrontation over the Jamison fiasco.

A few weeks later, Michael Kessler, the partner who chaired the hiring committee, asked Mungin why he had resigned. Mungin said he was angry that the minority clerkship program had failed. He also said he was worried that he hadn't been getting any credit from Chicago for his membership on the committee, and therefore was doing harm to his career.

Kessler nodded, agreeing that the minority clerkship had been a bust. Better not to have such a program than to have a bad one that alienates blacks, he added.

Large law firms recruit entry-level attorneys from the groups of law students they hire as "summer associates." The three summer associates in Katten Muchin's Washington office in 1993 included Antonio Barros, a promising black law student from the University of Pennsylvania. He performed well during the tryout period. Mungin praised him to others in the office and anticipated that Barros would get a full-time job offer. "He really looked out for me," Barros said later. In August, however, when Barros returned to Philadelphia for his third and final year of law school, there was an unexplained delay of several weeks in his being sent a formal job offer from Katten Muchin.

In late October, Mungin learned that an offer had finally gone out to Barros that month, but that the Penn student had turned it down. Barros told Mungin at the time that he was disappointed in Katten Muchin because of the delay and uncertainty. Most Washington firms sent job offers in September. But Barros later said in a deposition that a more important reason he didn't take the Katten Muchin job was that Dombroff planned to raise the billing minimum for Insurance Department lawyers to 2,300 hours a year, up from the 2,000 that other parts of the firm required. Barros also worried about the stability of the office and whether his job would be secure there.

Barros's not joining Katten Muchin full time was far from a tragedy. He later ended up as a real estate attorney at another prosperous firm in Washington. Mungin, however, interpreted the Barros episode in racial terms. "I believe that they didn't want to have to deal with such a talented black associate [who would be my natural friend and ally] so they made him an 'unacceptable offer' by delaying," he wrote in his diary. "I also believe that because the firm had one black already (me) they didn't want another."

The experiences of Boswell, Jamison, and Barros formed a pattern, as far as Mungin was concerned. The pattern reflected a subtle resistance to treating black lawyers or would-be lawyers with the same regard as whites. The fact that his perception wasn't supported by overt evidence of racial animus didn't concern Mungin.

As the number of what Mungin considered to be affronts mounted, his sensitivity to passing comments and seemingly trivial events increased. He resented, for example, Gilmore's saccharine compliments on his appearance. When she was in a good mood, Gilmore distributed cloying praise to many associates, secretaries, and paralegals. And Mungin did pay careful attention to his clothes and physique. So it shouldn't have been a surprise that one day she stopped him as he walked by her and said, "You know, Larry, you are the best-dressed person in this office."

Mungin hesitated for a moment, embarrassed. Gilmore had been talking to a paralegal, who now waited expectantly for his response.

"Thank you, Patty," Mungin finally said, thinking to himself, Here I am, battling for respect, and she sees me as decoration: the well-dressed black guy.

Gilmore's condescending opinion of him was confirmed in Mungin's mind by her announcement that he would be in charge of overseeing a new computerized filing system in the Washington office. That meant he was at the conference table when a group of technical support people from the Chicago office arrived to explain the new system, which would be used mostly by paralegals and secretaries. When Mungin identified himself as the Washington contact for the project, the support staff looked confused. "But you're a lawyer," said one of the visitors.

"I know I am," Mungin said glumly.

Mungin met Ed Shealy in the spring of 1993, when the black administrator was visiting from Katten Muchin's Chicago office. After some pleasantries, they began a guarded discussion about Elaine Williams, the black income partner who had sued the firm and who was a friend of Shealy's. Having now experienced his own troubles, Mungin ached to learn more about Williams, but he didn't want to probe for fear of word getting out that he, too, was a problem black. Shealy volunteered that Mungin might like to speak to Williams. He gave Mungin her home phone number.

When Mungin called the next night, Williams was friendly, asking how Katten Muchin was treating him.

"Oh, you know, the usual big-firm stuff," he answered cautiously. "I'm really sorry to hear about your lawsuit."

Yes, it was very trying, Williams said, but she had an excellent case and her lawyers were confident.

He wanted badly to ask about the details of her case, but resisted, still unsure that he could trust her. Instead, he told her that he was up for partnership that year and was worried about his chances.

"You'll be a cinch, Larry," she responded.

He appreciated the moral support. They agreed to stay in touch. In fact, they didn't speak again for more than a year. Mungin stuck to his pattern of avoiding personal entanglements.

Another person with whom Mungin shared his worries was John Villa, the white non-lawyer office manager of the Washington branch. Mungin saw Villa as a peripheral figure and therefore safe to complain to. "Doesn't the firm give a damn about this situation?" Mungin asked him one day. "You've got Elaine Williams's suit, my situation. I'm the only black lawyer here in D.C. There are no black males in Chicago."

"There are plenty of blacks in the mailroom and in administration," Villa responded. "And the firm did hire you."

Although Villa was generally friendly, Mungin took this comment as an insult. Mungin had been referring to lawyers (inaccurately, as it happened; there were two black male associates in Chicago at the time), and Villa's first response had to do with the mailroom.

Trying to make himself clear, Mungin said that he felt "uncomfortable working in an all-white firm. Would you be comfortable working in an all-black firm?"

"No."

"Why not?"

"That's different," Villa said.

Mungin gave up and went back to his own office. He didn't see why it was different.

Mungin almost never socialized with other lawyers in the office. He usually ate lunch alone. Other attorneys tended to stick with members of their practice groups. The insurance people ate with insurance people; the litigators with other litigators. Mungin neither received invitations to join these cliques, nor sought them. While the office had a pleasant, chatty veneer, each little group seemed to spend most of its time complaining about how it was being treated by Dombroff. When Mungin took a break and stopped by a colleague's office to ask about a holiday party or the weather, he often found that he interrupted a hushed conversation or a secretive telephone call.

Mungin's sense of disconnection was increasing. In March, Joseph Tomasetti, the Katten Muchin lawyer in Milan, had arranged for an Italian jurist visiting the U.S. to stop by the firm's Washington office for lunch. More than a dozen firm members attended. But no one invited Mungin, the one person who had spent his own money to visit the firm's Milan office. He heard about the lunch only at the last minute and decided to show up anyway. At Dombroff's instruction, Mungin sat next to the Italian visitor and translated for him.

Mungin was proud to show off his language skill and enjoyed conversing with the guest of honor. But when good-byes were said, a bitter taste remained for Mungin. Not being invited to the lunch was just one more indignity.

To some whites, Mungin's missed lunch invitation might seem a trifling oversight. But among black professionals, Mungin's reaction wasn't unusual. Black associates at most big law firms gripe that they tend to be left out of firm socializing, especially when it is informally arranged.

"You don't see the black associates forming the type of bonds with partners that white associates have, because the partners are white and don't automatically think of socializing with blacks," observes Elgin Clemons, a successful black lawyer and financier in Little Rock, Arkansas, who spent two summers and then two full years at the prestigious New York firm of Shearman & Sterling. Beyond hurt feelings, the absence of informal social contact denies blacks the practical advantage of relationships that boost careers. Clemons was an exception among blacks at Shearman & Sterling in that his natural charisma and self-confidence allowed him to bridge the racial gap. When a white partner suggested that he needed to pass the "white wine test," to show the firm that he could handle himself in social settings, Clemons took the comment as constructive advice, not a put-down. He did pass the test and readily admitted that he picked up some of his most interesting work assignments over drinks with partners. Blacks at Shearman & Sterling who were less at ease socially, or who were left out altogether, simply didn't have access to those assignments, according to Clemons and other African-Americans at the firm. Clemons left the firm on good terms to take an attractive job in his native city.

Mungin felt that his isolation at Katten Muchin—as reflected by incidents like the absent lunch invitation—reflected the firm's forgetting about him as a person. He was there to do menial work, but otherwise, he believed, they looked right through him.

* * *

Since he had arrived in Washington from Atlanta in 1990, Mungin and I had met for lunch every three months or so. I had soured on the idea of lawyering before I even tried it. Fortunately, I had some journalism experience and landed in the Washington bureau of the *Wall Street Journal*, where I covered legal issues. After our first year of law school, Mungin and I had gone our separate ways, remaining friendly, but never becoming close friends. We stayed in touch over the years with occasional postcards, so I was able to follow his progress from firm to firm. When Powell Goldstein transferred him to its Washington office, we renewed our relationship in person.

Mungin typically met me at my office on Connecticut Avenue, where his good looks always caused a small stir among the female receptionists. From the *Journal* office, we walked to a Chinese restaurant on K Street. Social conversation with Mungin consisted mostly of his talking about his career and view of the world. It had been much the same in law school. I always found his observations interesting, and so didn't mind listening. Reporters, after all, are trained to listen. In our early get-togethers in Washington, when he was still at Powell Goldstein, I was under the impression that Mungin's law school scheme of achieving economic security by means of a law firm partnership was still in place. He seemed to be the same ambitious, garrulous person I had known in Cambridge.

Then one day in the spring of 1992, Mungin surprised me by announcing he was leaving Powell Goldstein for Katten Muchin, a law firm with which I wasn't familiar. I was worried about his moving as such a senior associate.

Mungin assured me that such leaps had become routine, that I had an old-fashioned view of law firm careers.

But there was more to it than that. At the time, I didn't understand the powerful streak of restlessness that ran through my former roommate's adult life. There was a pattern in the decision to join the Navy in the middle of college, the move to Houston, the writing of his savagely introspective memoir, and the ambivalence over family relationships re-

flected in his awkward reunion with his father. With these
events as backdrop, the jump to Katten Muchin later appeared to be in keeping with Mungin's uneasy journey since
leaving Woodside.

Mungin's first reports about Katten Muchin in the summer
and fall of 1992 were relatively positive. He told me that he
expected to be made income partner the following year. He
praised this opportunity for a promotion above associate
status—but short of equity partnership—as suiting someone
like him who didn't have his own clients, but was a skilled
practitioner. (He had briefly explored trying to bring the
FDIC with him as a client, but it hadn't worked out, partly because the agency wasn't familiar with Katten Muchin's still-
new Washington office.)

It wasn't until late winter of 1993 that I heard ambivalence
creeping into Mungin's lunchtime soliloquies. He spoke of
the death of Thurgood Marshall that January and how moved
he was by the obituaries recounting the first black Supreme
Court justice's days as a civil rights lawyer. I had covered Marshall's magnificent funeral at the National Cathedral, and
Mungin wanted to hear every detail. I also recounted my
one interview with the great man. He had told me of traveling alone to hostile courthouses in small southern county
seats. From local lawmen, Marshall sometimes received half-
friendly, half-menacing advice that it would be best if he
caught the train out of town by sundown. He always took that
advice, Marshall told me.

"I really am standing on the shoulders of giants like Thurgood," Mungin said after I had exhausted my repertoire of
Marshall anecdotes. "Life for me is so much easier because of
what he went through. I have to make it count somehow."

This tone of respect—for someone other than his mother
or grandmother—wasn't familiar to me. Neither was the notion that he had to make his life "count" in some way beyond
achieving material success. What he said next was even more
startling: Mungin asked for recommendations of civil rights
groups he might contact about possible staff lawyer's posi-

tions. He said he didn't think that in the long run, working at a big firm would be fulfilling enough. The money, while nice, didn't make up for a sense of emptiness he had been feeling. "This isn't something new," he added. "I've been thinking about it for a while."

I offered him some ideas, trying not to show my surprise. Was this the same Larry Mungin who never once in law school spoke of doing public interest work?

In the end, he didn't pursue any of my suggestions of civil rights groups, but it was easy to see that his frustration was growing steadily. Without providing any details, Mungin said that Katten Muchin had changed the terms of his job. He wasn't getting the sort of assignments he had expected. The partners ignored him or saw him as a grunt. He said he felt humiliated, but in our conversations, he never put this in racial terms.

He sounded as if he had lost hope—something else I hadn't heard from him previously. His gloom seemed so severe that at one of our lunches, I suggested he consider seeing a psychiatrist to make sure that he wasn't suffering from clinical depression. Mungin demurred, saying things weren't that bad. He agreed to monitor his moods for signs of serious downswings.

Not long after that exchange in mid-1993, Mungin called me at work with another request. This time, he asked for the name of a lawyer who specialized in employment litigation. He wanted to know his rights.

Was he going to sue? I asked, incredulous.

He didn't know, but felt he had "to protect" himself.

I was puzzled over his even considering such a step. Filing a lawsuit would effectively end his career in big-time corporate law. I never pictured my former roommate as that kind of rebel. He wanted to belong to the system, I thought, not challenge it. Pondering civil rights work was one thing; becoming a plaintiff and attacking your own law firm was quite another. But his harried manner indicated that he wasn't much interested in discussion, so I offered the name of an attorney.

In retrospect, two things were striking about the conversation. First, Mungin, though himself a practicing lawyer, came to a journalist for an attorney referral—much as he had come to me for the names of civil rights groups. Granted, I had many acquaintances in the field, but Mungin was notably detached from the legal scene in Washington.

Second, and more important, he didn't refer explicitly to race, and I didn't automatically conclude that discrimination was the problem. Based on my long-standing impression of Mungin as someone who resisted being identified by his skin color, I assumed he had in mind some kind of breach-of-contract claim against Katten Muchin. (Although if I had remembered my contract law, I would have realized that he was probably an "at-will" employee, who would have no contractual rights.) I referred Mungin to an attorney at a premier downtown litigation firm, Williams & Connolly.

Mungin was more explicit with the Williams & Connolly man than with me. He told the litigator that he was exploring the idea of bringing a race-bias suit against Katten Muchin. The Williams & Connolly man said this wasn't the sort of case he ordinarily handled; in fact, the phone call turned out to be Mungin's one and only contact with him. But the Williams & Connolly partner did suggest that Mungin wait until after partnership decisions were made in the fall. If the firm mistreated him in that process, the lawyer said, Mungin might then consider taking legal action.

CHAPTER TEN

"You Fell Between the Cracks"

LATE 1993

Seeing his job situation deteriorate, Mungin faced a conundrum. There was a strong argument for cutting his losses and quitting. But if he left Katten Muchin in his partnership year, other firms might spurn him as too old to hire as an associate and too expensive for a lawyer who didn't have his own "book of business." He felt he had to try to survive at Katten Muchin, even though his faith in the firm was waning fast.

"I may have made a big mistake," he admitted to Deborah in a phone call in the summer of 1993. He rarely conceded weakness to his siblings.

His sister, a former postal worker who now raised three children and sold Tupperware, had trouble imagining her brother as anything other than a success. Wasn't this the job that looked so good only a year earlier?

Yes, Larry conceded, "but now I'm worried that it might get ugly."

Deborah steered her family through the dangers of a Woodside that was poorer and rougher than when she and her brothers grew up there. But she wasn't in a position to offer much advice about corporate law firms. Following the example of their late mother, neither of them referred aloud to how Larry's troubles might be related to race.

In April 1993, without much forethought, he had responded to an advertisement in a legal trade publication for an in-house lawyer's position at Coca-Cola Co. in Atlanta. Since Coca-Cola wanted someone with international experience, Mungin stressed his language skills, Navy service, and, in a misleading assertion, noted that Katten Muchin had "a Milan, Italy, office, with which I work on a variety of international issues." He added that he was "a single African-American who is available for travel."

Mungin never followed up on the letter, and nothing came of it. But it illustrated once again that he saw nothing wrong with trying to attract a potential employer by emphasizing his race. Big companies, like big law firms, wanted to hire blacks to show their commitment to equal opportunity.

In Katten Muchin's Chicago office, meanwhile, senior lawyers were thinking about Mungin in explicitly racial terms. When David Heller, an established bankruptcy attorney in Chicago, joined the firm in May 1993, Vince Sergi asked him to help Mungin. As Heller later described the conversation in a deposition, Sergi said "that we were hoping to get his hours up, [and] would I think about whether there was anything I could do to involve him in the Chicago work. . . . Vince did indicate to me that Larry was a minority professional and that we wanted him to succeed and to please think about anything I could do to help him along."

Heller was then asked in the deposition whether he referred any work to Mungin.

"None at all," he said. Heller maintained that he didn't have any bankruptcy assignments on the East Coast. He didn't see the sense in sending work to Washington that could be done more efficiently in Chicago.

Trying to help in some way, Heller suggested in a phone call to Mungin that the struggling lawyer draft a list of financial institutions in the Washington area that he would like to cultivate as potential clients. Heller had gone to law school in

Washington 20 years earlier and claimed to have business contacts there; perhaps he could introduce Mungin to lenders that had a need for local bankruptcy representation.

Heller's offer, though doubtless well intended, struck Mungin as an empty gesture. If Heller had business contacts in Washington, why didn't the Chicago lawyer take the initiative and call them directly, or turn their names over to Mungin, so he could try them? Why go through the motions of compiling a long list of Washington-area banks and commercial lenders when presumably Heller knew which ones he could help with? In addition, there was the problem of Dombroff's continuing hostility to the idea of any local bankruptcy practice under his roof.

It probably would have been a good idea for Mungin to take Heller up on his suggestion, however unlikely it was to pay off. But Mungin's well-grounded skepticism caused him to do nothing about the offer. So far as Mungin knew, Heller never independently picked up the phone to mine his purported Washington contacts for bankruptcy work.

On August 30, Heller and Sergi placed a conference call to Mungin, reiterating that they intended to find a way to involve him more in Chicago-based bankruptcy work. By this time, Mungin saw such promises as entirely insincere. Heller remarked that Mungin was the only person in the FAR Department he hadn't met, according to an entry in Mungin's diary. "Vince Sergi asked if I had clients yet," the entry continued, to which Mungin appended, "but which 7th year associates in major firms do?" And at a later time, Mungin scribbled a further annotation: "His sarcasm annoyed me." No one up to this point had suggested that Mungin relocate to Chicago, where the bankruptcy work was plentiful, Mungin later told me. He didn't volunteer for such a move because he knew it would anger Dombroff and Gilmore, who still needed him for low-level assignments in Washington.

On September 20, word went out unofficially in the Washington office that nominations for income partner had been made and that there were only two from D.C., both from the

Insurance Department. Mungin wasn't really shocked that he hadn't been nominated, but he was incensed that no one had even talked to him about the nomination process or evaluated his performance. Recalling the internal firm documents that referred to twice-annual evaluations, he went to Dombroff's office to complain about being neglected. But as had become his habit, Dombroff simply said that it was Vince Sergi's responsibility to evaluate Mungin and look after his interest in being promoted.

Two days later, Mungin began sending a stream of electronic-mail messages to Sergi and Heller (who had been made co-head of the FAR Department) requesting a face-to-face meeting. "I was going to hold them to their promise to evaluate me, and I was going to create a paper trail, just in case" things went bad, Mungin explained later. "I knew they couldn't look me in the eye and tell me I wasn't up to their standards," he added. "I figured I would wait until raises were announced in [November] and then see what they intended to do."

Paychecks distributed on November 16 included notice of salary increases for the following year, 1994, as well as bonuses for 1993. Mungin received a $4,000 bonus, which was modest for someone earning $100,000. In 1992, he had gotten the equivalent of a $10,000 bonus on a $92,000 salary. Much more important, he received no base-pay increase. He interpreted the bonus and salary news as a message: "They thought they could do whatever they wanted to me and get away with it. I wasn't going to let them get away with it. I had been through too much my whole life to let them."

Still, his e-mail to Sergi and Heller, dated November 16, 1993, 11:40 a.m., was conciliatory:

I noticed from my paycheck today that I did not receive a pay increase for 1994. . . . This surprises me. I believed that I was eligible for an increase and thought that I would receive one. I am now concerned that the same thing will happen in 1994 for 1995. Because I am in the Washington office and you are in Chicago, this may have been an oversight. If it was not, please tell me what I failed to do in 1993 and what I will need to do in

1994 in order to earn a raise for 1995. Thank you for your attention.
    LDM

As was his practice, Mungin presented a calm, almost passive public face, when in fact, he was seething. Katten Muchin thought it was dealing routinely with a single unremarkable employee; Mungin saw his treatment as disrespecting his entire life's mission to overcome disadvantage.

He kept leaving phone messages and typing e-mail. Sergi called back on November 24 but said he didn't see how he could evaluate Mungin, because he wasn't familiar with any of his work. Mungin insisted that he be evaluated formally—by *someone*. Sergi relented and asked Mungin for the names of other lawyers with whom he had worked—even fleetingly— and promised to send them all evaluation forms. Dombroff and Gilmore were, of course, at the top of that list, along with attorneys in Los Angeles and New York whom Mungin had assisted on a handful of projects.

As to the issue of a pay raise, Sergi blandly conceded that Mungin's name "never even came up" in compensation discussions among partners in Chicago. Sergi offered no explanation as to why Mungin had been forgotten. The senior lawyer agreed to meet with Mungin to discuss these matters on December 6 in Chicago. Sergi later recalled the voluminous exchanges of November 1993 as an example of his trying to *help* Mungin. "We [Sergi and Heller] were trying to arrange a meeting mainly to see what else we could do to help supply him with work," Sergi said in a deposition.

Mungin saw things quite differently. In his diary entry of November 24, he wrote, "I reminded him that I had never been reviewed and that I didn't see how a decision could have been made re: compensation w/o polling in writing the people I worked for."

As he and I reread the entry two and a half years later, Mungin's anger reignited over Sergi's blasé acknowledgment that the firm had ignored him. "It was hide-the-ball. It was amazing," he sputtered. "I was devastated. It was the worst thing you could do to somebody. . . . Obviously, they were trying to get me to quit."

The callous treatment that Mungin encountered at Katten Muchin had become more common at law firms generally, and for associates of all ethnic groups, I pointed out to Mungin. There were many white attorneys—members of our Harvard Law class, in fact—who turned away from big firms, every bit as disgusted as he ultimately became. Moreover, he freely chose to go to work for Katten Muchin—not as a raw rookie, but after spending six years at other firms.

Mungin himself was willing to acknowledge that reasonable observers might ascribe his difficulties to firm behavior that had little, if anything, to do with race. One day, I asked him whether it had been a plain mistake to take the job from Dombroff in the first place. Hadn't there been hints that Katten Muchin's still-young Washington office might be unstable?

The question obviously nettled Mungin. He launched into a legalistic argument about broken promises and being treated differently from others. But the next day, he raised the subject himself.

"You asked about whether I made a mistake, whether I was just naive about Katten Muchin," he said. "Whatever you do, don't describe me as naive, some helpless innocent who didn't know any better. I went in with my eyes open. We had a deal, and I was going to hold them to it. . . . They harmed me. They excluded me. . . . It was a fight. They hit me. I looked around for the best weapon I could. And I hit them back with everything I could. I leveled the playing field. I play to win."

In the D.C. office in the fall of 1993, Mungin felt there was no one he could talk to about his troubles. "There were no blacks there. Who was going to understand?" he said later.

He did record in his diary one hallway exchange on December 3 with Michael Kessler, a partner who represented energy interests and with whom he occasionally chatted. Kessler, who had an irreverent streak, listened to Mungin's woes and then said jokingly to a third attorney who was listening, "Why are they fucking Larry? Because they thought they could get away with it." Although intended as a wry expression of sympathy, the comment didn't make Mungin feel better. It sounded to him more like a factual statement than a jest.

Mungin set out early on December 6 for Baltimore-Washington International Airport, where he could get a cheaper flight to Chicago than if he flew from the more convenient Washington National. Katten Muchin was paying for the tickets, but David Heller had instructed him to get the lowest fare possible. That meant driving to Baltimore. The firm saved a few bucks; Mungin wasted hours on clogged highways.

When he got to Katten Muchin's offices in the early afternoon, Sergi came out to meet him, looking impatient. He demanded to know where Mungin had been that morning.

Mungin wasn't sure what he meant.

Sounding like a cross schoolteacher, Sergi said that he had tried to call Mungin at the D.C. office to cancel the get-together. David Heller was out of town on last-minute business, and Sergi thought they should reschedule.

Mungin felt the anger rising in his chest. This morning, he told Sergi in a flat, low voice, he had been driving to Baltimore to catch a cheap flight, as instructed.

Heller hadn't even shown up, Mungin thought, after all the e-mails and phone calls? Sergi had the audacity to suggest canceling? This was absurd.

Mungin sat on a low couch in Sergi's large office, next to piles of legal documents. His host got a few sheets of paper from his desk and sat down in an adjacent chair. Files, folders, and bound financing documents were strewn everywhere.

"I'm worried," Mungin began, "and I can't get anyone in either Chicago or Washington to give me an explanation" as to why he hadn't been evaluated and hadn't received a raise.

Sergi responded in a mild, apologetic tone. "You fell between the cracks," he said. "I'm sorry."

Fell between the cracks? As in disappeared? How could an experienced lawyer, hired with such enthusiasm 18 months earlier, become invisible? Especially when there hadn't been a word of criticism about the quality of his work?

Mungin began again, speaking firmly. "I don't know why I have to come all the way to Chicago to beg for a performance review," he said. "And I don't understand how you can make a decision one way or another about my compensation if you haven't evaluated me. And I don't understand how I could 'fall between the cracks' and not even be thought of for partnership."

Sergi reiterated that he couldn't have evaluated Mungin because he wasn't familiar with his work. He had asked six lawyers to fill out evaluation forms. Only two had done so: Dombroff and Gilmore. But frankly, they didn't have much to say, Sergi observed. He handed Mungin the evaluations. Dombroff had scribbled a few sentences on the bottom of his evaluation form. He wasn't "in a position to judge the quality of Larry's work," he said. But Mungin "always appeared cooperative and willing to get the job done." Gilmore, whose comments were typed, had praised him in similarly superficial terms, saying he accomplished his rare challenging assignments "with great skill," but that most of his work was "routine."

In any event, Sergi continued, the low-level tasks Mungin had been doing weren't the sort that qualified someone for partnership. That had never been in the picture. Sergi again said he was sorry.

Sorry? Mungin erupted. "How can you do this to me? This is my *life*!" He was yelling, to his own surprise. "I've done everything asked of me. Promises were made." Dombroff had said he would have a real shot at partnership. That promise was broken. "I've been *humiliated*!"

Mungin's outburst was eloquent; his body language, vaguely threatening, as he leaned his well-muscled frame in Sergi's direction. Abruptly, the younger man caught himself. It was unusual and unwise for an associate to shout at a partner. Mungin prided himself on never losing his temper. This was what they reduced him to.

But Sergi had barely blinked. Without a word, he got up and

closed the door to his office. He settled himself back in his chair and told Mungin he sympathized, but there wasn't anything he could do about partnership. Mungin wasn't anywhere close. The firm did want him to stay, though. Sergi could arrange for Mungin to get an 8 percent raise for 1994, which was what other senior associates were getting. That would boost Mungin's salary to $108,000.

Mungin accepted without implying gratitude or apology. He felt he owed neither. He asked whether he would be considered for partnership the next year.

Yes.

Would Sergi try to steer more challenging work his way?

Yes. Don't worry, Sergi told him. Mungin was still "on track."

In the days after this encounter, Sergi discussed the $8,000 raise with David Schulman. Another veteran partner in Chicago, Schulman recounted Sergi's comments in a deposition: "He said he wanted to keep him in the firm. He said he was a minority. And he said that while objectively he agreed with the [initial] compensation decision [to give Mungin no raise], he wanted to try to extend ourselves to give Mr. Mungin something more." Schulman added: "I believe he used the word 'save' Mr. Mungin."

On the flight back to Baltimore, Mungin found that he felt calmer than before he had vented his fury in Sergi's office. He didn't worry that his outburst would result in any sort of discipline. He thought that while Sergi had power over him in most ways, the Chicago lawyer was actually afraid of him at some basic level. Even in business suits, aggressive black men intimidated many whites. It wasn't Mungin's style to exploit this reality; ordinarily he resented stereotypes about black men. But on this occasion, he couldn't help savoring the confrontation.

Mungin didn't deceive himself into thinking that he was genuinely "on track" for partnership consideration. He didn't know exactly how things would play out, but he didn't see a bright future for himself at Katten Muchin.

A month *before* flying to Chicago, he had moved out of his two-bedroom suburban apartment, which he had rented for $1,100 a month. He had transported his belongings and Tommie, his black cat, to a different part of the complex and jammed them into a small one-bedroom apartment that cost only $740. He discovered that his king-sized bed didn't fit into his new bedroom, so he put it in the living room. It was almost impossible to move around the place, but Mungin didn't give it much thought. He had lived in close quarters before, as a kid in Queens, not to mention in the Navy. He saw trouble on the horizon and was lowering his overhead. He was writing things down, sending e-mails to create a paper trail. He was girding for battle.

CHAPTER ELEVEN

"As Long as You Get a Paycheck, You Do as You're Told"

1994

On January 7, 1994, Katten Muchin's computer produced a seven-page summary of Mungin's billable legal work for the previous year, sliced into 15-minute chunks. The tally told a great deal. There was evidence that Mungin had responded to Vince Sergi's scolding on the need to boost his hours. He had gradually increased his monthly billable total until he was exceeding the required 167 hours. For the year, he still fell 120 hours short of the 2,000 mark. But he was clearly moving in the right direction. Far more striking, though, was the sheer number of bankruptcy cases he had worked on: 155, many for only a few hours each. His billing records resembled those of a paralegal who coordinates, cross-tabulates, and affixes Post-it stickers, not a senior associate, who ought to be helping negotiate loan workouts and litigate Chapter 11 bankruptcy cases.

Mungin did have some assignments that were more complex. On behalf of a local Washington bank, for instance, he pushed a borrower into involuntary bankruptcy—a procedure that required his going before a judge, putting on witnesses, and arguing that the debtor couldn't pay even a fraction of his bills. On a few occasions, Mungin made appearances in bankruptcy courts in New York and Baltimore on behalf of Katten

Muchin partners whose clients had an interest in East Coast cases. But even these more challenging assignments tended to devolve into what Mungin described in his diary as "minor minion work."

In May 1994, Gilmore ordered that the lawyers working under her sign out of the office for any absences other than one hour at lunchtime. Mungin thought this was absurd; sophisticated law firms didn't impose such rules. Where was he working, at a supermarket? He *had* worked at a supermarket as a teenager, bagging groceries, and hated it. One of the cashiers had told him, "You don't look like you belong here," Mungin remembered, adding, "And she was right. I'm not supposed to be packing." Mungin never tried to disguise the sense of superiority his mother had nurtured in him as a device to catapult her son up and away from the dangers of the inner city.

Now, as an attorney in practice for almost eight years, he felt he was being treated as the equivalent of a grocery bag–stuffer. Since his pride was bound up with overcoming the potential hazards of race, a wound to his pride inevitably seemed in Mungin's eyes to have a racial aspect.

He wasn't the only anxious person in Katten Muchin's Washington office. TURMOIL BESETS KATTEN MUCHIN'S D.C. OUT-POST declared a front-page headline in the Washington *Legal Times* of May 16, 1994. "The anxiety level is so high here, we're afraid somebody is going to break down and come in and run around with a gun," one Katten Muchin employee told the *Legal Times*.

The marriage between Katten Muchin and Mark Dombroff was foundering. Katten Muchin had fallen in love with Dombroff's cash flow, but not with his personality or business methods. The cash was still coming in, but Dombroff had alienated his partners in Chicago. Catering to the insurance industry, which offered high volume but expected discount rates, he insisted on employing a higher ratio of associates per partner, even if that meant associates received less supervision. He demanded more billable hours from associates than Katten Muchin required, and he set lower hourly rates for Insurance Department associates. Sergi had allowed Mungin to be swept into the Dombroff discount-rate movement, even though Mungin wasn't an insurance lawyer. But Katten Muchin wasn't willing, across the board, to tolerate Dombroff's divergence from standard practices. Katten Muchin fancied itself a national firm, not a cut-rate insurance defense shop.

In late April, Michael Zavis made a day-long visit to the D.C. office to brief partners and associates on their future. By late morning, Mungin realized he hadn't been invited to any meetings. He complained to John Villa, the office manager. It wasn't until 6 p.m. that Gilmore, alerted by Villa, appeared at Mungin's office door and offered him a recap of the news that a spin-off of the Dombroff-Gilmore insurance practice was being seriously studied. "I still don't understand why I was not invited to the meetings," Mungin wrote in his diary that night. "I was the only one in the office not invited to anything."

What made Mungin different from everyone else? Why, to use Sergi's words, did he tend to fall between the cracks? Mungin's thinking on this question always circled back to his being the only black lawyer in the office. Although there were never any nasty words or overt discriminatory acts, he had come to believe he was an afterthought, a racial token, someone not seen as a real lawyer.

From Chicago's perspective, he was certainly a source of annoyance: an associate who Sergi thought never should have been hired. There wasn't any evidence that Dombroff, who had promised Mungin eligibility for partnership, had given much thought to fulfilling that promise. In 1992 Dombroff had bragged of discovering a new hybrid practice combining bankruptcy and insurance. Only three years later, he said in a deposition that Mungin had been hired merely to "put out . . . fires." Once AIG's big bankruptcy blazes had been doused, or had become the responsibility of the rival New York firm, Mungin, the $108,000-a-year fireman, became expendable, as far as Dombroff was concerned. There was no one in a position of authority at Katten Muchin who had any stake in doing the decent thing, namely, reorienting Mungin toward a new role within the firm, or making arrangements for an honorable separation.

The impending disaster in D.C. didn't dampen Katten Muchin's long-planned 20th anniversary bash that May. Despite the turmoil in Washington, Dombroff and a number of other lawyers from Washington, including Mungin, were flown to Chicago for the affair, which lasted several days. The firm rented the grand main hall of Chicago's Field Museum of Natural History for a black-tie banquet. Lawyers and their guests dined among towering dinosaur skeletons, the world's largest globe, and full-scale reproductions of African elephants. Standing on a raised platform but still dwarfed by the brachiasaurus, senior partners spoke of Katten Muchin's heroic ascent from a band of hardy pioneers. Longtime clients were thanked and new ones welcomed. One new account in particular elicited oohs and ahhs: Katten Muchin had been retained by the primary executor of the $1.2 billion estate of tobacco heiress Doris Duke. This was the biggest probate matter that Katten Muchin had ever handled. A will contest was already crackling and promised to generate millions in legal fees.

Listening to the self-congratulation, Mungin wondered how Michael Zavis and the others could pat themselves on the back when the Washington office was collapsing. They pretended to be such savvy businessmen, yet their mismanagement damaged people's lives. Mungin wasn't a total innocent; he had gone into law to make money, not save widows and orphans. But he was sickened by the gleeful, predatory atmosphere.

Seated next to Mungin was Howard Bernstein, a partner who represented employers against unions. Mungin began explaining what had happened to him in Washington. Bernstein seemed taken aback, but Mungin couldn't contain the words. When he finally stopped, expecting some reaction from his listener, he got none. Bernstein turned back to his meal. Reflecting on the encounter later, Mungin said, "I'm clearly freaking out, and sending a signal, I guess unconsciously, but they do nothing. Weil Gotshal would have taken action. They would have called me up the next day and said 'Larry, we heard you've got a problem. What is it?' This firm—nothing."

Dombroff confirmed everyone's expectations in July, when he and Gilmore left Katten Muchin, only five years after joining the firm. He immediately formed a new firm, Dombroff & Gilmore, and took about 30 of his Katten Muchin subordinates with him, cutting loose about a half-dozen attorneys from what had been the Katten Muchin Insurance Department. A dozen non-insurance attorneys remained in Katten Muchin's decimated D.C. branch. No one in Washington knew where Mungin fit, if anywhere.

Katten Muchin partners in Chicago weren't sure what to do with Mungin either, but they didn't want him in Washington after the Dombroff exodus. They discussed sending him to the firm's tiny New York office, or bringing him to Chicago. Sergi didn't want the firm to lay off a black attorney, especially one who hadn't demonstrably failed. Richard Waller, the Chicago partner who was coordinating the Dombroff departure, later recalled in testimony that he and Sergi discussed "offering Mr. Mungin a job in one of our other offices, because his situation was different from other people's."

Sergi called Mungin, hoping to sound him out. The conversation turned into a case study of passive-aggressive non-engagement on the part of both boss and employee. Sergi began by asking Mungin what was new in Washington.

"Nobody tells me anything," Mungin said.

When Dombroff left, there would be no work for Mungin, Sergi said. What were his plans?

"I don't want to speculate, since I don't have all the facts about Mark and Patty's plans."

Was Mark taking Mungin with him?

"I'm not in their department, and I don't expect to be asked. Vince, I'm in *your* department."

Sergi raised the idea of Mungin's moving to the New York office, which had only a few lawyers.

Mungin said he couldn't respond. He knew practically nothing about the New York office.

Sergi said they would talk again. But he never called back. This was the last time he and Mungin ever spoke. Sergi still saw himself as Mungin's advocate in Chicago. He told his partner Dick Waller that if Dombroff didn't have a place for Mungin, Katten Muchin should find him one, because of his unhappy experience with Dombroff and Gilmore. "We owed it to Mr. Mungin," Sergi remembered telling Waller. But Sergi, in fact, didn't extend himself to reassure a justifiably wary Mungin that the firm really wanted to keep him. Sergi had to know that the prospect of being the lone bankruptcy lawyer in a New York office that existed primarily to give the firm the appearance of a Wall Street presence wouldn't be attractive to Mungin, or any other sensible attorney. Significantly, Sergi didn't even suggest bringing Mungin to Chicago. That silence sent a message: Mungin was not particularly welcome in his own department.

Dick Waller called Mungin several days later to prod him about New York.

Mungin balked. "I have no idea what this is all about," he said. "I need specifics. I need to know exactly what the opportunities are in New York."

Waller switched direction. What about coming to Chicago?

Mungin was confused. Why hadn't Sergi mentioned Chicago? Was this a serious option? If Sergi, the head of his department, wasn't enthusiastic about it, would Mungin really fit in?

Waller said Mungin should "think very hard about" moving to New York or Chicago, that either would offer a good opportunity. He reminded Mungin that he was an at-will employee, meaning that he could be let go at will by Katten Muchin. Three months' severance pay was available if Mungin chose to leave, Waller said.

Mungin responded that three months' pay wasn't very much, considering that he wasn't being fired "for cause," meaning as a result of some failing.

Waller reiterated that associates were at-will workers. He

said he would get back to Mungin with more information. But he didn't.

In Chicago, Sergi discussed Mungin's fate with David Heller. "Vince indicated to me that Larry was somebody that . . . we were trying to create a situation for," Heller said in a deposition. "Larry had not reacted well to going to either New York or Chicago, that in New York [his hesitation had to do with] compensation and that in Chicago he may not be comfortable." Heller said he would like to pitch in somehow. "I asked Vince to let me go home and talk to my wife. I came back the next day and told Vince that Larry could stay with us to visit Chicago if that would help." But the notion of Mungin's staying with the Hellers was never communicated to Mungin. The Katten Muchin partners in Chicago later remembered themselves being greatly concerned about helping Mungin because he hadn't gotten a fair chance in Washington. The truth was that however concerned they were in conversation among themselves, they didn't take any strong *action* to signal to Mungin that they wanted him to remain and thrive at the firm.

Mungin's uncertain status in the Washington office caused confusion there. Nancy Luque, an assertive litigation partner, called him to her office one day in July because she had been asked to take some depositions in a bankruptcy case. Luque didn't know why she was being dragged into the case; she wanted Mungin to take the depositions. He explained that he was in the process of leaving the firm. But Luque wasn't interested in excuses. "As long as you get a paycheck," she said sharply, "you do as you're told."

Insulted, he turned and left her office without responding. As he walked down the hall, he heard her yell, "Come back here, you!" He didn't even turn around. In his diary, Mungin wrote that Luque was the first lawyer ever to chew him out in that fashion. "Her response sums up the firm's attitude toward me [and other blacks]—as long as I get a check, I'm supposed to do as I'm told." It wasn't clear which other blacks Mungin was referring to, since he hadn't worked with any in

Washington, and barely knew Elaine Williams in Chicago. (Luque confirmed the essence of Mungin's account but insisted that her language had been less harsh than he recalled.)

After the Luque blowup, Mungin returned to his office and wrote an e-mail message to Waller:

Unfortunately, due to personal constraints and other considerations I cannot possibly move to New York or Chicago at this time. Because you have made it clear that there is not enough work in the D.C. office to keep me busy and that my only alternative is to be laid off, I would like to discuss an appropriate amount of time to search for a job and an appropriate departure date. Please call me at your earliest convenience.
LDM

Mungin later told me that the strikingly mild tone of his e-mail reflected an expectation that, despite his mounting bitterness, he still might ask Katten Muchin for a job reference. He assumed that someone at the firm eventually would sit down with him to learn why he declined to switch offices. There weren't really "personal constraints"; Mungin just didn't want to work for Katten Muchin anymore. The firm had misled him and hurt his career. Now, it should repair the damage. He had in mind an apology, help in finding a new job, and an especially generous severance to encourage him to go away quietly. "It's the way decent people deal with each other after things go bad," he said.

Katten Muchin didn't understand Mungin's encrypted message, or ignored it. When Waller received the e-mail, he picked up the phone and informed Mungin of the rules for leaving the firm: Mungin would get the standard severance package, and that was it—no apology, no special settlement. There would be no more efforts to "save" Mungin.

It was at this juncture that Mungin discovered he wasn't the only African-American member of the Harvard Law School Class of 1986 who had problems with a law firm employer. Andargachew "Andy" Zelleke, like Mungin, had a sparkling résumé, with two Harvard degrees. Zelleke, the son of an Ethiopian United Nations official, lived in the same Harvard dormitory as Mungin and I. He and Mungin were friendly acquaintances, although Mungin viewed the caramel-skinned Zelleke with a touch of envy. "He was bright and so-phisticated, sure, but didn't come up the hard way, like I did," Mungin said.

Zelleke went to work for the 50-lawyer Los Angeles office of an old-line New York firm, White & Case. At first things went smoothly, but soon he began hearing that a fellow associate was bad-mouthing him behind his back. Zelleke shrugged off the insults, until he heard that this associate was referring to him as a "lazy black." He complained to partners in Los An-geles, who seemed indifferent, and then to the firm's manage-ment in New York, which fired the other associate (despite his denial that he made the demeaning comments). But things didn't get better for Zelleke. After he spoke up, a pair of part-ners in L.A., who were close to the fired associate, allegedly punished Zelleke by giving him fewer good work assignments. He sued White & Case for race discrimination and retaliation, gathering a stack of sworn statements that racist comments went beyond the fired associate. The two L.A. partners who he felt had punished him had themselves allegedly referred to blacks as "niggers" and "spear chuckers." (The partners de-nied saying these things.)

Mungin read about the Zelleke case in *The American Lawyer*. The magazine reported that after a year of legal skirmishing and only two weeks before trial, White & Case offered Zelleke $505,000 to settle. He took it, but refused to go along with the firm's desire to keep the settlement confidential. The firm continued to protest its innocence, but its leadership realized that it would be lunacy for a rich, white, out-of-town law firm to go to trial against an attractive black plaintiff in racially charged Los Angeles.

Mungin was stunned. This was the first time he had heard of a successful discrimination lawsuit filed by a black lawyer against a law firm. There weren't any in the law books. But if that was "all it took" to put together such a case, he thought, he would sue, too. And that was how Mungin made his decision to go to war against Katten Muchin.

Mungin thought he could mount a case as strong as, or stronger than, Zelleke's. This conclusion, however, was palpably incorrect. The racist comments at White & Case were better evidence of racial hostility than anything Mungin could realistically hope to find. White & Case itself had conceded it had a problem when it fired the wayward associate. But Mungin's sense that he had been wronged was so powerful that he made little of this distinction.

Helen Mungin had taught her children to be proud: "Shoulders back, head up high . . . You treat people well, and you'll be respected," Deborah recalled. Larry was not getting respect at Katten Muchin. "They devalued him, treated him like crap on the floor," she said.

"As a kid," she told me, Larry "didn't forget slights. He wasn't a fighter, exactly. But he remembered insults, and he reminded you." In a favorite family story, Kenneth, age six, came in from the playground one day, crying that Chuckie, a known bully, had been picking on him. While Helen comforted her younger son, Larry, 12, wordlessly closed a schoolbook he had been reading, marched out to the playground, and walloped Chuckie. Larry then returned to the apartment, opened his book, and resumed reading without saying a thing. "He was sure about right and wrong," Kenneth remembered a quarter-century later.

Still on the Katten Muchin payroll during his severance period, Mungin became a fixture in the firm library, where he researched discrimination law, a subject he hadn't studied at Harvard. Surprised to see him, other lawyers asked what he was doing. He told them he was thinking about taking Katten Muchin to court. Their smiles indicated they didn't take him seriously.

Mungin took his research very seriously. He began to think of himself as part of the tradition of black lawyers struggling against racism. He had arrived at what he called his "Thurgood Marshall moment." He later said of the civil rights titan,

"He wasn't brilliant. He was an executor. He made the arguments, got things done. On the Supreme Court, he wasn't the most brilliant. He had a role, and he played it and got it done." Of himself, Mungin continued, "I had a role. When they took advantage of me, uh-uh. No. I'll fight back. I'll make you pay. This is my time to fight. And I had the information. I had the evidence. I had the documents. I may not have a lot of money, but I have my reputation. Reputation is my currency."

On a wet Monday morning, August 29, Mungin arrived at the reddish-brown marble headquarters of the Equal Employment Opportunity Commission in downtown Washington. Before filing a federal job-discrimination suit, a potential plaintiff has to have his claim reviewed by the EEOC. The bespectacled black bureaucrat who interviewed Mungin played variations on a single theme: "How were you treated differently?" Mungin recited his frustrations over pay, work assignments, and promotion. Race wasn't there on the surface, perhaps. But race had to be the explanation. By process of elimination: What else was there?

He wasn't naive; he expected to encounter extra hurdles because of his skin color. He had been jumping over them for three decades. But now he was tired of jumping. After 20 minutes, the EEOC man put down his pen. "It sounds like you have a case," he said.

Outside on L Street, the rain was so fine it was almost mist. Mungin felt relief but also shame. In a sense, he had failed. He had worked all these years to "make it," and now he would be typecast as a complaining black—precisely what he had tried to avoid. But that was just what made the situation so unfair: After a lifetime of keeping his head low and following the rules, he had been deceived and cast aside.

But maybe, he worried, he just hadn't made the grade. Was he a fraud? Would he get laughed out of court?

As he walked away from the EEOC, preoccupied by these thoughts, Mungin happened to cross paths with my father and me, on our way back to our respective offices after sharing lunch. Downtown Washington is a very small place.

The three of us stopped, shook hands, exchanged a few words, and then moved on. My father, who had met Mungin on only a few occasions, was curious about how he was faring. He'd had some tough times with his law firm, I explained, but I was sure he would come out fine. I had been out of touch with Mungin for several months and didn't know he had decided to sue. In our brief sidewalk encounter, he revealed nothing.

For Mungin, the momentary meeting was torture. All he could think about was what someone like my father—late 50s, Jewish, moderate politics—would think if he knew that Mungin was going to court, claiming race bias. "He would think . . . that I'm one of *those* blacks," Mungin said later. He viewed my father, the successful son of a postal worker, as a model of hard work and achievement, someone for whom respectability was a central value. Many whites, including those basically sympathetic to the black civil rights movement, had grown suspicious by the 1990s of demands based on racial victimhood. Until now, Mungin felt he had avoided that suspicion. Now, he had severed the Harvard-woven tethers to respectability. He was on his own in a new way.

CHAPTER TWELVE

"They Promised You the World; They Gave You the Street Corner"

FALL 1994

Mungin was struck by the scene in the eighth-floor corner office. At a small circular conference table, he and two other attorneys were gathered for important business. All three were sophisticated and well educated, and all three were black. In the white corporate law world, he had never seen such a thing—not three in one room.

It was the Saturday before Labor Day, 1994, and Mungin had come to meet Koteles Alexander, the managing partner of Alexander, Aponte & Marks. Also at the table in Alexander's office was Abbey Hairston, a member of Alexander's mostly minority firm. Mungin didn't have to tell them he was there to talk about filing a discrimination suit; that was understood.

An attorney representing himself has a fool for a client, the saying goes, and Mungin saw the wisdom in it. To be effective, a lawyer needs emotional distance from a case. But having decided not to represent himself, Mungin realized he didn't know that many trial lawyers. He'd returned to the Katten Muchin office from his visit to the EEOC on that damp late August afternoon wondering where to turn for help.

That week's issue of the Washington *Legal Times* had the answer. MULTICULTURAL LAW FIRM BIDS FOR THE BIG TIME, the front-page headline declared. Reading the article in the Katten Muchin library, Mungin learned about Koteles Alexander's ambition of building a law firm owned by minorities that would compete with mainstream Washington firms. Mungin noted Alexander's unabashed desire to promote himself. A discrimination suit with a Harvard-trained attorney as the plaintiff would appeal to him, Mungin thought. Black lawyers "would have an incentive to really go all out to win a case that would make a name for themselves," he said later. "We could all win."

Koteles Alexander gave the impression of someone capable of achieving his immense goals. In the office, he dressed in dark pinstriped suits with suspenders and monogrammed shirts. Attentive as he was to his wardrobe, Alexander, a handsome man of medium build, almost always needed a visit to the barber. He worked long hours but arrived late for most meetings. He had been married and divorced four times. "I've been obsessed about making something of myself, providing an example for others," he told me, sounding weary and older than his 40 years. "It's had costs. I recognize that."

The son of a career Army enlisted man, Alexander announced in the seventh grade that someday he would be a lawyer. He attended law school at historically black Texas Southern in Houston, where he served as editor-in-chief of the law review. After graduating, he landed a highly prestigious clerkship with the U.S. Court of Appeals in Atlanta.

As a law student, Alexander had worked one summer for one of Houston's premier corporate law firms. "It was like another world," he said of Vinson & Elkins. The partners, though distant, were worldly, powerful, and wealthy. But a few years later, even with the appeals court clerkship on his résumé, Alexander couldn't even get an appointment to discuss a full-time job at Vinson & Elkins. He applied to two dozen big firms from Houston to Miami; not one indicated any interest. "These law firms were taking a few blacks in the early 1980s,

but the blacks they took were only the cream of the cream—
the Harvards and Yales and Stanfords," he said.

Alexander and his wife at the time decided to try their luck
in the Washington area. For eight months after arriving in
1985, he couldn't find any legal work. He delivered packages
and documents for a courier service. Eventually one of his
customers helped him get in the door at a small black firm. A
few years later, he audaciously formed his own firm, envi-
sioning a partnership with the standards he had seen at
Vinson & Elkins, but whose ranks were integrated. Located in
suburban Silver Spring, where rents were cheaper, the new
firm grew quickly, becoming the biggest minority-owned firm
in Maryland.

Still, Alexander Aponte struggled. Banks and real estate
companies wondered about its stability and capabilities. They
asked flat out: "Do you have any white partners?" Alexander
answered evenly that he did. "But on the inside, I [was]
seething," he told me. He felt like firing back: "You're not
asking majority law firms about whether they have any
black lawyers, are you?" Without steady corporate business,
Alexander Aponte's finances were perennially shaky. Koteles
Alexander's strength was vision, not cost control. Lenders
provided credit grudgingly. Partners came and left. Still, as
black-owned firms went, Alexander's was successful, drawing
the attention of the *Legal Times*, and Larry Mungin.

Alexander assigned the Mungin case to his star litigator,
Abbey Hairston. "She has an edge on her because she has had
some personal experiences of her own with racism," he explained. "She doesn't take shit, not off associates, not off partners, certainly not off this Chicago law firm."

Growing up in Chicago in the early 1960s, Abbey Hairston
was one of the few black children sent to an integrated private
Lutheran school. "I remember in the first grade, kids asked
me, 'Why are you a different color?' " One classmate told her,
" 'My mom says you're a different color because you don't take
baths.' " Hairston's cousins, who attended the mostly black
Chicago public schools, teased her for "talking white."

In high school, she was the first black member of the home-coming court and the first to be in the top 10 academically. She remembered being "very popular," and was voted the female "class comic" as a senior. Her mother was a payroll clerk, her father an electrician and insurance salesman. Neither had gone to college. At the University of Iowa Law School, she was one of only four blacks in a class of 180; race soon became a distraction. In her small evening study group, each student shared outlines of their classes. Hairston, the only black in the group, produced an outline for one course that was considered "very good," she told me. But when grades were posted for that class at the end of the first semester, it was Hairston who had the lowest score in the group. "They had used *my* outline, but [they] did better. Why?" she wondered. Her fellow blacks had similar experiences. Even though exams were supposed to be reviewed without students' names known to the graders, the four blacks suspected they were being singled out somehow. "How could it be," she reflected, "that . . . there were other black students there like me, who had gone to white schools, to private schools, and had done really well, and now we come to law school and all of a sudden we're dummies?"

With a less-than-stellar academic record, Hairston couldn't find a law firm job. "None of us made it," she said, referring to her black classmates. She ended up taking a position with a Legal Services office in Florida, where a friend worked. Paid $13,000 a year, she learned to litigate by handling social security, disability, and immigration cases. She felt she didn't get respect from white lawyers and judges. "The perception was that you weren't as smart as your white counterparts," she said. Even her destitute clients, she felt, were suspicious of her because she was black.

After a few years, she moved to a staff attorney's job with the Palm Beach County school system and climbed the ladder impressively to become the top lawyer at an organization with a $1 billion budget. But when the time came to leave the government because of a switch in school superintendents, no significant private firm in the area wanted to bring her in as a partner. "It was very disturbing to me that I could not command what a white male who had been in my position would have been able to," she said. Hairston moved to the Washington area, where she met Koteles Alexander, who hired her in an "of counsel" position, with the understanding that, if she built a successful practice, she would rise to partner.

Alexander and Hairston had a volatile relationship. He valued her self-confidence and familiarity with employment law. He also couldn't help noticing Hairston's regal good looks. She favored brightly colored dresses and business suits and wore her hair in a fashionable close-shaved "fade." Her wit could sting. She was single. Hairston appreciated Alexander's backing, although she found him annoyingly disorganized. Deeply devoted to her work, she admired his dream to build a lasting black-owned law firm that included all races. But she thought it was just that—a dream, which Alexander wasn't likely to accomplish. She worried that his overreaching would be Alexander's undoing.

On the Labor Day weekend that Mungin visited the Alexander Aponte office, Koteles Alexander couldn't help thinking that in Mungin, he saw himself "with the Harvard degrees added on." What had happened to Mungin was an outrage, Alexander thought. "We were told in the sixties, 'Get educated; your time will come,' " Alexander said later. "Well, we've gotten educated; we expect to get our due."

Mungin presented a genuine African-American Horatio Alger story, Alexander marveled. Alexander had met many minority employees over the years with grievances against their employers; he couldn't recall a biography like Mungin's. Alexander didn't specialize in trial work, but he was sure Mungin would dazzle a jury—if Katten Muchin was dumb enough to let the case go to trial.

Hairston was less sanguine. She was the one who would actually go to court if Mungin became a client. She found Mungin's manner self-righteous. He referred to his impressive credentials a lot. Did he think he was smarter than her just because he went to Harvard and she went to Iowa? Juries didn't like that sort of smugness. Neither did she.

Before Hairston could decide how to raise these questions, Mungin did it for her. He asked whether 30-attorney Alexander Aponte was up to the task of suing a 400-lawyer firm that had more experience, connections, and money. "I could take this case to any white firm in town," Mungin said.

The boast wasn't accurate; most white firms would be unwilling to attack another member of the established legal fraternity. But whether or not Mungin believed what he said, his goal was to provoke his hosts. He had come to Alexander Aponte because he thought it would intuitively understand his experience. Now he wanted to know whether Alexander and Hairston were willing to go all the way to trial—an expensive process that could take years. He didn't want lawyers who would sell him out for a quick settlement. Katten Muchin, accused of racism, could be counted on to fight long and hard.

Hairston lost patience. Yes, she interjected, she had conducted complicated trials and negotiations, and was well qualified to handle this case. "I know what I'm doing," she told Mungin. Her worries about him were confirmed. She was ready to say no thanks and boot the Harvard snob out of the office.

Alexander saw that Mungin was testing them. "You're a lawyer, a Harvard-trained lawyer," he said. "Lawyers are difficult clients. Abbey is a damn good trial lawyer. You have to trust her. We can handle this, but we don't need to be second-guessed."

That forceful response appeared to mollify Mungin. He agreed to allow Alexander and Hairston to prepare a "retention agreement," or contract, which they would review when they met again the day after Labor Day.

Hairston still had reservations. "Is he going to think that I don't know what I'm doing?" she asked her boss. "And then, if I lose, is he going to blame me, even though I have done everything I possibly could do?"

"But Abbey," Alexander pleaded, "it's a great case." A big weakness of the typical job-bias suit is that the plaintiff has a blemish on his record—a forged résumé or a fudged expense account—that undercuts his credibility. "But here," Alexander said, "you've got someone who's clean."

Hairston agreed to suspend judgment until they met Mungin again. He seemed emotional, she observed. Maybe he would never come back.

Mungin returned on Tuesday. After grilling Hairston some more about her credentials, he said he was ready to hire her and the firm. He signed the retention agreement and wrote a check for $3,000 to cover initial expenses. Once more, he asked, was Hairston *sure* she could handle the case?

"We can do it," she answered. "We can do it."

The faxes started within days. "It's a Mungin fax!" Hairston would announce, walking into the office of her associate, Adrian Nelson. She would lay several pages of Mungin's barely legible script on Nelson's desk. "What did we do now?" she would ask sarcastically.

A typical Mungin missive read: "I am experiencing *great frustration* because I have not heard from you a coherent litigation strategy. . . . As discussed from day one, my law firm will fight this action vigorously. Accordingly, we have to have a forceful strategy."

Hairston assigned Nelson the task of monitoring Mungin's prolific communications. "Right now, Larry has nothing to do," she told her associate. "Right now, all he's doing is focusing on what happened to him, reliving it over and over."

Hairston was correct. Mungin had ceased going to the Katten Muchin office and had time on his hands. He did make one final, quiet appearance at his former workplace in late October, though. He nodded hello to a couple of secretaries and avoided conversation with the handful of lawyers still on staff. He was there to write one last memo to Sergi. "It is my understanding that consistent with firm practice and policy, I am eligible for a bonus pro-rated for 1994," he wrote, requesting that the check be sent to his Alexandria apartment.

Mungin didn't see his unlikely entreaty—made at the same

time that he was suing the firm for millions—as a joke or taunt. In his mind, it was merely an extension of what he had been doing since he first walked in the door to meet Dombroff: playing by the rules and demanding that the firm do the same. The memo was a defiant reminder that he intended to fight the small points as well as the big ones. He left it with office manager John Villa and walked out of the red-brick building in Georgetown for the last time.

The bonus, needless to say, wasn't forthcoming.

Hairston knew from past clients how lonely the lot of a discrimination plaintiff could be. "He has no money, he's scared about the future," she told Nelson. "Right now, he's throwing everything to us. He's relying on us. I know he's a pain, but . . . until he gets a comfort level with us, we are just going to have to eat it."

Nelson, as he put it, "did not relish this assignment." A formal young man with a dry sense of humor, Nelson believed his client had a good case, but he didn't care for Mungin's personality. "He speaks like, and looks like, what the majority law firm wants, what I think of when I think of Ivy League, white or black." This was not a compliment from Nelson, who received his college degree from historically black Hampton Institute and his law degree from William & Mary, both in Virginia. "I mean, he came on with that Harvard stuff, and I said, 'Oh, boy, what's this?' "

Mungin's main fear was that Hairston, either because of indifference or incompetence, would settle too easily. He would have entertained a settlement offer that bespoke real victory—one, say, that put $1 million in his pocket, after attorneys' fees. But he also relished having a chance to confront Katten Muchin in court. And since he made a "contingent-fee" agreement with his lawyers, he had to help pay only a portion of certain expenses, not for the time spent preparing the suit. The agreement discouraged quick compromise. His lawyers were entitled to 33 percent of any winnings at trial, but only 10 percent of a pre-trial settlement. They received nothing if they lost at trial. So his point couldn't be missed, Mungin lectured Hairston that she "should *not* expect a settlement but look forward to a trial by jury. . . . My *only* difficulty in awaiting trial is that I fear that *you prefer* to settle and will *resist* going to trial."

Despite Mungin's bellicose stance, Hairston had to open communications with the other side. In early October, she learned that her counterpart defending Katten Muchin was Michael Warner, a partner at Seyfarth, Shaw, Fairweather & Geraldson in Chicago. Seyfarth happened to be one of the fancy Chicago firms that snubbed a young Abbey Hairston when she came home, looking for a job after law school. She hadn't forgotten. Michael Warner was the same Warner who published the April 1992 article in *Chicago Lawyer*, warning of more lawsuits against employers. His prediction had proved accurate. Warner had been a busy man.

Katten Muchin wasn't impressed by Hairston's alert that Mungin was planning to file suit. "It was a bullshit lawsuit that would go away," was how one former Katten Muchin partner remembered it being received within the firm. "There was the sense from Zavis and Sergi that this was just piggybacking on the other side"—Elaine Williams's suit, filed the previous summer. Another former partner agreed: "It didn't make a big splash at the firm. The Washington office was falling apart, and this was some minority lawyer blaming his troubles on discrimination—that's what you heard." Vincent Sergi was said to be in a huff that Mungin would go to court "after all the firm had done for him," said another lawyer familiar with the situation. But Sergi also thought the Mungin suit wasn't a real threat.

David Heller, the Katten Muchin bankruptcy lawyer, felt frustrated at being drawn into a race-discrimination case. He had never met Mungin. "I was a little upset at having been named a defendant," he said in a deposition. Mungin had singled out four individuals—Mark Dombroff, Patricia Gilmore, Vincent Sergi, and David Heller—and sued them personally, along with the firm as a whole. "Vince and I talked about the fact that I knew Vince to be one of the primary advocates within the firm of the importance of hiring and retaining

minority professionals and non-professionals," Heller continued, "and we kind of commiserated about the fact that I
thought it was ironic that he had been sued. . . . I was just, you
know, disappointed to be a defendant and disappointed that
Larry saw things this way."

Co-managing partner Michael Zavis thought the suit was
garbage. They had tried to help a black lawyer whose hours
were low, and this is what they got. No good turn went unpun-
ished. He was confident it would never get to trial because
there was nothing to it. They'd get it dismissed long before
any jury was impaneled. In Washington, Mark Dombroff, busy
setting up his new firm, couldn't understand what had
prompted the suit. Mungin hadn't been shy about complaining, but he hadn't said anything about discrimination to
Dombroff, who later stated in a deposition that he never cate-
gorized subordinates by race.

This was Katten Muchin's settlement offer: Mungin would
be allowed to relocate to the firm's Chicago office and would
be reimbursed for any related expenses. No cash payment, no
promises as to his status, salary, or future.

Mungin refused. He told his lawyers: "Under no circumstances will I accept a move from one *plantation* in Washington
to another in Chicago. The firm is racist & I plan to tell that to
the jury." On October 21, Hairston filed a civil action,
Lawrence D. Mungin v. *Katten Muchin & Zavis et al.*, in U.S. District Court in Washington.

Abbey Hairston said that she "never doubted" the core of
Mungin's story, but she did have one critical concern. "It was
questionable," she told me, whether there was persuasive evidence of race-based discrimination. "There's a difference,
you know, between being screwed and being able to prove that
a statute has been violated, that you have been treated differently, based on your race, from 'similarly situated' white co-
workers." And there, expressed with admirable brevity, is the
main issue in any case in which intentional discrimination is
alleged.

* * *

At the beginning, a lawsuit is a bare-bones affair. The plaintiff need only identify the laws that he alleges the defendant violated, the harm that resulted, and a skeletal version of the evidence that he could produce at trial. The defendant then gets a chance to argue that the complaint is so inadequate that it ought to be thrown out before the trial even begins.

Mungin's lawyers claimed that Katten Muchin violated two federal statutes: the Civil Rights Acts of 1964 and 1866. With the 1866 Act, Congress forbade bias against blacks in the making of contracts, but like much of the Reconstruction Era legal apparatus set up to abolish the effects of slavery, the 1866 Act lay dormant for nearly a century. Only under pressure from the black civil rights movement and the intrepid lawyers of the NAACP did the federal courts give meaning to the 1866 Act and other long-ignored laws.

The 1964 Act was the premier 20th-century legislative effort to promote racial equality. Its roots can be traced to Rosa Parks's refusal in 1955 to give up her bus seat to a white passenger and the waves of protest—and violent white resistance—that her brave action ignited. Pressured by the unrest, President John F. Kennedy urged Congress to ban discrimination in public accommodations, education, and private employment. His recommendations became law after his death.

As they have been interpreted by the courts, the overlapping protections provided by Title VII of the 1964 Act and Section 1981 of the 1866 Act cover the entire employment relationship, forbidding discrimination from hiring to firing. The provisions on money damages under the two laws are complicated, but for minority employees who can invoke both statutes, the bottom line is that potential recoveries are unlimited. And, critically, someone in Mungin's position is automatically entitled to a jury trial, as opposed to a judge determining the outcome on his own.

With Mungin's full support, Hairston fashioned a kitchen-sink complaint into which she dumped every conceivable accusation against Katten Muchin. Mungin, the suit alleged, had suffered from "disparate treatment," "constructive dis-charge," "a hostile work environment," and "retaliatory con-duct." The complaint also said Katten Muchin had breached an "implied covenant of good faith and fair dealing," inflicted "emotional distress," and injured Mungin's reputation.

"You put a lot of stuff in, and you see what works," Hairston explained later.

Of the various causes of action, disparate treatment and constructive discharge were by far the simplest to understand. They formed the core of Mungin's claim: first, that Katten Muchin treated Mungin differently from whites who were, in the legal jargon, "similarly situated"; and, second, that the firm effectively forced him to leave by making his job unrea-sonable. To support the claim of disparate treatment, the complaint asserted that Mungin was worse off than whites in terms of salary, "mentoring," work assignments, and consid-eration for promotion.

Hairston believed that another theory—that Mungin was subjected to a "hostile work environment"—would prove the most effective. A hostile work environment is one "perme-ated" with "intimidation, ridicule, and insult" so severe that it becomes impossible for the victim to work normally. The com-plaint said Mungin was "isolated" as the only black in the Washington office and that the firm "condoned the humili-ating and degrading comments" of supervisors and coworkers. These remarks included Gilmore's saying to him, "You have a job, a paycheck, no wife and kids; what's the problem?" and office manager John Villa's comment that there were plenty of blacks in the mailroom and in administration. It was far from obvious, however, that these comments amounted to perva-sive intimidation or insult.

As for damages, Abbey Hairston thought she could win $1 million, at most. "We're talking about a black male; let's be re-alistic," she reminded Koteles Alexander. The harsh rule of thumb among trial lawyers is that juries award white women far bigger discrimination verdicts than black men. Jurors, white and black, tend to assume that black men have less promising professional prospects and therefore, if they are hindered by bias, have less to lose in the way of opportunities and future earnings.

"Don't sell it short," Alexander responded. "You're talking about someone whose life was the embodiment of the American Dream."

Despite their difference over what a jury might ultimately award Mungin if he won, Hairston and Alexander agreed that for purposes of the complaint, they would seek an amount that would turn heads. Totaling the maximum potential awards under various statutes, they came up with $11.3 million. "We wanted to give Katten Muchin something to think about," Hairston said later.

Mungin's immediate thoughts about money were on a smaller scale. He had collected his regular Katten Muchin salary of $2,250 a week during the three-month severance period, but that ended in late October 1994. He couldn't face applying for a new job with another big law firm. How could he get back into a double-breasted suit to play the good black around a bunch of white lawyers? The question was academic, anyway; once other firms heard about what had happened at Katten Muchin, they wouldn't offer him a job under any circumstances.

Could he take unemployment compensation? The idea made him cringe. But the old formula about working hard and following the rules had malfunctioned. His mother would have understood. So, he went one day to a shabby office near the Greyhound Bus Terminal in northwest Washington and got on line. The other people there looked tired and defeated. He thought of pictures of Ellis Island. Was he really one of them? He filled out some forms and soon began receiving a check for $330 each week.

By the time the unemployment checks ran out six months later, he had signed up with several temporary-employment agencies that provided attorneys for short-term projects. A typical assignment was going to a corporate headquarters in the Virginia suburbs, where he would sit in a conference room, organizing and coding documents for easy computer retrieval.

The starting pay was $11 an hour. The jobs lasted a week or two, sometimes more. The advantage was that no one knew who he was, or that he had gone to Harvard. He didn't wear a suit and tie to these jobs; it seemed too ludicrous. As a result, he encountered more often than usual the problem of white women being obviously uneasy around him in elevators and parking lots. "No more am I in Georgetown, dressed like a professional and at least getting some respect on the street," he said. "I'm out in Chantilly, Virginia, or wherever, and the secretaries are afraid I'm going to attack them as they go to get in their cars."

Mungin had been out of law school for eight years, earning a healthy salary the whole time. But he had saved only about $5,000. He was still paying off loans on college and law school, and every year he paid some bills for his brother and sister. He had an expensive wardrobe. He took vacations in Europe and the Caribbean. He had always assumed that he would have a Harvard lawyer's pay and that he would start saving in his 40s. Now, everything changed. Travel abroad was over. He had no health or dental insurance. A year earlier, he had moved to a smaller apartment. As things broke—CD player, microwave, vacuum cleaner—they weren't fixed or replaced. He kept his Mustang in the garage to save on gas. He paid Kenneth $40 for an old ten-speed bike, which Larry used for local commuting.

He had trouble sleeping. His thoughts jumped. If not a lawyer, then maybe he should be a doctor. He registered for pre-med science courses at a community college. But he never showed up for the first class. He was 37, and the medical-training road was just too long.

He toyed with opening a one-man consulting firm out of his apartment. He would provide advice on everything from wills (which he would first have to learn about) to small-business financing. He discussed the idea with Kenneth, who ran his own business installing and servicing computerized cash registers at New York restaurants. "He wanted to know some nuts and bolts about wiring for a computer and putting in extra phone lines," Kenneth told me. Larry's thrashing around bespoke "a lot of pain," in Kenneth's view, but also some positive changes. The experience at Katten Muchin "lowered" Larry, his brother said, and "brought him closer to the family." Kenneth lived with his wife and three young children on the top floor of a small two-family house in a working-class Queens neighborhood. He tried to reinforce his brother's resolve. "They promised you the world," he told Larry. "They gave you the street corner."

In a fax to Hairston on February 20, 1995, Mungin passed along this tidbit: "You will be interested to know that last week the head of KM&Z's Tax Department was expelled from the partnership for embezzling client funds." The tax lawyer was forced to resign after an internal audit turned up allegedly questionable billing of expenses to a client. *The American Lawyer* branded the incident "a pathetic scenario that is becoming all too common: a well-respected senior lawyer at a top firm watching his career unravel amid allegations of what amounts to petty theft." As the magazine indicated, such revelations were becoming almost routine as traditional law firm mores gave way to unabashed profit-maximization.

Of more acute embarrassment to Katten Muchin, the Doris Duke case had become a national public relations disaster. Sorting out Duke's affairs had deteriorated into a tawdry melodrama, featuring a motley pack of hangers-on scratching at the heiress's pile of cash. Rather than remaining above the fray, Katten Muchin found itself under attack, in part because of how much money the firm itself raked off. By February 1995, Katten Muchin had been paid a breathtaking $9 million by the estate for some 14 months of work, and was seeking another $4.5 million, according to press accounts. There were allegations—never proven and stiffly denied by Katten Muchin—that the firm had aided its client, the alcoholic, pony-tailed Duke butler, Bernard Lafferty, in exercising undue influence over the dying heiress. The case got coast-to-coast media coverage, and Katten Muchin was held out as a prime example of the law profession having gone off the rails. "The grand prize for sticker shock went to the lawyers at

KMZ," *People* magazine reported. The firm said it had done nothing wrong. "Everybody wants a piece of this money. It's all about money," Katten Muchin partner Howard Weitzman told the *Los Angeles Times*.

Noting the firm's troubles, Mungin told his attorneys that they had a chance to catch the enemy in disarray. Mungin thought from the outset that the firm would underestimate his determination. Now, he faxed his lawyers, "I believe the walls are starting to crumble" at Katten Muchin.

CHAPTER THIRTEEN

"I Am a Whistle-Blower"

SPRING AND SUMMER 1995

Michael Warner offered no greeting as Larry Mungin and his two attorneys entered the conference room at the downtown Washington office of Seyfarth, Shaw, Fairweather & Geraldson. A tall man with a full head of white hair and horn-rimmed glasses, Warner asked impatiently how late the plaintiff's team could go on this first day of Mungin's deposition. Tomorrow, he said, he expected to be on a mid-afternoon flight back to Chicago.

This would be the first face-to-face confrontation of the lawsuit. Mungin thought it strange that Warner tipped his hand about wanting to sprint through the questioning. Did he have more important things to do? Whatever plans Warner had, Mungin decided to gum up the works. He would provide as little information as he could, and do it as slowly as possible. Mungin thought of this lawsuit as the equivalent of war. But his plan to be uncooperative in the deposition wasn't simply a reflection of hostility. A deposition is also an audition of sorts for a witness. Warner would be evaluating Mungin's performance with an eye toward a future meeting in court.

"Isn't it an advantage to have your opponent underestimate

you?" Mungin asked rhetorically when he and I later discussed his conduct in the deposition.

Depositions are a part of the "discovery" process, which is designed to prevent parties from holding back relevant evidence or attempting to spring a trap at trial. Discovery conducted in good faith lets each side see what it's up against and may encourage combatants to settle, rather than face the expense and uncertainty of trial. Inevitably, though, some litigants turn discovery itself into a highly confrontational process. The Mungin case didn't bog down nearly as badly as many lawsuits do, but the plaintiff turned his own deposition into a strange, vitriolic session.

Warner quickly sparked Mungin's anger by probing his economic situation.

"I am poor. I do not have any investments," Mungin said.

"You own no stocks?"

"I am poor. I do not own any stocks."

"You own no bonds?

"I am poor. I do not own any bonds, municipal, or otherwise."

"Do you own any real estate?

"No. I am poor. I do not own real estate." Mungin sounded incensed.

How much money had he given over the years to his siblings?

"I never had any reason to keep track. I wouldn't even want to know. I'm their survivor. I'm the one who got out. I will give them whatever they ask for without counting."

Mungin, who had recounted for his own attorneys a detailed history of his time at Katten Muchin, now claimed great gaps in his memory. "I don't remember," he said over and over, sounding a little bit like Ronald Reagan during his forgetful testimony in the late-1980s Iran-Contra affair. "I don't remember specifically. . . . No. I don't remember specifically."

"One way or another?"

"No. I don't remember specifically. . . ."

"You have no specific recollection?"

"No, I don't."

At one point, Warner asked whether during his interview with Dombroff, Mungin told his prospective employer why he had left the Houston office of Weil Gotshal.

"If he asked, I'm sure I did."

"Do you have a recollection of whether you told him at all about that?"

"I have no recollection as to whether he asked, and I have no recollection as to whether I answered the question that he may or may not have asked," Mungin said.

Even Hairston lost her patience. During a break, she took her client into another room and said, "Larry, just answer the questions. Quit messing around."

"They're getting on my nerves," he responded. "They're acting like I'm the one on trial here, when I'm not." That wasn't so, of course. As Hairston knew, her client's behavior and background were just as much on trial as Katten Muchin's actions. And she had another concern: The judge would review the transcript of this deposition when he considered the inevitable defense request to throw the suit out before trial. If Mungin appeared to be obstinate from the transcript, that wouldn't help his cause.

The deposition resumed. Warner wanted to get Mungin to admit that there hadn't been any promises that he would ever be made partner. What had Dombroff said at the interview, Warner asked, "about what it would take to be made partner?"

"He didn't give me specifics as to what it would take to be made partner."

"Did you ask?"

"There is an understanding when you're interviewing at a certain level, that unless you're looking for a demotion, that you're on track and that you will be eligible."

Warner thought he was beginning to gain a little traction. The picture Mungin offered of how a law firm worked was patently inaccurate, in Warner's view. Firms didn't have to guarantee associates some sort of procedural fairness—a right to be considered seriously—which seemed to be what Mungin was demanding. Mungin clearly didn't deserve a promotion and *that* was why he wasn't considered seriously, Warner thought. Race had nothing to do with it. Lawyers in a corporate firm were more like independent contractors than employees of a bureaucratic company. They had to make their own way and prove they would bring in business. Katten Muchin wasn't a friendship society, and it didn't have a structured system of mentors and evaluations. Mungin had demanded something that didn't exist. Sure, he got some bad breaks, Warner would have acknowledged. The disintegration of the Washington office wasn't his fault. But he had failed to advance for legitimate reasons.

Warner went on the offensive. What *harm* had the whole experience really caused Mungin? "So. you have an additional two and a half years of experience over what you had at Powell Goldstein. Isn't that correct?"

Apparently furious, Mungin said, "I have had two and a half years' worth of work that has devalued me in the marketplace as a bankruptcy attorney, sir, that is what I have."

Fighting Katten Muchin had ended his big firm law career, Mungin correctly believed. "I have sued a major law firm. [Other firms] may admire me, but they won't hire me. I am a whistle-blower. I am a troublemaker. I am persona non grata. My career is dead. That is what I think. That is what I found. That is what I know."

Warner produced a copy of a June 10, 1994, memo, in which Mungin had listed his grievances with Katten Muchin. (It was unclear whether Mungin had ever sent the memo to anyone at the firm.) The defense lawyer read the first sentence, which accused Katten Muchin of "offer[ing] to fire" Mungin if he didn't "accept a permanent move to New York or Chicago." "It is true, is it not," Warner asked, "that as of June 10, 1994, you understood that you were being given an opportunity to transfer to either the New York or Chicago office?"

"Of course not," Mungin said.

"Well, how do you explain that sentence . . . ?"

Mungin rambled a bit about no one in Chicago getting back to him and then said of the memorandum, "This was my professional way of asking the firm what their position was with respect to getting me out. . . . I never got a response from this."

"It is true, is it not," Warner repeated, "that as of June 10, 1994, you understood that you had been offered the opportunity to move to New York or Chicago with the firm?"

"I just *answered* that question!" Mungin shouted. "I'm not going to answer it again. It is no. It is no, a *thousand* times no! This was written by someone who was told to get out of this office, okay?"

If this was the way he was going to perform on the stand, they were not going to make it, Hairston thought to herself.

The Seyfarth lawyers came away thinking that Mungin was either a pathetic loser or a flake, or both. It seemed to them that he couldn't discuss his case without getting emotional. Warner was confident he could persuade the judge to throw the suit out by means of summary judgment.

One person who at the time kept his own counsel about Mungin's performance was Mungin himself. Later, he told me that he had known exactly how he appeared to the other side. Seyfarth and Katten Muchin would think he would make a poor witness at trial, and he could catch them off guard by performing well in front of the jury. "Warner didn't know what to think," after the deposition, Mungin said.

But from my reading of the deposition transcript, Mungin had seemed to genuinely lose his composure. Was that an act?

He smiled and shrugged.

Usually, sophisticated litigants want to impress and intimidate the opposition by showing how *good* a witness they would make. Mungin claimed to have done the opposite. In the end, I chose to believe him. I concluded that he probably could have controlled his anger, but as part of a risky and bizarre plan to mislead Warner, he had self-consciously exposed his rage and bitterness.

Adrian Nelson disagreed with my belief that Mungin had turned the deposition into a giant bluff. Mungin was just a difficult person, Nelson said. "Larry doesn't seem natural. He doesn't seem to have the ability to just answer a question in a natural way."

* * *

Word that Junior Mungin had fallen seriously ill reached his son in the early summer of 1995, as depositions in the lawsuit continued. Relatives in South Carolina had called Deborah to say that Junior was coughing up blood—worse than before. He was in a hospital in Charleston. Surgeons removed a lung. His long-term prospects were unclear. Junior's medical history was clouded by inadequate records and his own secretiveness. He had suffered from chronic infections, which caused internal bleeding that got more severe over the years. In the past, he would check himself into the hospital but leave as soon as he felt better, always sooner than he should have. This time, Junior couldn't leave.

The Mungin cousins in South Carolina, while of course concerned about Junior, suggested strongly that his children should help oversee his hospital care and get his personal affairs in order. Deborah, who had flown to Charleston when she learned of the crisis, couldn't be away from home for too long; she had a husband and three children—including twin grade-schoolers—to look after. Kenneth also had heavy domestic burdens. Larry didn't. He resisted going south for a whole month, but his relatives there insisted and eventually he gave in.

He had started a new job at the Securities and Exchange Commission and couldn't afford to miss a day of work, so he made the eight-hour drive down I-95 on a Friday night that spilled over into Saturday morning. The SEC job, arranged through a temporary-employment agency, paid $12 an hour. It involved transcribing and coding tape recordings of stockbrokers under investigation by the agency. Like the other temp jobs he had had, it was boring and nothing he was very proud of. He worked in a cramped basement room at the SEC's Washington headquarters, not far from the federal courthouse where his lawsuit was on file. There were no secretaries in the SEC basement, no fine leather furniture, no thick carpeting. He shared a single phone line with several other temps. But the job was low stress and allowed him to be anonymous. He needed the money to pay his rent.

Although only 61 years old, Junior Mungin had lived hard. For long periods in Junior's life, "he drank his meals," as his Aunt Florence Kentuck of Beaufort put it. After their encounters in the late 1980s, Larry had cut off contact again. They hadn't seen each other for six years. Larry didn't know what to expect, from his father or from himself.

As he drove through Virginia and North Carolina, he had time to think about his disorienting existence in Washington. He was consumed by the legal fight and lacked a permanent job or a plan for the future. Everything had come unattached. He wondered sometimes how he kept his sanity.

Just weeks before he heard about his father's hospitalization, Larry had mused about taking a weekend trip to Germantown, Pennsylvania, where his mother's natural mother, a white woman, was said to have been from. He imagined himself walking the streets in Germantown, looking for people who resembled Helen Mungin. What he would do if he found a resemblance, he wasn't sure. Declare their blood tie and give the startled white person a big hug? His meditations about Germantown had been interrupted by the news about Junior, and now, despite past misgivings, Larry realized he was curious in a wary sort of way to see the old man.

Synthia Glover, a cousin who lived in Charleston, accompanied Larry to St. Francis Hospital. A soft-spoken lawyer and health food enthusiast, Glover brought a container of carrot juice for Junior. She went into the hospital room first, while Larry waited outside in the hall, the door ajar.

"Guess who's here," Synthia asked the patient.

"Who? Is there somebody else outside there?"

"No, guess who's here."

Junior refused to play her game.

Still stubborn, this old man, Larry thought to himself. He peeked his head in and said, "It's me! Are you surprised?"

It wasn't clear whether anyone had told Junior his son was on the way, but he recognized Larry immediately and broke into a big smile. They hugged, and Larry kissed his father on the cheek. The old man was emaciated and weak, with tubes running from several places on his body. But he sat up in bed, and his mind seemed clear enough. "Well, well, look here!" he said. "My son, my son!"

Larry didn't bring up the lawsuit. It embarrassed him. Junior was happy to talk about little things, like what kind of car his son drove.

A Mustang, Larry told him, failing to mention that it was nine years old and showing its age.

Junior wanted to know how much it cost, where it was parked. "He had to know everything," Larry told me. "That's just the way he is. That's the way I am, too. I've got to know everything."

After the visit, Larry realized he had almost no memory at all of his parents early in their marriage. There must have been happy times, he thought. He had to dig out black-and-white photographs from Easter 1960 to recover an image of his father from that period. He found one in which Junior, slim and dark, dressed in a black suit and white shirt, sat on a couch with a flower-pattern slipcover and playfully squeezed little Deborah and Larry, one in each arm. The squirmy children, dressed in their Sunday best, were obviously delighted by the gentle roughhousing. His mouth wide open, crew-cut Larry seemed to shout with joy.

Larry remembered that after Helen threw Junior out, his father still came around occasionally for dinner or to wish someone happy birthday. On evenings when he was especially charming, as Junior was very capable of being, Helen would remark, "That's the Lawrence I remember." Then she wouldn't say anything for a while.

Now, as Junior lay in his hospital bed, probably dying, his son discovered a desire to learn more about the man for whom his mother had once fallen and who, after leaving New York, had lived, apparently peaceably, for another two decades on the lush island of Edisto. Cousin Synthia Glover began that weekend to introduce Larry to a seemingly endless web of relatives who knew Junior and had heard of his famous son, the lawyer from up north. He got to know many of these people as he made what turned out to be numerous trips south.

He met Uncle Teddy Mungin, 85 years old, a bit hunched with age but broad-shouldered, taut, and powerful. Uncle Teddy still took his boat out on the creek and returned with heaps of fish and crabs. He spoke of root doctors and ancient superstitions, and he still referred to Rebels and Yankees, as if the Civil War hadn't ended all that long ago. Junior was okay by Teddy, because he was family.

Cousin Laird Scott was especially close to Junior. "But you know Daddy was no good," Larry said to her during one visit. "You do know that he left Ma with three kids in New York, and we hardly saw him after that."

"But that was before he came back down here, back home, Dwayne," Cousin Laird said. "He's changed."

Junior's relatively comfortable life on Edisto was due in no small part to the death of his father, Lawrence Lucas Mungin, Sr., two years after Junior's return. Lucas had been a wealthy man, by island standards. He was said to have owned 75 acres, which he diligently farmed. He also did quite a bit of fishing, operated a couple of small general stores, and sold illegal corn liquor to whites from Charleston. Lucas was said to have been distilling a batch when he expired of a heart attack. At the wake, Junior declared, "I went to bed a poor man and woke up a rich man." He inherited the stores, three trucks, two boats, a tractor and interests in several sizable plots of land. He moved into Lucas's house and installed indoor plumbing. Junior began his "retirement" at age 50, by all accounts a contented man.

Larry learned that his family was descended from the Gullahs, former slaves from plantations in coastal Carolina who for generations had preserved distinctive customs, language, and spiritual beliefs that could be traced to West Africa, by way of the Caribbean. Some Mungins, like Uncle Teddy, still spoke with a lilting cadence and antique vocabulary. Much more striking to Larry than quaint speech patterns or wizardry with straw baskets was the Gullahs' relationship with the land itself on Edisto, St. Helena, and the other barrier islands. In the early days of freedom after the Civil War, some of the more enterprising former slaves in the region, including the Mungins and related families, managed to acquire modest pieces of land. Some plantations that had been foreclosed upon or simply seized by Union troops were sold off cheaply by the federal government. Other tracts were scooped up by Yankee speculators and resold or leased to local blacks. Struggling to keep up their loan and tax payments, many slave descendants lost their recently acquired property. But some of the Mungins held on to theirs, even when Jim Crow reared his hateful head. In time, Larry's relatives bought additional plots, and the extended family thrived.

Growing up, Larry had heard little about his relatives in South Carolina and saw them only at the occasional summer picnic up north. He remembered them as loud and affectionate. Decades later, these same people accepted him simply because he was Junior's son. The Sea Island Mungins and related families seemed strikingly proud, even if they weren't rich. Larry believed it had to do with their owning their own land, or at least knowing people who owned their own land. Whites had come lately to build houses on the beach, and even to sniff around inland real estate. But the Mungins of Edisto and St. Helena lived in a cohesive community of African-Americans that stretched back to slave times. In the 18th and early 19th centuries, the islands were isolated from the mainland, allowing island slaves to retain more of their African culture than most mainland slaves. That heritage survived into the 20th century and became known as Gullah.

"They didn't grow up around a lot of white people," Larry said of his southern relatives. His perspective on integration had shifted dramatically since the Katten Muchin fight had begun. His relatives "didn't have to feel inferior to anyone . . . They know where they came from. There's none of this rootlessness, lack of identity." He was referring to the rootlessness associated with the black urban underclass. But to my ear, it could just as easily have been the rootlessness of a black Harvard graduate who once had seemed to personify the optimism of 1960s integrationism.

Larry exaggerated about his relatives, of course. They hadn't escaped racism altogether. As late as the 1960s, there were separate public facilities and whites-only lunch counters on the mainland.

But on some of the islands, they were even today physically and psychologically insulated from whites. This wasn't so in resort areas, such as Hilton Head, where heavy development displaced many blacks. But to the north, on Edisto and St. Helena, where much of the Mungin clan lived, blacks still controlled their communities. Whites were the outsiders—wealthier, of course, but less certain of their place.

Junior enjoyed telling of the whites who built vacation houses right on the ocean, even though once every few years, a hurricane came along and knocked some of them down. After a big storm, blacks would jump in their boats, motor around to the ocean side, and scoop up the perfectly fine wood floating in the water. Many blacks on Edisto have sturdy wooden sheds built behind their inland bungalows, courtesy of storm-wrecked beach houses.

In Junior's hospital room, the two Mungin men passed the time talking about Edisto, or they sat quietly and watched television. On some visits, Junior asked his son to shave him. Larry carefully applied the cream and scraped off the tough whiskers. The old man had a heavy beard, like his son.

"When are you coming next?" Junior would ask when they were through.

Larry didn't pity his father. The old man had lived life pretty much as he wanted. Larry enjoyed imagining his father wearing a wide-brimmed straw hat, pulling in nets filled with shrimp and then selling his haul to the white people from Charleston. "That was a real skill . . . going into that creek, knowing where those shrimp and crabs are and how to get them out," the son said proudly. Junior had never dedicated himself to one job. He lost the stores his own father left to him and did only a modest bit of farming on the family land he inherited. He told people he was a private investigator, although it wasn't clear what there was to investigate on Edisto.

"He sounds like a stereotype: couldn't hold down a job and

do one thing," Larry later said of his father. But "he was a guy who survived, who took whatever job he could get. . . . You could work in the post office—what my sister ended up doing until she stayed home with her kids and sold Tupperware—or you could hustle, be a con man. He [Junior] was a con man. . . . Blacks had to be sharp. You had to outwit the white guy. It's a tradition down there." As Junior himself put it during one of their hospital visits, he "wouldn't work for $1 an hour, carrying someone's bag."

The clash with Katten Muchin transformed Mungin. Or maybe it merely freed ideas and emotions that previously he had kept locked away. He came to see the lawsuit as the culmination of all of his past frustrations, large and small, related to race. That he had been raised to look away from these frustrations—that he *wasn't* a complainer—only made his anger over being mistreated all the more powerful. Mungin felt he had sacrificed greatly to transcend race, only to find that in the end, he still felt vulnerable in the face of forces he couldn't control. Provoked by Katten Muchin's indifference, he allowed bottled-up fury over earlier slights to erupt. "They didn't realize that when they say I don't matter, they're saying my whole life doesn't matter, everything I've invested doesn't matter, my family doesn't matter," Mungin told me.

"When I was younger, it was 'Take it to another level' by working within the system. Show them in the 60s that you're not going to get involved with the Black Panthers, that you're more a Martin Luther King than a Malcolm X, and go to the schools and show them that you can do it, and do this, and do that. . . . Now, what I want to show is that I did it *my* way, okay? I played by the rules. But there's nothing genetically or inherently inferior about me, and if you insist on it, I'm going to rub your nose in it. It's an anger, but it's a place I feel that I've earned. It's an in-your-face position that I feel that I really did earn."

The black author Shelby Steele has written that in modern America, there have been two models for black behavior: "bargaining" and "challenging." According to Steele, retired

General Colin Powell and actor Bill Cosby are classic bargainers. Shelby paraphrases Cosby's message to whites as: "I will confirm your racial innocence if you accept me." Cosby subscribes "to the American identity, and his subscription confirms his belief in its fairmindedness."

A challenger, on the other hand, says to whites, "If you are innocent, then prove it." Malcolm X was a challenger, as is one of his old rivals, Louis Farrakhan, leader of the controversial Nation of Islam. The Reverends Jesse Jackson and Al Sharpton, though sometimes willing to bargain within the Democratic Party, are challengers when they lend support to the anti-white ravings of a Farrakhan or the conspiracy tales of a Tawana Brawley, or they attack the corporate establishment as monolithically racist.

Mungin had gone from being a bargainer—a "good black" in white eyes, as he sardonically put it—to being a challenger. He came to believe that for his entire life, he had been disingenuous "by focusing on getting some security, getting shielded from poverty, and getting to a kind of class position that at least would psychologically shield me and make me more acceptable [to whites]. But at heart, that was incredibly dishonest. I was going to have to be more publicly honest about the lie that I was living. It wasn't that I was around people who were open minded, who thought blacks are terrific. It's that I was bending over backward all the time to avoid making white people uncomfortable. Like my neighbors [in Alexandria]: Now I'm just tired of making them feel comfortable, I don't even talk to them. If they say hello, I'll say hello, but I don't even bother anymore making them feel comfortable late at night. It's too much work."

As Mungin spent more time in South Carolina, he viewed his law firm years and what he called his "whole yuppie existence" in ever harsher light. In South Carolina, among less-educated blacks who accepted him not for his accomplishments but because of his membership in a family, he felt at home. Mungin spent long hours questioning his relatives about how the bloodlines traced back over the generations, who owned which land, how cotton was picked in the old days.

He even sought out descendants of the white planters who had owned his ancestors. The whites were gracious and glad for his interest. He began taking notes and sketching a family tree. Then, on one visit, he discovered that a now-deceased white Sea Islander had published a novel in 1942 about the rise of Joe Lincoln Mungin, a fictional post–Civil War black. The book, *Here Come Joe Mungin,* clearly was based on experiences of real Mungins, and others like them. Larry realized, with great pride, that his forebears were seen as a model family, typifying black society on the Sea Islands.

Discovery continued in the lawsuit as each side interrogated potential trial witnesses. Mungin and Hairston believed the depositions of current and former Katten Muchin attorneys—Vince Sergi, David Heller, Mark Dombroff, and Patricia Gilmore—were revealing a pomposity and obliviousness that would offend a jury. "And yes, of course, I was thinking that it would be a black or mostly black jury in D.C.," Mungin told me. "If [Katten Muchin] didn't want to face reality, tough."

Hairston agreed with her client. After deposing current and former Katten Muchin partners, she told Koteles Alexander, "Now I know what racism is. It's arrogance." She continued, "It's people who just believe they are so much better than you are, they write you off. They're just so condescending."

Of course, she also found her own client condescending, but his superior attitude seemed to her to apply equally to people of all races and creeds.

Offhand remarks rankled Hairston. Mark Dombroff in his deposition insisted—disingenuously, Hairston fumed—that because he didn't think of lawyers in racial terms, he couldn't say whether any of the 15 or so associates in his new firm were African-American. "I just . . . don't focus on it that way," he said. A month later, in a separate deposition, former Katten Muchin bankruptcy associate Charles Thomson gave a similar answer when asked how many black lawyers worked at his current seven-person firm in Chicago. "I don't know. I have never inquired into their ethnic background," Thomson told Adrian Nelson, who was handling the questioning.

"Do you know whether or not *I'm* African-American?" asked Nelson, whose medium-tone brown skin and facial features betrayed the answer.

"I assume that you are," Thomson said, "but I don't know."

"I think taking the depositions is what really gave me the drive to take this case to the end," Hairston said later. "If they hadn't been so condescending to me and to Adrian . . . I probably would have worked harder to settle it."

Mungin applauded his lawyers, predicting that the opposition would underestimate their abilities. By fax, he cheered: "Now we're rocking!"

CHAPTER FOURTEEN

"There Will Be a Trial"

January 1996

Michael Warner began with a stumble. Abbey Hairston had made her formal introductions of the plaintiff's side at the January 5, 1996, hearing on Katten Muchin's motion for summary judgment—the firm's request that the suit be thrown out before trial. Now it was Warner's turn to introduce his team to the judge.

Warner: Michael Warner, Michele Phillips, and Susan Gallagher for the defendant.

The Court: Michele *Roberts*, you certainly mean.

Warner: Michele Roberts.

Roberts: Good afternoon, Your Honor.

Michele Roberts was supposed to be Katten Muchin's big gun, but Warner couldn't even remember her name. (He may have had music on his mind; Michelle *Phillips* and her husband, John, were members of the 60s folk-rock group The Mamas and the Papas.)

Roberts was a prominent criminal defense attorney in Washington, and she also was black. Her name had first surfaced in the case in September. The defense side had grown worried about pale Michael Warner standing in front of a predominantly black Washington jury, questioning Mungin's character and veracity. So Seyfarth launched a search for a local black lawyer willing to lend his or her complexion to the defendants' cause.

The talent hunt caused a stir in Washington-area black legal circles. Koteles Alexander learned of it at a July Fourth picnic sponsored by a black men's civic organization. An acquaintance, who was an attorney, mentioned in passing that he was considering doing some employment discrimination work for a big Chicago law firm that wanted a local black to handle a trial.

"That wouldn't happen to be Katten Muchin & Zavis, would it?" Alexander asked.

"Yeah, how did you know that?"

"We're representing the plaintiff in that case," Alexander answered. "We're the good guys."

Alexander's acquaintance didn't get the job. Katten Muchin's first choice had been Kenneth Mundy, a courtroom virtuoso who a few years earlier had extricated Washington mayor Marion Barry from a broad federal drug indictment with only a single misdemeanor conviction. Mundy, whose other past clients included U.S. House Speaker Dan Rostenkowski and Congresswoman Mary Rose Oakar, accepted the Katten Muchin assignment, but before he got deeply involved in the case, the 63-year-old attorney suffered a heart attack and died. Searching for a replacement in the summer of 1995, Katten Muchin heard that Michele Roberts was a younger female version of Mundy. She got the nod.

Roughly the same age as Mungin, Roberts also grew up in a New York housing project. She attended Wesleyan University and went to Berkeley for law school. Unlike Mungin, she was idealistic about representing the downtrodden. At the highly regarded Washington Public Defender Service, she relished doing combat for accused killers and drug dealers. It was like the "Romans versus the Christians" in Roberts's mind. In 1991, she served on the legal team that advised Anita Hill during the Clarence Thomas sex-harassment controversy before the Senate Judiciary Committee. But Roberts joked about folks back home in the Bronx asking her when she would become a "real" lawyer and make some money. Eventually, she formed a small firm with a fellow veteran defender and tried to broaden her portfolio to include civil cases. Roberts had never before represented a defendant in a race discrimination case. She felt certain that her client in this one hadn't harmed Mungin based on his race.

"I had to satisfy myself, as an African-American, that there was no discrimination in this law firm," she told me. "I looked at the facts, the case file, and saw it wasn't there. Management issues? Maybe. But not discrimination." Roberts said that "no one ever told [me]" that she had been hired because of her race, although she didn't deny reality. Some of her African-American friends demanded an explanation. "They said, 'Well? Did they discriminate against him?' The answer was, 'No.' That was pretty much it. Were there conversations behind my back? I'm sure there were. But I had no doubts that anyone I represented was racist."

There was nothing unethical about Roberts being hired based on her race. In cities with big minority populations, it isn't unusual. Parties to a lawsuit are entitled to choose lawyers to whom potential jurors will relate. And it would be unfair, to say the least, to prevent black lawyers from capitalizing on the sort of advantage that white attorneys have in front of all-white juries. But that isn't to say that all blacks would be willing to be used as a front by a rich white law firm that was representing another rich white law firm. Many black lawyers would worry that they would be viewed as a mere prop—that their clients might not even remember their name when introducing them to the judge, for example.

Warner further underscored the nature of Roberts's role by stepping forward and arguing the summary judgment motion himself. For the jury, if there was to be one, Seyfarth had a black woman. For the white male judge, they had a white man.

In its motion for summary judgment, Katten Muchin told Judge James Robertson that he should throw the case out because nothing that Mungin complained about could have violated the civil rights laws. Robertson was skeptical from the start. As soon as he had reproved Warner for forgetting his co-counsel's name, the judge told the Chicago lawyer, "Motions for summary judgment in Title VII cases are tough. You knew that when you filed it."

Robertson looked the part of the judge: silver-gray hair turning to white and a handsome tanned face with a prominent chin. He was relatively new on the bench but had spent decades trying cases as a lawyer. He had no shortage of confidence in his instincts. Although he didn't explain himself, all of the lawyers in the courtroom, including Mungin, understood his clipped comment about summary judgment in discrimination cases. Many white-collar discrimination cases turn on the meaning of comments and actions that are subject to differing interpretations. Did Katten Muchin *hurt* Mungin or *help* him when it gave him basic bankruptcy work to boost his billable hours? Lawyers would call that a classic "question of fact," to be determined by a jury. Robertson, who had already read briefs from both sides and had scanned transcripts of the depositions in the case, made it clear that Warner had a difficult task in front of him.

The Mungin team was thrilled by the judge's preliminary comment. If they could get past summary judgment, they would be able to make Mungin's case to jurors, nonexperts who would be far less concerned about technical legal standards. "Getting to the jury was all I was focused on," Mungin said later. "Then we were home."

Trying to confound the standard imagery of victimhood, Warner stressed in his argument that it had been *his* clients—the law firm and the four individual defendants—who'd been harmed and had "a right to be freed from this litigation as soon as possible." Continuing in this vein, Warner pretended to have Mungin's interests at heart. "I accept that he genuinely believes that the treatment may well have been a product of his race," Warner said. But he was wrong, and "it may well be in Mr. Mungin's interest to have this case end now so that he can proceed looking forward instead of backwards."

"Oh, *please*," Mungin said under his breath.

Warner devoted most of his argument to singing the praises of the individual defendants. Mark Dombroff, he said, willingly hired the plaintiff, "knowing Mr. Mungin was an African-American." It didn't make sense that Dombroff would later treat Mungin poorly because of his race. Vincent Sergi, meanwhile, was "one of the last people who should be charged with discrimination."

Rather than counter Warner defendant by defendant, Abbey Hairston decided to rest her argument on the theory that Katten Muchin was a workplace animated by racial hostility. "This is really a case about callous indifference, a very willful indifference on the part of the defendants," Hairston said. "None of those individuals on their own came to Mr. Mungin and encouraged and worked with him or supported him in any efforts to be in a position where he could be considered and perhaps even made a partner in the firm, which was the reason why he took the position in the first place. . . . [T]he gravamen of the situation in this case was the creation of a hostile work environment for Mr. Mungin."

The judge seemed doubtful. "Surely," he said, "you are not going to try this case, Ms. Hairston, on the premise that all Mr. Mungin had to do was get hired, and then everything would be given to him, mentors and salary and work and everything."

"Absolutely not," Hairston said. Realizing she was in trouble, she fired off a jumbled burst of lawyer-talk; the judge silenced her with a crisp, "Okay."

"Let me tell you what I know about the hostile workplace case, or what I think I know about it," Robertson said. He ticked off the comments that had offended Mungin: Gilmore's "You have a job, a paycheck . . ."; Villa's observation that there were plenty of blacks in the mailroom; and Nancy Luque's "As long as you get a paycheck, you do as you're told."

"What else?" he demanded of Hairston.

She offered for his consideration Mungin's frustration in bringing younger black lawyers into the Washington office and the difficulties Elaine Williams had in Chicago.

"But it has to be a hostile workplace not for [others] but for *Mr. Mungin*," Robertson insisted.

Hairston moved on to other claims, but the judge didn't warm to those, either. When she sat down, Robertson announced, "I want to tell counsel where I am right now." He didn't dress pronouncements in unneeded verbiage.

"There will be a trial unless you settle this case," he said. "The motion for summary judgment will not be granted entirely, but it will be granted in part."

There will be a trial. Mungin would get his day before a jury.

The judge said he saw the Mungin case as a narrow one. The question was whether Mungin had been treated differently from white colleagues and whether he had been effectively forced to leave his job by the mistreatment. "The hostile work environment claim," Robertson said, "does not come close to meeting" the established standard of pervasive intimidation or ridicule. No "reasonable jury could find a hostile work environment," he added, "and that element of the complaint will be dismissed." He hadn't fully made up his mind, but Robertson said he was inclined to dismiss the individual lawyers as defendants, as well. "I have a feeling that the trial of this case may be somewhat more streamlined than the plaintiffs had in mind," the judge concluded.

Hairston wasn't terribly troubled. She figured that she would get to put on much the same evidence, whatever theory the judge permitted. Jurors weren't law professors who would parse the differences between "disparate treatment" and "hostile work environment." Jurors want a good story, and Mungin had one.

"We're going to trial, buddy!" Hairston said to Nelson as they left the courthouse and headed for their car. It would be Nelson's first trial. He considered himself lucky that they had a plaintiff who would impress a jury—if only Mungin would control himself.

"You're going to get your million," Hairston told her client as they parted. Mungin thought he might do even better. Summary judgment had been the most threatening obstacle. Now Katten Muchin would have to play in a court where he would be seen as the hometown favorite. Mungin walked by himself to the Judiciary Square subway station and caught the train home to Alexandria. He took a nap and then went to the gym.

The television was dark in his father's hospital room when Mungin arrived. Larry suddenly realized this might be his last visit. Junior was on a ventilator and couldn't talk; he could barely move. But his eyes seemed to open wider when his son came to the bedside. Larry stood there for a long time, speaking to him softly.

"It was sad," Larry told me. "But I think he knew there had been some forgiveness and that gave him peace."

Junior died on January 23, 1996.

It was the general consensus at Edisto's New First Baptist Church that the funeral went well. A soul, once thought lost, had returned to the fold. Junior had followed a path not uncommon among the male members of New First Baptist. Footloose into middle age, many men circled back to the church in their 50s, as they began to contemplate their mortality and worry about who would tend their graves. Junior had become a steady presence within the congregation.

The Spartan whitewashed church was filled with at least 150 people, and there were a couple of dozen more who stood outside, content to talk and greet. The choir sang a gospel dirge as the immediate family filed in and sat in the front pew. The closed casket, covered with flowers, stood in front of the simple wooden altar. The deacons looked on sternly from their place of honor at the preacher's right. From the lectern, Assistant Pastor Charles "Chick" Morrison spoke warmly of his friend, Lawrence Lucas Mungin, Jr. Junior had told Morrison that he would die a happy man because "the family has come home." Pastor Toney Dease added in his eulogy that "Brother Mungin had his life in order. He knew he made some mistakes. He atoned for them. Brother Mungin came to the church."

Junior's high school classmates were asked to stand. He had

been a member of the last graduating class of Penn Center, a famous school started by northern abolitionists to educate newly freed slaves. Four Penn Center graduates got to their feet. A testimonial was read. Junior was part of history here, his son thought.

With a flourish of prayer and song, the casket was opened, and worshippers paraded past to say a last farewell. Larry was relieved that there weren't any histrionics; no one collapsed or tried to climb into the coffin. Everyone agreed that the mortician had done a fine job. Junior looked almost like his old self. The choir sang an upbeat hymn as everyone left the sanctuary.

They buried Junior in the pleasingly overgrown graveyard behind the church, near many other Mungins, going all the way back to slave times. In the end, Larry thought, his father redeemed himself. "He drew me into this place. Through his illness and death, I met these people. I saw this land, some of which was now my land, and I got a sense there was some decency in him. . . . He knew he was lucky to have saved face, that I showed up, that I was going to take over. He didn't have to say, 'I was a terrible father.' "

CHAPTER FIFTEEN

"Racism: When It's There, You Can See It"

MARCH 1996

"This case is about a claim of racial discrimination," Judge Robertson declared in a tone suddenly grave. His silver glasses perched low on his nose, he said: "The only thing [the jury would] use as a basis for deciding this case is the evidence in this courtroom."

Robertson evidently was concerned that some potential jurors might be swayed by a feeling of racial solidarity in making sense of the confrontation that was about to unfold. Earlier, he had interrupted the jury-selection process to ask the nearly all-black group of 30 prospects: Given that the plaintiff, Mungin, was African-American, and the defendant law firm was white, did any members of the pool think they would have difficulty rendering "a fair and impartial verdict, without giving favoritism to one side or another?"

Silence answered the judge. Some people in the pool shifted on the courtroom's uncomfortable wooden benches. Robertson searched their faces for a moment, then resumed the winnowing process.

Inevitably, the O.J. Simpson case came up. In a trial about race, albeit a civil trial, how could there not be some allusion to the polarizing spectacle that had ended only five months earlier with Simpson's acquittal on murder charges? During jury selection, one potential juror in the Mungin case, a retired school principal, confessed to being familiar with Michele Roberts because he had seen her on television providing expert O.J. commentary.

Would you hold that against her? the judge asked.

No, the former educator said.

Would you weigh it in her favor? Hairston wanted to know.

"Sure, to her favor," the ex-principal answered cheerfully. "Glad to see her on the tube."

It may have been no more than enthusiasm for a hometown lawyer getting some air time, but the comment was enough to get the ex-principal bounced from the Mungin jury. Judge Robertson was determined that Simpsonmania not infect his courtroom. The lack of a bloody murder, a celebrity defendant, or a violent interracial marriage helped, of course. But another important distinction between the two cases was that in place of the hapless Judge Lance Ito, who allowed preening lawyers to walk all over him on nationwide television, the Mungin case had a firm taskmaster in Judge Robertson. TV cameras were banned from the Mungin case, as they are in almost all federal court proceedings. Robertson told Hairston and Roberts that they would have only 10 hours each to put on testimony and cross-examine the other side's witnesses. He even brandished a large double clock of the sort used in chess matches. The trial would last a week—no longer—the judge vowed.

Robertson took only a couple of hours to select a panel of six jurors, plus two alternates, who also sat in the jury box. Federal judges have discretion to try civil cases with as few as six jurors, in the interest of saving time and expense. Robertson worked skillfully with the lawyers from each side to cull problem cases. One candidate mentioned that he took an array of medication and had recently been the target of what he called a "speed hijacking." The judge politely sent him away. The jurors selected were mostly in their 60s or older and working class:

- Gladys Morrison, 66, a retired clerical worker for the federal government.
- Phyllis Allen, 62, a retired counselor of abused and HIV-positive children.
- Evelyn Sligh, 51, a former McDonald's manager. "Did you ever have to fire anyone?" Hairston asked her. "Quite a few times," Sligh said. Hairston didn't object to her taking a seat.
- Sylvia Carroll, 46, a federal grant manager.
- Elwood Vaughn, 74, a retired warehouse worker at Walter Reed Hospital. Under questioning, he appeared not to understand the difference between civil and criminal trials but was seated anyway.
- Robert Lucky, 66, a retired steward at the exclusive Cosmos Club.
- Catherine Matthews, also 66, a health aide, who clearly didn't want to be on the jury. She glared at Robertson when her turn came to be questioned. "It took you a long time to get up here," the judge apologized, referring to a momentary delay. "You can send me back out, too," Matthews said.
- Anna Marks, 64, a retired Capitol Hill secretary, and the only white juror. She said she had been fired from two jobs over the course of her career. "Did you file any complaints?" Robertson asked. "No," Marks said, matter-of-factly. "It was in the fifties," long before unhappy employees sued.

Marks and Matthews took their seats as the two alternates; at the trial's conclusion, Judge Robertson would allow them to deliberate and vote, even though he didn't need to remove any of the first six.

Defense attorney Michele Roberts had the same concern about race that the judge had, although from a partisan perspective. The former public defender, herself African-American, feared that the seven black Washingtonians on the jury would be suspicious of a white corporate law firm. That was why Michael Warner, the white Chicago lawyer who had directed Katten Muchin's defense until the trial, now sat in the third row of the spectators' section.

An angular, combative woman who practiced tae kwon do as a hobby, Roberts flipped through documents at the defense table while loudly crunching on ice from the water pitcher provided by the courtroom clerk. Close by, Vince Sergi sat quietly. Next to the trial-toughened Roberts, Sergi looked soft, vulnerable. But he didn't appear embarrassed or contrite. While the Mungin mess ought to have reflected badly on Sergi's management abilities, his status within Katten Muchin hadn't suffered noticeably. Quite the contrary: Since the filing of the lawsuit, Sergi had been elevated to co-managing partner, a promotion that could be read as the firm's defiant refusal to admit that Sergi had done anything wrong.

Still, for at least a few days, Sergi, a lawyer used to practicing law in private conference rooms, would be out of his element, exposed to public inspection by jurors who hadn't a clue how important he was back home in Chicago. He occupied himself writing page after page of notes on a long white legal pad.

Sitting at the plaintiff's table, only 15 feet from Sergi, Mungin whispered to Abbey Hairston. He looked like a man of accomplishment and privilege, dressed in a light-gray double-breasted suit and fashionable wire-rimmed glasses. Portraying him as the victim, despite his obvious success, and despite the absence of stark evidence of racism in the case, would be Hairston's central challenge.

"The plaintiff, represented by Ms. Hairston, goes first with the opening statements," said Judge Robertson. Hairston, who wore a tapered charcoal-gray business suit, turned the wooden lectern toward the jury and began.

She immediately confronted the potential problem of her client coming off as thin-skinned, the sort of person who, when thrown in with whites, was quick to blame problems on race. "Larry's case is a little unusual, because you have a lawyer suing a law firm," Hairston said. But "you will learn through Larry's testimony that he was not unfamiliar or uncomfortable with living in a situation where he was either the only, or one of a few blacks." She clasped her hands behind her back and bowed slightly at the waist to emphasize a word or phrase. "In high school, he was in advanced classes where he was the only black. When he went to Harvard, he had no black roommates. When he was in the Navy . . . he was one of two blacks out of six hundred to serve as a Russian linguist." At the several law firms that had employed him, the story was the same: "the only black within his department and one of a few blacks in the firm.

"So we are not talking about an individual who made a habit of filing discrimination claims everywhere he worked or had a discomfort with working with white people. Instead, we're talking about just the opposite kind of individual, who had spent the majority of his lifetime working in an environment where he expected adversity, but not injustice."

As Hairston outlined her case, she verbally italicized certain racially charged words. "You will hear Larry describe how, ultimately, he was *segregated* in the Washington, D.C., office. He was the only black attorney in that office." Mungin, who sat facing the jury, worked with Hairston, nodding slightly as she hit key images. Later, when he took the witness stand, Mungin would himself engage in provocative wordplay.

Hairston wasn't a consistently smooth speaker. She got tangled at times in clunky legalisms. But periodically, she broke free with a perfect metaphor: "Larry became a basketball," she said. "He was passed off between Vince Sergi, who is sitting at defendant's table . . . and Mark Dombroff, who was the managing partner in the District of Columbia." When she had them in the witness box, Hairston planned to goad the current and former Katten Muchin partners into blaming each other for Mungin's poor treatment.

Hairston acknowledged that the evidence wouldn't be sensational. "This is not a case where you're going to hear blatant racial slurs, cruel jokes. It's not direct. It has to be inferred." And the surface facts about Katten Muchin's business problems wouldn't tell the whole story, she warned. "You have to look beyond and see what is the truth." Compare my client to his antagonists, and choose a side, she urged. "You have to assess the credibility of each person who gets up on that stand and make a determination as to whether or not you believe more likely than not they're being honest. The most important issue in this case is credibility, because you're going to hear a lot of difference in testimony as to the reasons why Larry was treated the way he was treated."

Hairston intelligently kept her opening argument short and didn't make many specific promises about the testimony she would present. Experienced litigators believe that jurors punish few mistakes as severely as unkept promises in a flamboyant opening. Hairston concluded with a deft distillation. "Ladies and gentlemen," she said, "this case is about fairness. That's all it is. Was Larry treated fairly under the circumstances? And if [not], why not? It's our hope that you will conclude that the reason why he was not treated fairly was because of his race."

Michele Roberts was eager to steer the jurors in a different direction, but first she worried about the spectators in the courtroom. There were only three of us: Michael Warner, Andy Marcus, a former Katten Muchin paralegal and Mungin friend; and me. Uncertain of who Marcus and I were, Roberts demanded to know whether Hairston intended to have us testify, in which case she wanted to invoke the rule banning witnesses from hearing testimony before they take the stand.

No, Hairston told the judge, we weren't witnesses. "That's Paul Barrett from the *Wall Street Journal* and Andy Marcus, who is just a friend."

Marcus soon left, so for most of the five-day trial, Michael Warner and I were the only regular spectators. Even Warner disappeared before the end. The only other observers were the young law clerks and casually dressed tourists who wandered in from time to time. Facing the toughest fight of his life, Mungin drew no steady supporters.

"You know, ladies and gentlemen," Michele Roberts said from the lectern, "it's been said that when it's there, you know it. Racism. When it's there, you know it. When it's there, you can see it." As Hairston had done, Roberts appealed to the jurors' special expertise on the topic. But she reminded them that they were also experts at sniffing out frauds. They had all known people who used race as an excuse. Slipping into a preacher's rhythm, Roberts continued: "Sometimes it's subtle. But whether overt or obvious, when it's there, ladies and gentlemen, you *know* it. It's *clear*. You don't have to *guess* about it or assume that's what it is. If it's there, you *see* it.

"Well, ladies and gentlemen, from this case, on this record, with respect to Lawrence Mungin and Katten Muchin & Zavis, it ain't there." Roberts knew she couldn't make her client seem entirely appealing, but she genuinely believed—and was being paid handsomely to make the jury believe—that the firm hadn't violated any laws. How to convey this distinction? Roberts had decided to make a virtue of Katten Muchin's tendency to handle its associates shabbily: She would assert that this was just the way things were done in big corporate law firms. "You'll learn that Mr. Mungin may have had reasons to complain," she told the jury. "But, ladies and gentlemen, you'll learn that Mr. Mungin's unhappiness and his reasons to complain had nothing whatsoever to do with race. . . . How are you going to know, ladies and gentlemen, that Mr. Mungin's complaints, reasons to be unhappy, had nothing to do with race? I'll tell you how you're going to know. . . . Mr. Mungin wasn't alone. You know why? Mr. Mungin wasn't the only person to complain. You know why? Mr. Mungin wasn't the only person that was unhappy. He had company. A whole *heap* of company.

"Do you know how that company looked to Mr. Mungin? White, white. As my grandmother used to say, *lily white*. White attorneys, white support staff, all had the same complaints. All treated the same way." Roberts committed herself to displaying at least some of this heap of unhappy white company, in a defense strategy reminiscent of that sometimes chosen by wayward government contractors. Weapons manufacturers caught padding bills will often argue, in essence, Well sure, we charge a lot of overhead, but that's just the way we do things in this industry."

In contrast to Hairston's more formal style, Roberts was casual, colloquial. As she spoke, she chopped at the air with her left hand and even continued to crunch ice between words. There really weren't significant disputes on the facts, she seemed to say. On the topic of client contact, for example, she promised the jury it would "hear from other attorneys . . . that worked with the same partners that Mr. Mungin worked with. And they're going to tell you that they, too, had to suffer the *nonsense* of those partners who refused to allow them client contact." The others who were cut off were white, she added. "Racism, it ain't there. You won't see it."

Mungin peered at the jurors, shaking his head sorrowfully, as you might over a child not telling the truth. At least several jurors glanced directly back at him. Communication in this trial wouldn't be limited to dry words uttered from the lawyers' lectern and the witness box, regardless of Judge Robertson's instructions.

Roberts was reaching her final chorus. "When it's there, ladies and gentlemen, you don't have to guess about it. When it's there, you don't have to assume about it. When it's there, you can see it."

Judge James Robertson, 56, had seen it in the raw: racism without apology or nuance. Although he had spent most of his legal career as a partner with one of Washington's top corporate law firms, he had left the conventional career track to do civil rights work in the late 1960s and early 1970s. He served in Jackson, Mississippi, as chief counsel for the Lawyers Committee for Civil Rights Under Law, filing suit on behalf of black clients struggling with everything from job discrimination to police brutality. His first taste of this sort of work had come in 1968, when downtown Washington went up in flames after Martin Luther King's assassination. The riots stunned Robertson, a young associate who had kept his head down for most of the tumultuous 1960s. He joined others from his law firm, Wilmer, Cutler & Pickering, who volunteered to represent blacks prosecuted for rioting. Then he took a sabbatical from commercial litigation to work for the Lawyers Committee, which deployed many northern attorneys to fight racism across the South. Explaining his motivation years later, Robertson noted modestly that he had gone to law school with the vague notion of making "a contribution." Here was his chance.

Robertson returned to the Wilmer firm in 1972 and soon made partner. His clients were automobile and pharmaceutical manufacturers, television networks and insurance companies. He joined elite social clubs, made a handsome living, and was elected president of the D.C. bar association. His rationale for choosing to labor in the higher reaches of the legal-corporate establishment was that from that position he could afford to continue to push liberal causes. Which he did. He represented the NAACP, for example, in a major U.S. Supreme Court case that resulted in a 1982 ruling protecting civil rights protesters from being sued by white businesses they had boycotted.

As blacks made great gains from the 1960s through the 1980s, Robertson saw the issue of race relations migrate from the streets to office suites. In his role as leader of the D.C. bar, he gave speeches and convened conferences on how to promote the careers of minority lawyers. As a working lawyer, though, he had much in common with partners at Katten Muchin. (In fact, in one case in 1984, Robertson teamed with a Katten Muchin attorney to defend a government contractor accused of fraud.) At the Wilmer firm, Robertson was aware of black associates who felt less comfortable than their white colleagues. He sympathized but didn't believe such discomfort was necessarily the result of racism, whether conscious or unconscious. The problem was complicated. There weren't easy answers.

Robertson came to the Mungin case, then, with the sympathies of a civil rights lawyer, but also those of a former big-firm partner. He knew that even well-intentioned employers could be blamed unfairly for ordinary career problems.

* * *

Ideally, Mungin's dispute with Katten Muchin ought to have been resolved privately, in Robertson's view. He signaled on several occasions before the trial that the attorneys should try to work out a compromise. But Robertson, who was appointed by President Bill Clinton in 1994, was still new to the bench and uneasy about knocking heads to get lawyers to settle—a skill some judges gain with experience.

Hairston had put a price on the case three times. Just prior to filing suit, she had told Warner that Mungin would settle for $3 million; later she dropped that amount to $1 million, plus her fees. On the eve of trial, Hairston said she dropped the figure to $675,000, although Mungin told me that he hadn't signed off on the last offer. In any event, Katten Muchin never offered more than about $250,000. The firm was adamant: It hadn't done anything wrong.

There was nothing more Robertson could do except run the trial as tightly as possible and try to keep the jurors focused on the evidence. In addition to trimming Hairston's case at the summary judgment stage by throwing out a number of claims, including the hostile work environment theory, he also had dismissed the individual defendants: Dombroff, Gilmore, Sergi, and Heller. Only the law firm as a whole remained as a defendant. Although technically defeats for the plaintiff's side, these actions were actually favors to Hairston and her client. She would have had to strain to prove all of the allegations in her original complaint. Demonizing the individual defendants—showing them to have personally treated Mungin differently from whites—would have been far more difficult than arguing that he was harmed by the cumulative actions of the firm. Judge Robertson focused Hairston's attention and limited her target.

By midday, all of the preliminaries were finished. The judge announced a lunch break, advising the jurors to eat lightly, so they wouldn't get sleepy in the warm, windowless courtroom.

When court reconvened an hour later, he announced, "We had a nice light lunch. We're ready to go."

"Real light," juror Matthews answered, catching the judge by surprise.

"Hungry already?" he asked her.

"Hungry already," she said.

Robertson paused, staring at Matthews, who stared back. Then the judge smiled and told Hairston to call her first witness.

CHAPTER SIXTEEN

"It's My Party; I'll Cry If I Want To"

Mungin looked enormous in the witness box, as if he were wearing football shoulder pads beneath his suit jacket. Hairston had called him as the first witness. She knew her chances turned largely on whether the jury liked and believed her client. The jurors were fresh, and doubtless curious about what sort of man Mungin was. Hairston wanted to grab their attention. Sitting ramrod straight, Mungin did just that.

His message was that he was one of them. He presently lived in "a little apartment" in Alexandria, he said in answer to Hairston's biographical inquiry. "I was born in New York City, Sydenham Hospital, in Harlem, U.S.A."

His siblings?

"Just hard-working people trying to make it."

School?

"Well, I worked hard. You know, that was the way out. . . . I did very well. I had a good mom."

He was one of them, a loyal son, the sort they could be proud of. He listed his many high school accolades and spoke of Harvard. His race didn't hinder him in the Navy, he said. "I grew up in the sixties and the seventies, when it was a time of opportunity. . . . I was not looking for things to hold me back."

A week before the trial, Hairston had organized a dress rehearsal for Mungin's testimony. About a dozen associates with Alexander, Aponte & Marks gathered in a conference room to play the jury. An experienced litigator with another small firm served as judge. Once Hairston had put Mungin through his paces, the others made suggestions: Mungin should slow down his answers and avoid mumbling. Don't get testy, as he had in the deposition. "If you show them who you are, what you've done with your life, the jury will understand," Hairston told him afterward. He listened. His performance before the real jury was brilliant: understated yet proud.

Hairston and Mungin wanted his testimony to illustrate that Katten Muchin's treatment of him diverged from standard law firm procedures. The challenge was to discuss how *other* law firms did things, without having the testimony excluded as irrelevant. Hairston asked Mungin about his summer job with a New York firm after his first year of law school. Was he evaluated at summer's end?

"Sure," Mungin answered quickly.

A second too late, Michele Roberts rose to object. His being evaluated elsewhere had no bearing on Katten Muchin.

"Sustained," the judge said. But Mungin had already made his point. "My performance was reviewed at the end of the summer," Mungin repeated, blatantly disobeying the judge.

"Objection!" Roberts said.

"Sustained." The judge glared at Mungin.

Asked to describe his first full-time job in Houston, Mungin testified that he had drafted documents and done a lot of library work. But he also worked closely with partners and met their clients.

"Can we approach?" Roberts interrupted. Mungin was obviously laying the foundation for asserting that Katten Muchin cut him off from clients. Lawyers from both sides and the court reporter gathered at the side of the judge's bench, out of the jury's hearing.

Roberts accused Mungin of trying to "backdoor," or sneak in, irrelevant evidence about his experiences at other firms.

The judge agreed. He warned Hairston against further backdooring.

Mungin testified that upon arriving at Katten Muchin, he immersed himself in the various firm documents about the promotion process. Hairston had him read aloud at length from the documents. "Each associate receives regular semiannual reviews based on evaluations from those senior attorneys with whom he or she recently worked," Mungin read. "Initial assignments will include direct client contact."

Hairston took a sharp turn away from this line of questioning to try to slip in a reference to Elaine Williams and her race-bias suit. Judge Robertson had said before trial that he would not allow any testimony about the Williams case. Mungin couldn't argue that because one African-American in Chicago felt aggrieved, another in Washington was more likely to have been victimized. So, Roberts quickly objected when Hairston asked Mungin to testify about reading an internal firm memo about Williams's suit in the summer of 1992. The judge ordered the lawyers back to his sidebar.

"So we've got a memo about somebody else's problems. So what?" the judge demanded.

"It gave him some concerns about whether or not the firm was going to be fair in the treatment of him when the only black partner had filed suit," Hairston said.

"I'll sustain that objection," Robertson said.

When Mungin retook the stand after the mid-afternoon break, he turned to the issue of race. Hairston asked about his brief service on the Washington office's hiring committee and the special effort to recruit blacks.

"Yes," Mungin said, he had participated "because I was the only black in the office and there was some concern expressed on my part and there was some concern because of the history—"

"Objection, Your Honor!" Roberts was on her feet.

"Sustained," Robertson said. "Let's start that answer over again." Mungin's version of Katten Muchin's "history" on race wasn't legally relevant. But he had succeeded in hinting that there was a history and that it was an unflattering one.

"There was a minority recruitment program that was established to recruit blacks," Mungin said.

Who was primarily responsible? Hairston asked.

"I believe I took more of a leadership role in it since I was the black, the *token*—the *token* on the committee and in the office."

"Objection, Your Honor." Roberts was up again, looking exasperated.

"Sustained," the judge said. "The jury will disregard that last statement of the witness." Robertson, arms crossed, shot Mungin another silent warning.

Hairston guided Mungin to the hiring of Janice Jamison, the part-time black student clerk from George Washington University. Mungin explained why he refused to be both mentor and work-assignment coordinator to Jamison. "I argued that that would *ghettoize* the whole program, if a black is completely in charge of her. So it would be fairer to her if she—"

"I object to that and ask it be stricken," Roberts interrupted. "Your Honor, just the term *ghettoize*."

"Yeah. I think it's an unfortunate choice of words," Robertson said. "But I'll overrule the objection."

"That it would *ghettoize* the entire program," Mungin restated, "because the purpose of it was for her to integrate, to be working with other partners." Mungin used every inch of leeway Robertson allowed him.

Hairston bounced on the balls of her feet, hands clasped behind her. This was all going very, very well. She and Mungin had annoyed the judge, but not quite enough to make him genuinely angry at them. And anyway, a plaintiff's lawyer wasn't doing her job unless she tested the judge. The jury, meantime, almost certainly would understand that the defense objections kept out negative information about Katten Muchin.

Hairston moved Mungin along to the period in 1993, when circumstances changed for the worse at Katten Muchin. He described how he sought guidance from Dombroff and Gilmore. "I wanted to make sure, since that was my partner-

ship year, that everything was in place, that I would get re-
warded for the work that I was doing, and that it was clear
what department I was in."

What did they say? Hairston asked.

"They made it unequivocally clear that I was not in their department, that I was in Vince Sergi's department, that I would
have to look to him for anything dealing with promotion,
marketing, ultimate evaluations for promotion." Dombroff
and Gilmore passed the basketball to Sergi.

A few minutes later, Mungin testified about Sergi's saying
he couldn't possibly evaluate Mungin, because he didn't know
anything about his work. "Regarding partnership, because I
asked him about partnership, he said, 'You slipped through
the cracks.'" Sergi dropped the basketball.

Mungin sewed silk purses from sows' ears. Of his misfired
"marketing" trip to Milan, he said: "I also took it upon myself
to go to Milan, Italy, for four days, jet lag and all, to meet the
partner in the Milan, Italy, office . . . [and] some people there
who wanted to work with me in the future in terms of developing possible business through the Milan office." In exchange for this fruitless extracurricular exertion, Mungin
complained to the jury, he was denied reimbursement of his
expenses.

A little while later, the firm told him that it had cut his
billing rate. "I was shocked, a little dumbfounded, and a little
intimidated," he said.

Did you quit? Hairston asked.

"Oh, no. I'm not a quitter," Mungin said. "It was getting
very difficult. I was in my partnership year. I didn't want to
give up. I was getting very worried. But Vince Sergi had told
me that I was doing fine." Sergi had told him so, Mungin explained, during their talk about the rate reduction. Sergi had
complained about his hours, Mungin conceded. "I was not
going to argue. If billables were important to him—this was
the first time he had ever said anything to me. I was in my
partnership year. I'm not a troublemaker. The billables will be
there."

Mungin described his sagging spirit. Why didn't he complain, Hairston asked, about being left out of the August 1993 seminar for airport operators? That was the one where Charlie Thomson, the white associate from Chicago, came in to give a talk on bankruptcy law.

"I didn't find out about it for another month or two," Mungin said, "and by that time, I was so humiliated, I didn't ask."

Hairston questioned at a deliberate pace, pausing for effect as she shifted from one incident to the next. The courtroom, a large drab space, would fall completely silent at the pauses, except for the buzzing of the fluorescent lights on the high vaulted ceiling. Most of the jurors looked intently at Mungin, even during the short lulls. He gazed back, smiling slightly.

Hairston had Mungin carefully re-create his December 1993 confrontation with Sergi in Chicago. Here, Hairston believed, the jurors could see how badly Mungin wanted to be taken seriously, and how casually the firm shunted him aside. She asked whether Mungin really thought that his receiving no raise in November had been an "oversight," as he suggested in an e-mail to Sergi and Heller.

"That was my polite, professional way of opening the topic," Mungin said. "I certainly didn't believe it was an oversight." He described how he insisted on a face-to-face meeting, despite Sergi's seeming resistance. "It was the most important meeting of my life," Mungin told the jury. "I confirmed it. It was very important to me."

Hairston had him read his torrent of e-mails, including the one mentioning that he would drive out of his way to Baltimore to take the cheapest possible flight. Mungin set the scene in Chicago: Heller's failure to show up, Sergi's desire to cancel the whole thing before it started, Mungin's own determination that they follow the agreed-upon agenda and that he receive his evaluation.

The only evaluations Sergi could produce were Dombroff's and Gilmore's, and those weren't much to speak of. Hairston asked Mungin to read aloud Gilmore's half-page performance review. Mungin found the document in the black loose-leaf notebook of trial exhibits Hairston had put in front of him. He began to read:

"Larry does not work with me in a traditional partner-associate setting, and accordingly, the standard evaluation form is inappropriate. Rather, Larry, in conjunction with Carlos Acosta [a first-year associate] and Cyndie Baughman [a paralegal] coordinates the routine oversight of responsibilities of approximately 100 bankruptcies. Much of Larry's time is consumed by routine tasks such as drafting status letters to our clients."

At the word *clients*, Mungin's voice caught. He took a sharp breath. Then he drew another quick gulp of air and released a clearly audible sob. His shoulders heaved and collapsed. He covered his eyes with his left hand.

"Your Honor, can we take a break, please?" Hairston asked.

"Yes, we'll take a break," Robertson said, peering down at Mungin. The courtroom clerk promptly led the jury out.

"Do you have some water there, Mr. Mungin?" the judge asked, looking concerned.

"Thank you," Mungin said softly. From the spectators' gallery, I couldn't tell whether he had actually shed tears. Hairston looked just as disconcerted as her client. Roberts sat silently at the defense table, an incredulous expression on her face. Within a few minutes, Mungin had composed himself. The clerk brought the jury back. Mungin cleared his throat and calmly read the rest of Gilmore's evaluation.

"Occasionally we receive a challenging assignment from AIG, which Larry accomplishes with great skill. AIG is a very difficult client, and Larry's ongoing efforts to coordinate with me have made a potentially troublesome situation relatively easy. I do not believe that, for the most part, AIG offers challenging work to Larry. Larry, nonetheless, accomplishes the tasks for AIG with a helpful attitude and a willingness to tackle the unique problems this client presents."

As he read the document, the question floated like a neon sign above Mungin's head: Had he faked the sob?

"I was shocked," Hairston told me later. "I thought, Larry,

you're getting carried away." Hairston worried that the jury would think Mungin contrived the demonstration.

Mungin apologized to Hairston at the next break but denied fabricating the response. Having to read an account of his mostly basic duties in public "just got to me," he told his lawyer. She reassured him; they both needed to keep their cool. Hairston told me later that what she was wondering was whether the jurors would see that even though the evaluation praised Mungin overall, it harmed him by confirming how rudimentary his responsibilities were.

At least one juror saw Mungin in a new light. "At first I didn't take him seriously because he was smiling so," Catherine Matthews said in a post-trial interview with *The American Lawyer*. "But he was smiling to hide the hurt. . . . When a man cries, you have to look at him. I started really looking."

When I later asked Mungin about the sob, he smiled. " 'It's my party; I'll cry if I want to,' " he said, quoting the old rock-and-roll song. I didn't know what to think. Later, he said flatly that the sob was genuine. I concluded that, just as he had consciously allowed himself to lose his temper in his deposition, Mungin let himself react to the anguish stirred by Gilmore's accurate account of his lowly role. Could he have kept his composure? Perhaps. But he thought it was to his advantage not to.

Wrapping up Mungin's testimony on the first day of trial, Hairston asked him, "Did Mr. Sergi, during the [December 1993] meeting, indicate to you any concerns he had with your work performance, personally?"

"None whatsoever," Mungin said. "We reconfirmed that I was still on track, that I should continue doing as I was doing, that he would ensure that I got credit for the value to the firm that I was giving."

Mungin left the courtroom as confident as a heavyweight champion who has spent the first round softening up a hack challenger. "I've been preparing for something like this my whole life," he said to me. "The jury is listening."

* * *

Mungin seemed to enjoy the confrontation and the opportunity to dramatize his frustrations at Katten Muchin. His direct testimony, which continued on the second day of trial, was fluent, even playful at times.

Hairston resumed her questioning by prompting him to describe the chaotic atmosphere in which Dombroff and Gilmore split from Katten Muchin. Mungin portrayed himself as helplessly adrift: "I saw people go into meetings. It was embarrassing for me. No one was including me." He testified that he didn't understand why Sergi insisted that after the spin-off, Mungin wouldn't have anything to do in Washington. "I said, 'Of course there will be something for me to do.'" He ticked off scattered examples of non-insurance work he had done, adding that he was also building his "own little practice."

Mungin's assertion was misleading, although he made it with such authority that it sounded credible. In fact, the non-insurance tasks he mentioned weren't enough to keep him busy, and his "own little practice" consisted of only a handful of hours of billable work. Katten Muchin conceivably could have accommodated Mungin by retraining him in another specialty and routing new assignments to him from Chicago. But some realignment of this sort would have been needed to allow him to remain productive in Washington after the Dombroff-Gilmore departure.

Repeatedly, Mungin said he was told that his choice was to transfer, or "be fired." He feared he was "getting squeezed out," he told the jury, because the transfer offers never included any specific information on what he would do in Chicago or New York. "I need something to give me some security that this firm wants me to stay," he recalled telling partner Richard Waller.

Mungin read from his own e-mails to illustrate his efforts to prod Katten Muchin into being more explicit about his potential new role in Chicago or New York. "I am not rejecting the New York option," he said in one message. "It's just that it is not entirely clear to me exactly what my other options are, especially when events are unfolding so rapidly and I have so little information." No one from Chicago ever responded to Mungin's plea for specifics, he told the jury.

Hairston asked Mungin to read his July 7, 1994, e-mail, in which he said that "personal constraints and other considerations" prevented him from moving to New York or Chicago. What did he mean?

"That's professional talk when you want to make sure you can have a reference," Mungin said. "It's being polite when you have no power." With evocative statements like this, Mungin successfully conveyed the unfair position that Katten Muchin had put him in. Sergi and other partners asked him to agree to a transfer based on the vaguest of assurances; Mungin had no reason to trust them, considering his prior experience with the firm.

An obvious weakness in Mungin's presentation was his dubious claim that he could have remained happy and busy in the Washington office. But at this point in the testimony, the jury had no reason to question that statement.

Some of Mungin's carefully crafted testimony—his use of the word *ghettoize*, for example—irritated Judge Robertson. Hairston asked her client whom he had told about filing his EEOC complaint. "By then," Mungin answered, "I was pretty well isolated. And I was talking to some of the support staff—"

"Could you just say who you told, sir," Robertson interrupted sharply.

"Okay," Mungin answered, his mission already accomplished.

At a break, Mungin and I spoke in the hallway. "I think they're buying the story," he said of the jury. He looked for my reaction.

I nodded noncommittally. I couldn't read the jurors, other than to observe that they were paying close attention.

"They see I'm for real, where I'm from," Mungin continued. "Katten didn't even give me a chance."

He seemed surprisingly calm, I told him.

"It just feels right," he said. He drew connections that I didn't fully understand. "My father's illness and death, burying my mother before that—I'm supposed to make a mark."

Mungin appeared to view the trial as the denouement of the first half of his life, a life he certainly thought of in dramatic terms.

Hairston concluded Mungin's direct testimony by eliciting some of his current circumstances. He had earned $9,000 a month as a Katten Muchin lawyer. That amount fell to about $1,300 on unemployment compensation.

How much was he now earning at the SEC?

"I got a raise in October. It's $14.17 [an hour] now," which worked out to about $2,300 a month. But he hadn't been able to work 40-hour weeks until recently.

Why was that?

Mungin explained that he had taken some days off to care for his dying father in South Carolina.

Did he intend to work 40-hour weeks now?

"I have to," Mungin said. His father had left $312,000 in medical bills.

Prior to this suit, had he ever filed a discrimination action against another employer?

"Of *course* not," Mungin said.

Michele Roberts rose from the defense table to start her cross-examination. In the public defender's office, before she went into private practice, Roberts was known for her skill in jabbing holes in the stories told by policemen and snitches. "I like dominating the courtroom . . . questioning a witness, the more hostile, the better," she once told the *Washington Post*.

She opened with a flurry of fast questions, peppering Mungin with the names of former Katten Muchin lawyers. After each name, she asked, "And he is a white male, right?" or "And she was a white woman; is that right?"

Mungin answered yes to each query, indicating by his tone a growing puzzlement over Roberts's point. *All* of the lawyers in the Washington office except him were white; that had been acknowledged by both sides.

The point, of course, related to Roberts's opening argument, in which she promised to show that Mungin "wasn't the only person" who was unhappy in Katten Muchin's Washington office, that he had "a whole heap of company." But after Roberts confirmed the race of 10 of Mungin's former co-workers, she unceremoniously moved on to another topic, failing to follow through with evidence that these white lawyers were "unhappy."

What could the jury possibly have made of the defense's opening thrust? It established nothing of substance. Roberts was off to a bad start.

She wanted to show the jury that Mungin had been mistaken or had lied about a whole range of small matters. This is a standard method of undermining a witness's credibility. It didn't work with Mungin. He politely insisted that his recollections were accurate, or that there were only trivial differences between his memory and Roberts's version of the truth. They tussled over the precise date of his interview with Dombroff. She said he got a raise just before leaving Powell Goldstein; he said it was a cost-of-living adjustment. The real question was: Who cares?

Roberts made the mistake of failing to provide any context for her jumpy questioning. She hopped from topic to topic, never seriously bruising Mungin.

At times, Roberts inadvertently reinforced the plaintiff's contention about Katten Muchin's uncivil behavior. She wanted Mungin to concede that he accepted the job without having met Sergi, although the significance of this point was unclear. "You didn't go to Chicago until June of 1992, correct?" Roberts asked.

"Right. Because he agreed that, after I started, I could go to Chicago."

"You didn't—"

"That if I accepted—"

"Mr. Mungin—"

"I'm sorry."

"—we'll be here *all day*. My question is: You didn't go to Chicago until June of 1992, correct?"

"Right."

"And, indeed, as you told us yesterday, when you got to Chicago, Mr. Sergi wasn't present, was he?"

"Right. He didn't show up."

In fact, Mungin didn't meet Sergi until he had been at the firm for six months, Roberts noted.

"Yes. And it bothered me."

"You didn't complain about it, did you?"

"I was working. I wasn't complaining."

Upshot: Mungin, the associate, was working, not complaining. Sergi, the partner, failed to show for an important meeting.

Roberts frequently asked questions with a cup of water poised near her lips. She continued to chew noisily on ice. This achieved the air of casual confidence she apparently sought, but her desultory interrogation appeared to do Mungin little, if any, damage.

Each time she made a modest point in Katten Muchin's favor, Mungin managed to turn it around. Roberts asked whether Mungin ever specifically inquired about getting a mentor at the firm.

"I didn't specifically ask [Dombroff]; that's correct."

"Thank you, Mr. Mungin. You also . . . did not discuss any evaluation system for associates with Mark Dombroff, did you?"

"Right. And I didn't discuss if I [would] have a desk and a chair. It comes. I expected to be evaluated."

His expectation surely would seem reasonable to a jury that had heard him read at length from the firm's internal documents, promising monitoring and evaluation of associates.

Eventually, the defense attorney seemed to realize that she wasn't getting anywhere. She began pacing while Mungin offered long, involved answers to her niggling questions. "Are you *done*?" she asked Mungin after one filibuster-length answer.

"Yeah," he said.

Roberts shifted to the cut in his billing rate. "You understood, Mr Mungin, that the reason for the reduction in your billable rate was because the insurance clients were not happy paying those big-firm fees? You understood that, right?"

"No, I didn't understand that."

"That's what you were told, isn't it?"

"That's what I was told—"

"All right."

"—but I didn't *believe* it."

Roberts seemed not to have anticipated that answer and had no response to Mungin's introducing the notion that Katten Muchin may have been deceiving him about the true reason for the rate cut.

Roberts moved on. She did establish some components of her client's defense. Mungin admitted that he spent most of his time on assignments from Dombroff and Gilmore and that they took all of that work with them when they left Katten Muchin. Roberts also effectively raised questions about Mungin's contention that he was hindered in marketing himself. She forced him to describe his misbegotten business trip to Milan, which the firm declined to pay for, and another, equally unprofitable venture in Los Angeles, which the firm did underwrite.

But on the core issue of his being treated differently from white attorneys, Mungin thwarted Roberts by casting doubt on whether he had "a whole heap" of white company when Katten Muchin mishandled him. He agreed, for example, that Jeff Sherman and some other white attorneys in Washington were barred from directly contacting Dombroff-Gilmore clients. But he suggested that there were other more-favored Dombroff underlings who *did* deal with the insurance clients on their own. Roberts didn't contradict him.

Was Mungin aware, Roberts asked, that a white woman attorney from the Washington office, whom neither Dombroff nor Katten Muchin wanted, was laid off, while Mungin was offered a transfer?

"But there was no work" for that attorney, Mungin answered blandly. Roberts had no follow-up question. Instead, she noted ambiguously that Katten Muchin offered to keep only two lawyers who had done work for Dombroff but whom he left behind. Mungin was one of them.

Mungin shrugged, unimpressed.

Without more information about the fates of the other junior lawyers in Washington, this exchange couldn't have meant much to the jury.

Roberts was glancing frequently at her notes. Had Mungin half-heartedly inquired in 1993 about a job at Coca-Cola in Atlanta?

Yes.

Did Mungin understand that he was an at-will employee and could have been fired at any time?

Yes.

"I'm winding down, Mr. Mungin," Roberts said, sounding strangely apologetic. "Just a few other questions." She sat down after less than three hours of cross-examination.

Hairston looked at her associate, Adrian Nelson. They had the same thought, Nelson recalled later: Is this it?

The plaintiff's lawyers were elated. "We were waiting for dirt," Nelson said. "There was no dirt. They had nothing on Larry. There was no real defense."

Roberts had failed to tag Mungin with more than glancing blows. There would be more chances and other witnesses. But the plaintiff's testimony would clearly be the most important of the trial, and he left the stand the victor over Roberts. Mungin was more nimble. Roberts failed to organize her interrogation in a way that would make her contentions clear to the jury. She underestimated Mungin's ability to dodge and feint. Having studied the transcript of his deposition, she likely thought he would lose his temper. But Mungin was a different witness in the courtroom, in front of the jury—when it really counted.

CHAPTER SEVENTEEN

"Afraid We Would Lose Him"

David Schulman was the keeper of Katten Muchin's charts and rules. The balding, soft-spoken partner from Chicago hadn't dealt with Mungin directly, but Hairston wanted to use him to explain the firm's internal workings and establish that procedures that benefited other associates weren't in place for Mungin.

Schulman gamely described the elaborate promotion process. The subject-area departments—Corporate, Litigation, Finance and Reorganization, and so on—recommended potential partners to the department heads committee, which passed names along to the partnership review committee, which filtered them to the board of directors, which received advice from the executive committee. Smiling and apologizing for the complexity, Schulman appeared to revel in his mastery of firm bureaucracy.

Hairston turned Schulman's attention to the minutes of an October 1992 firm meeting. She had obtained this document and others like it as part of the discovery process. The minutes recorded that the executive committee approved the promotion to income partner of a white associate, James Baer, even though, according to the minutes, "there may not be enough work to keep him fully occupied." Hairston methodically elicited that although he lacked enough clients of his own, Baer was promoted and given a salary of $170,000 because he was highly thought of and had backers among the partners. The rules, in other words, were flexible in this regard.

Schulman squirmed a little, but agreed.

Hairston offered another such case, involving a white estate-planning associate who was promoted to income partnership without clients of his own and without much expectation that he would ever achieve full-fledged capital partner status. This associate was elevated because the firm "needed to have a person with his skill and experience," Schulman explained. "Every decision about partnership is a specific one made with reference to a specific individual."

"Okay, so, again, it depends," Hairston coaxed.

"It depends," the witness conceded. Hairston had established that Mungin's lack of clients, in and of itself, shouldn't have been an automatic basis for failing to consider him for partnership.

She next delved into the knotty subject of Mungin's salary. She put up on an easel in front of the jury a series of oversized charts drawn from the law firm's own records. The charts showed the salaries of all lawyers at the firm who, like Mungin, graduated from law school in 1986. Several of the jurors leaned forward in their seats to get a better look, as Hairston questioned Schulman about the numbers.

In 1992, his first year, Mungin made less than the four white insurance associates in Washington who graduated in 1986. His total compensation of $102,000 (prorated to reflect his May 1 starting date) was $4,000 less than that of three of the comparable lawyers and $13,000 less than one of them. The charts showed that of 14 class of 1986 associates working in Chicago, only one, a white man, received lower total compensation than Mungin.

For 1993, Mungin was listed as making the same total compensation—$104,000—as one Washington associate, a new hire named John Enerson, and less than the other four. The next-highest-paid associate received $106,000. Pay for Chicago associates of similar seniority was higher across the board in 1993. For 1994, Mungin received an $8,000 raise in salary, to $108,000, but he left without getting a bonus, making comparisons difficult. (Also, the firm hadn't provided complete 1994 information on some other associates.)

Hairston didn't challenge Schulman as to why Mungin was at, or near, the bottom of the salary charts for 1992 and 1993. She had shaded her client's name in gray, however, so the jury could not miss the point.

Schulman explained that when Katten Muchin hired experienced associates from lower-paying firms, it generally split the difference between the associate's former salary and what his Katten Muchin classmates were making. The new hire would feel like he got a raise, while Katten Muchin saved some money. In any event, Schulman pointed out, potential new recruits didn't have to take the offer; they could work somewhere else if they thought Katten Muchin was short-changing them.

This, of course, is exactly what happened to Mungin. In early 1992, when he moved to Katten Muchin, he agreed to what amounted to a $5,000 raise over his $87,000 Powell Goldstein salary. Dombroff never offered to bring him up to the $95,000 (or higher) base salary that other 1986 associates in the Washington office were receiving. Mungin freely agreed to accept $92,000.

Schulman's testimony that the firm's general practice appeared to have been followed in Mungin's case seemed to deflate Hairston's argument that his starting salary was discriminatory. Amazingly, neither Hairston nor Schulman appeared to realize the significance of what he said. Hairston didn't seem surprised by Schulman's answers and didn't try to undercut the witness. For his part, Schulman testified as if he were engaged in an academic inquiry into law firm salary practices, rather than a race-discrimination lawsuit. He failed to draw any connections between his testimony and Mungin's experience.

Lacking a road map to Schulman's winding testimony, the jury, in all likelihood, never realized the significance of what it heard—beyond the raw fact of Mungin's being paid less than white colleagues.

In an equally odd series of questions, Hairston prodded Schulman to recount how Mungin received the $8,000 raise for 1994. Sergi came to Schulman's office and told him that "he wanted to save Mr. Mungin, that we had kept his base salary flat, and he wanted to provide an increase because he wanted to keep him in the firm, and he wanted to save him," Schulman said. "He was afraid we would lose him if we didn't."

This testimony raised the question of why Hairston would invite a loyal Katten Muchin partner to narrate alleged efforts to help her client.

The question was never answered, but Hairston recovered some ground with an almost offhand inquiry shortly before finishing with Schulman. Was there "a performance review process for income partners?" she asked.

"Oh, yes," said the expert on firm procedure.

"Was there a performance review process for associates?"

"The answer is yes."

Mungin, according to this testimony, wasn't foolish or naive to expect that he would be evaluated. Hairston nodded with satisfaction and took her seat.

Roberts now had the strange assignment of cross-examining a member of her client firm. She might have tailored her questions to explain to the jury the importance of what Schulman had said about salary matters. But Roberts didn't do that. She instead encouraged Schulman to expostulate endlessly about the firm's Byzantine process of determining salaries and bonuses. He made it sound like the partners in Chicago spent three-quarters of their time worrying about who would be paid how much. At one point late in the afternoon, Roberts, bogged down in the wording of one of her own questions, interrupted herself to sigh, "I'm so tired."

Hairston saw an opening and rose for "redirect" examination, a second crack at her own witness. Roberts had prompted

Schulman to discuss a sample white attorney who was turned down for income partnership in late 1993. But this attorney "at least was *considered*," for promotion, "would you agree?" Hairston asked.

"Yeah. He was nominated."

"And he was discussed and reviewed, correct?"

"Oh, yes."

"And Mr. Mungin, to your recall, was never considered; is that correct?"

"That's correct. He was not nominated. That's correct."

"I have nothing further, Your Honor," Hairston said.

Before the Mungin trial, Hairston was best known in Washington legal circles for having represented Benjamin Chavis in a 1994 lawsuit against the NAACP. Chavis, a controversial black leader, had challenged his ouster as the group's executive director. That dispute grew out of another, in which Chavis was accused of improperly spending NAACP money to settle a sexual-harassment complaint. The Chavis case had helped put Alexander, Aponte & Marks on the legal map, but at a personal cost to Hairston. Suing the venerable NAACP didn't win her a lot of new friends, black or white. The Mungin case, by contrast, was an opportunity to emphasize her preferred role as an advocate for minorities and women, fighting long odds and white male authority.

At the conclusion of the second day of testimony, Judge Robertson cautioned Hairston that by his chess-clock calculations, she might run out of time needed to cross-examine some of her opponent's witnesses. "That's a pretty high-risk operation," the judge observed.

"Well, I take risks," Hairston said evenly.

The first time Mungin ever laid eyes on David Heller was on the third day of trial, Wednesday, March 20. The two men crossed paths in the central aisle of the spectators' section of Judge Robertson's fourth-floor courtroom. "Hi, Larry. How are you doing?" Heller asked, sticking out his hand.

"Hello," Mungin answered, shaking Heller's hand and

marveling at the attorney's cheerful demeanor. Sergi and Mungin hadn't exchanged a word and had been avoiding eye contact, even on those occasions when they had to brush past one another at the swinging wooden doors to the corridor.

On the stand, Heller claimed that at the time he joined the firm, he knew very little about Mungin. Was he aware that Mungin was part of the Finance and Reorganization Department, which Heller co-chaired?

"No."

"What was your understanding of the department that Larry was working in at that time?"

"I had no understanding of whether he was in a formal department or not, so to speak."

Hairston walked Heller up to the December 1993 confrontation in Chicago, including Mungin's e-mail, addressed to Sergi and Heller, confirming that he was traveling to the home office "for [his] written review."

"Did you have any knowledge that Mr. Mungin was . . . coming to Chicago to get a review of his work performance?" Hairston asked.

"No I did not."

"Did you . . . believe that it was your responsibility to provide Mr. Mungin with a review of his work performance?"

"No, I did not." Heller added that he thought Mungin had a beef only about his pay. Heller professed to know almost nothing about Mungin's problems.

Roberts tried to improve Heller's image on cross-examination, asking him about Sergi's suggestion that he find more complex work for Mungin. Then Roberts made a tactical mistake. She asked a "why" question without knowing how the witness would respond.

"Did Mr. Sergi ever explain to you *why* it was that he wanted you to make efforts to get some work for Mr. Mungin?"

"Yes. Among other reasons, we wanted to keep all of our lawyers busy. . . . And Mr. Sergi emphasized to me that Mr. Mungin was a minority candidate, and it was the firm's philosophy to advance minority candidates and retain them."

This seemingly innocuous answer arguably opened the door for Hairston to ask Heller and other witnesses about whether the firm's "philosophy" grew out of past difficulties in persuading blacks to stay at Katten Muchin—a topic that Judge Robertson had excluded from the trial on relevance grounds. If she had read the deposition transcripts carefully, Roberts would have known that Heller and Sergi discussed the firm's vague affirmative action policy in connection with Mungin. But in the courtroom, Roberts seemed to be taken by surprise. Before Hairston began her redirect examination of Heller, an anxious Roberts asked for a sidebar conference.

"I have never done this before," she whispered to the judge, "but I'm actually going to move to strike an answer that was in response to a question of mine because it was not expected." She told Robertson that she expected Heller to say, merely, that Sergi was "trying to get [Mungin] more complicated bankruptcy" work.

"And he volunteered the answer you're afraid opens the door," the judge said.

"Yes. And I'm prepared to have the court strike the answer. I didn't see it coming, clearly."

"It may not have been the answer you wanted, but he gave an honest answer," Hairston protested.

Robertson refused to strike the answer, but, to Roberts's relief, told Hairston that he still didn't want the jury to hear testimony about past problems with black associates.

On redirect, Hairston asked Heller two quick questions about "the firm's philosophy" on retaining blacks and didn't press the issue further. It couldn't have been apparent to the jury what the fuss at the sidebar was about. Certainly it wasn't obvious that Katten Muchin had suffered any sort of defeat. But Hairston was pleased that she had gotten the firm to concede that it thought of Mungin in racial terms—even if Katten Muchin claimed to have taken extra measures to *help* him. She would return to this theme later in the trial.

* * *

Hairston faced a fundamental dilemma in making Mungin's case. She had to put on witnesses who would testify to her client's being treated poorly. But the defense could then ask these same witnesses about their own experiences at the firm. If the testimony showed that Katten Muchin handled lawyers with roughly similar indifference, Roberts would have proved her point.

Hairston wanted to use Mark Thomas to establish that the Washington office had brought in the white partner from Chicago, along with associate Charlie Thomson, to handle complex bankruptcy assignments, without including Mungin. Following Heller to the stand, Thomas confirmed the basics of a 1993 aviation-insurance bankruptcy assignment he and Thomson worked on. Had Patricia Gilmore suggested that Thomas involve Mungin in the project? Hairston asked.

"No. We had two people on it, and that was sufficient." He and Thomson previously had done work for the same Dombroff-Gilmore client, so it made sense for them to get the 1993 assignment.

"Did you, at any time, have an understanding that the [finance] department in Chicago should provide Mr. Mungin with work assignments?"

"No. I never had that understanding."

The defense cross-examination focused not on Mungin's experience, but on Thomas's. He testified that, like Mungin, he was hired from another firm as an experienced associate, and that his starting pay was less than that of Katten Muchin associates in his class. There was no mentoring program when he was an associate, Thomas said, and he never felt he needed a mentor. The only evaluation he received as an associate was a verbal "Keep up the good work" that came with his bonus check one December.

Susan Gallagher, a white associate from the Seyfarth firm, handled the Thomas cross-examination. She asked him what it had been like to work with Dombroff and Gilmore.

"Very difficult," Thomas answered. They forbade him from talking to the insurance company client or to the lawyer for the corporate policy holder that had gone bankrupt. "To me, that was an impossible way to represent a client."

Gallagher guided Thomas toward describing the Finance and Reorganization Department under Sergi's leadership as unstructured.

"We were known for being quite loosely organized," he said. "I think the best example is we had a Christmas party in July, finally, one year. That's how organized we were."

Although Hairston was moving her case along smartly, Judge Robertson wanted even more speed. He complained about David Schulman's turgid testimony of the previous day and scolded Hairston for putting on repetitive evidence about how the firm operated. "I'm on hurry-up time here," he warned her.

The next three witnesses called by the plaintiff's side were black lawyers who had unhappy experiences of varying descriptions with Katten Muchin. The judge had sharply limited what they could talk about, telling Hairston that he wouldn't tolerate general aspersions about the firm's difficulties with blacks. Everything had to be tied to Mungin.

Janice Jamison, who had worked at Katten Muchin as a law student, told the jury that she had "concerns" about her experience at the firm.

Did she apply to work at Katten Muchin full time?

"No."

Why not?

"Objection," Roberts interjected.

"Sustained," Robertson said, telling Jamison to step down.

Anthony Boswell followed Jamison and told the jury about being interviewed for an associate's job at Katten Muchin's Washington office in 1993. Dombroff was impressed with him, Boswell reported. The applicant was promised another round of interviews in Chicago, he said, but that never happened. He never got an explanation.

Swiftly directing witnesses on and off the stand like a maître d' tending to patrons at a busy restaurant, Hairston next examined Elaine Williams. Dressed dramatically in black,

Williams was separately pursuing her own discrimination battle against Katten Muchin. If allowed, she could have attacked the firm as heartless and biased, adding weight to Mungin's claims. Williams spoke with clarity and intelligence. But Judge Robertson had ruled that her experiences in Chicago were irrelevant to Mungin's in Washington. Under the judge's forbidding gaze, Hairston didn't dare broach the subject of Williams's complaints. Instead, Williams told the jury about the firm's performance evaluation process, which she described as being far more formal and effective than her former Chicago colleagues had. The testimony was bland, but through her friendly body language, Williams indicated a connection to the plaintiff's team. And in a further demonstration of his courtroom savvy, Mungin, at the conclusion of Williams's testimony, followed her from the well of the court to the spectators' section, shook her hand and whispered a thank you—all within the jury's sight. Williams then sat down to watch the proceedings for several hours, underscoring her concern. In the jury's eyes, Williams's desire to lend support added to Mungin's credibility.

While we waited for court to resume that afternoon, Mungin introduced me to Hairston for the first time. Members of the defense team eyed us suspiciously as we spoke in the hallway outside of the courtroom.

"How do you think it's going?" Hairston asked me. She paced and bounced like an athlete at halftime. Tiny beads of perspiration lined her forehead.

I demurred, saying it was hard to know what the jury would think of someone like Larry, who made $108,000 but still complained about mistreatment. Would a retired Cosmos Club steward or former warehouse worker or federal government employee understand why partnership was so important, why Larry couldn't have just looked for another job?

"Yeah, exactly," said Hairston, sounding worried. That was the question.

We discussed the judge's tough rulings limiting testimony by Jamison, Boswell, and Williams. Robertson "knows the defendant is a law firm," said Mungin. "He knows they're going to hit him with an appeal." Mungin casually assumed he was going to win the trial. The judge, he continued, "is limiting the evidence" to give the firm fewer things to complain about on appeal.

Mungin seemed so unruffled he might have been a neutral observer, rather than a combatant. "I'm proud of how this is going," he told me after Hairston stepped away. "It's been totally clean and above board, no dirt. . . . Win or lose, I have no regrets, this was the right thing to do. Someone had to show them they can't just crush people and walk away."

Hairston still had one more witness to call, Mark Dombroff. But the Robertson rocket docket was moving more quickly than she anticipated. She hadn't asked Dombroff to be available until the next day, Thursday. Rather than end court for the day, the judge told Roberts to start her case; they would come back to Dombroff later.

Roberts began slowly—very slowly—with John Villa, the stout former administrator of Katten Muchin's Washington office. She laboriously walked Villa through firm records indicating two things: that Mungin did the vast majority of his work for Dombroff and Gilmore and that from 1992 through 1994, the firm reimbursed him a total of $1,585.92 for business lunches and marketing expenses. Roberts's point, of course, was that once Dombroff and Gilmore left, there was no work for Mungin. As for reimbursements, she wanted to demonstrate that Katten Muchin wasn't tightfisted with Mungin (although $1,600 spread over two years isn't a lavish amount by big law firm standards).

Next, Roberts asked Villa to confirm that four white junior lawyers whom Dombroff didn't take with him were let go by Katten Muchin. In each instance, the defense lawyer asked the race of the fired attorney. "White," Villa answered. Whites were terminated, while Mungin was given a chance to transfer.

* * *

On cross-examination, Hairston tried to show that the white attorneys Villa had testified about weren't "similarly situated" to Mungin. One had herself testified that she was a "staff lawyer," not a conventional associate, meaning that she had never been eligible for promotion to income partner. Another fired lawyer was a part-time employee; a third, while let go by Katten Muchin, was allowed to continue using space in the firm's office at no charge to pursue an immigration-law practice. The fourth attorney had actually been told to leave the firm in February 1994, months before the split-up, Hairston suggested. Villa said he didn't recall whether that was true.

Hairston's counterattack succeeded. Katten Muchin was comparing Mungin, a senior associate who was told he was eligible for partnership, to younger lawyers with a variety of attenuated relationships to the firm. Roberts's promise of a heap of unhappy white lawyers—who were "similarly situated" to Mungin—was turning out to be hollow.

Determined nevertheless to pursue this line of argument, Roberts turned to the duo of Sherman and Soberman, the two bankruptcy lawyers who worked with Mungin early in his tenure with Katten Muchin and were squeezed out by Dombroff in February 1993. Again working together for another firm, the pair cooperatively told the jury that they hadn't had much contact with Dombroff-Gilmore clients or with Katten Muchin's home office.

Stuart Soberman, wearing a brightly colored flower-print tie with his gray suit, described his only official performance evaluation: Somebody walked into his office, handed him a bonus check, and said, "Here you go." But then he added an important observation: "I worked with Jeff [Sherman] sort of one on one. And I think I got my feedback on a more direct basis from him on a daily basis as to individual projects."

This kind of informal mentor-apprentice relationship is a common method of bringing along younger lawyers. No partner ever gave Mungin the sort of guidance that Soberman

described Sherman giving him. That didn't necessarily indicate race bias, but race may have been part of the reason why
Mungin didn't forge closer bonds with white colleagues.

Jeff Sherman recounted the rise and quick deterioration of
Dombroff's insurance-bankruptcy practice. Sherman attributed part of the problem to Gilmore's jealously blocking him
from having contact with her insurance clients, making it difficult for him to provide timely bankruptcy advice to those
clients. By 1993, "my whole rationale for being there in the
first place, which was the [insurance] bankruptcy practice,
didn't apply anymore," Sherman said.

On cross-examination, Sherman commented on a topic
otherwise strangely absent from the trial: the quality of
Mungin's work. Asked by Hairston if he had any concerns in
that regard, he said, "The quality, no. As to the amount of
time that was spent on various matters, yeah, there were
times that I was concerned."

Hairston asked whether Sherman ever mentioned this
worry about timeliness to Mungin.

"I don't believe I ever did."

"So he would have no knowledge of that concern; is that
correct?

"I would doubt it." Not exactly the daily feedback that
Soberman said he got from Sherman.

Mungin grew more confident with each witness. Standing
in the hall during a break between Soberman's and Sherman's
testimony, he said to me sarcastically, "Well, you've heard the
devastating [defense] case. . . ."

At that moment, Soberman walked over to where we were
standing. "Howya doin', Larry?" he said.

"Howya doin'?" Mungin echoed. I couldn't tell if he was
putting Soberman on.

"Okay," Soberman replied. "Pushing paper. You practicing
law? What are you doing?"

"Surviving."

"Get out if you can," Soberman said, smiling and sounding like he meant it. "Take care. Good luck."

Mungin rolled his eyes. He had no interest in good wishes from this source.

Richard Waller, another of the senior Chicago lawyers, took the stand, looking highly irritated. His aura resembled that of Catherine Matthews, the grumpily reluctant health aide on the jury. They came to the courtroom from different worlds, but appeared equally put out by the intrusion on their lives.

Waller wore a well-tailored navy blue double-breasted suit. His answers to Roberts's questions came in circuitous grumbles. No longer a practicing lawyer, he served on administrative committees and had what he called an "indefinable role" coordinating the work of the firm's field offices on the coasts. At one point, Waller gave a candid hint of how unruly firm management was. Roberts asked him about his "specific responsibilities" related to the breakup of the Washington office.

"I think, yes, I—specifically—*specific* is a funny word sometimes, because I don't—responsibilities in our office sometimes shift from place to place, but I—there was—I was one of the two primary—preliminary negotiators in the separation agreement itself."

Waller recalled his phone conversations with Mungin in the summer of 1994. He'd urged the plaintiff to "think very hard about the idea of moving to New York or to Chicago," assuring him that a transfer to either city "would be a good opportunity."

Did Mungin ever question whether there would be enough work for him in New York or Chicago? Roberts asked. Did he express doubt about Katten Muchin's sincerity in making the offer? Did he say he wanted to stay in Washington because there was enough work there?

"No," Waller answered, to all three questions. All Mungin told him in the end, Waller insisted, was that moving "would be a very hard decision for him for personal reasons, and it just didn't seem to be a thing that he could work out."

* * *

Once Hairston completed some unenlightening cross-examination of Waller, the judge called the lawyers to the bench. "Where do we go from here?" he asked.

Both sides had decided to trim their witness lists, partly in response to Robertson's demand for expedition, partly so as not to bore the jury. Hairston said she had only Dombroff left to put on the stand. Roberts reported that she had two more minor players to interrogate, and then her big finale: Vince Sergi.

CHAPTER EIGHTEEN

"Shucking and Jiving"

Thursday morning at nine a.m., Robertson's courtroom had the cheerful atmosphere of a small business about to welcome the first customers of the day. The court reporter and clerk chattered at their stations on either side of the judge's blond wood bench. At the defense table, Sergi silently scanned a legal pad crammed with notes. Mungin sat at the plaintiff's table, his back to Sergi, reading the *Washington Post* "Style" section. He took out a pen and began working the crossword puzzle.

The previous night, Mungin had left a message on my home answering machine: "I don't feel bloodied or wounded or anything. I'd like to think it's because [the suit] has been so well planned out and executed." He sounded proud.

The judge and trial lawyers soon emerged from a private meeting on procedural matters. Mark Dombroff strode swiftly to the witness box, planted himself with authority, and greeted Robertson with a forceful "Good morning, sir." Hairston expected that Dombroff, while no ally of her client's, would cast some negative light on Katten Muchin.

Dombroff's dazzling yellow and blue horizontally striped silk tie appeared to be operating on 1,000 watts. A white handkerchief sprouted from the pocket of his handsome dark blue suit. He smiled relentlessly and never answered a question with one sentence when three would do.

As Hairston anticipated, Dombroff took every opportunity to remind his old comrades at Katten Muchin that if they expected loyalty, they were mistaken. Dombroff was for Dombroff. "I had never heard of the firm," he said of Katten Muchin when describing his joining up in 1989. He referred to Sergi as "a bankruptcy lawyer," adding unctuously, "I hope you'll forgive me." As Dombroff well knew, Sergi preferred to be known as a specialist in real estate finance.

Hairston wanted Dombroff to sketch the history of his insurance-bankruptcy group, but the witness couldn't resist endless digressions. Robertson eventually lost his patience and ordered Hairston to the sidebar. "Twenty minutes and we're still hiring Sherman," the judge fumed.

"I'm trying, Your Honor."

"You can ask him to confine it, to shorten up his answers."

"Okay."

"If you need some help, *I'll* do it," the judge offered.

Hairston did the best she could to obey. She prompted Dombroff to testify that he "was impressed with" Mungin. But Dombroff denied any direct responsibility for the black associate because Mungin wasn't part of the Insurance Department. Mungin repeatedly evinced concern about the direction of the insurance-bankruptcy practice, Dombroff confirmed. At Mungin's request, Dombroff called Sergi on more than one occasion to voice the associate's unhappiness over not being involved in bankruptcy activities in Chicago. While mostly atmospheric, this testimony could be seen as helpful to Mungin.

Dombroff resisted Hairston's question about Mungin's billing rate being reduced from $185 to $125 for his "work on simple bankruptcy matters." Having multiple rates wasn't unusual in the insurance-defense field, he insisted. But, as he himself had pointed out, Mungin wasn't a member of the insurance team. In the eyes of non-insurance lawyers, having one's rate suddenly slashed is a grim signal.

Since they weren't provided with any of this background,

the most the jurors could have gathered from Dombroff's testimony was that he didn't want to admit that Mungin's rate was indeed reduced for the bulk of his work. As Hairston had planned, the white lawyer's obtuseness almost certainly worked in her client's favor.

Did you evaluate your associates' performances? Hairston asked the witness.

"Irrelevant, Your Honor." Roberts rose from her seat at the defense table.

"Sustained."

"Your Honor, I think it goes to similarly situated," Hairston said, meaning that the insurance associates were similarly situated to Mungin. They all worked in Washington, taking orders from Dombroff and Gilmore. If they were evaluated and he wasn't, that was telling.

Judge Robertson shook his head no. Objection sustained.

But Hairston didn't give up. She put in front of Dombroff the 1992 promotional document published by Katten Muchin's Washington office. Does the brochure, she asked, "indicate that each associate receives regular semiannual reviews based on evaluations from senior attorneys?"

"Yes, ma'am," Dombroff admitted.

Did he follow the policy?

"I can only answer for the Insurance Department."

"Objection," said an angry Roberts.

The judge called the lawyers forward. "I take Ms. Hairston's point about similarly situated," Robertson now said. The judge was fed up with Dombroff. "The witness is doing a lot of kind of shucking and jiving here," the judge said. "I'm going to let him say what he did in the Insurance Department."

Hairston asked Dombroff whether he followed the policy in the brochure.

"Yes, ma'am."

Did you review all associates in the year that they were eligible to be made income partners?

"Yes, ma'am."

But as the jury knew, Mungin *wasn't* reviewed.

Hairston had won the skirmish. But how far did the victory

take her? Mungin was treated differently from insurance associates, but practices in the Finance and Reorganization Department seemed to have been looser. And where was the link to race?

Roberts didn't do much to recover on cross-examination. Dombroff testified that of the four white insurance associates who became eligible for income partnership during his time with Katten Muchin, he nominated only two. "And, in fact, Mr. Dombroff," Roberts said dramatically, "there were no African-American associates in your department at that time who had seven and a half to eight and a half years of experience; is that correct?"

"That's correct," Dombroff answered, sounding understandably confused. Who ever said there was a black lawyer in his department? Roberts seemed lost.

Before finishing, Roberts asked Dombroff in a by-the-way tone what his pay had been at Katten Muchin.

"Approximately the nine hundred fifty thousand range, slightly higher."

That fact, though arguably irrelevant, seemed like the sort of thing that Hairston would have wanted to tease out—to illustrate just how well off Mungin's adversaries were. Why the defense would put Dombroff's pay on the record was a puzzle.

More puzzling still was the defense team's decision to call Forrest Walpole to testify. Hairston had completed her evidence with Dombroff, and now it was Roberts's turn to finish off. She began with Walpole, an ordinary-looking midwesterner in his 50s who had joined Katten Muchin's Washington office in 1992, late in his career. He spoke highly of Mungin's bankruptcy-law abilities. Then, at the bidding of junior defense counsel Susan Gallagher, he told this strange story.

In late June 1994, an important client of the Washington office, Dan Clemente, said he might have a lucrative bankruptcy-law assignment for Katten Muchin: representing a group of creditors in a big local case. Eager for the work, Katten Muchin partners introduced Clemente to Mungin, whom they identified as the office's bankruptcy specialist.

But in a private conversation with Clemente, Mungin was equivocal about taking the assignment. Mungin's behavior potentially alienated the client. Later, Mungin complained to Walpole that the Washington partners should have cleared the assignment with Sergi in Chicago.

Walpole testified that Mungin seemed concerned about whether "we in the Washington office really had the manpower to staff a complicated bankruptcy transaction." Walpole was "surprised" that all Mungin "wanted to talk about was whether we formally assigned him, and whether he was going to get credit for this case, and whether he personally was going to advance his career, rather than thinking about how we can position ourselves to get business as a firm." Other Washington partners were similarly disturbed. On the stand, Walpole sounded like he was still shaken by what he saw as a show of disloyalty.

On cross-examination, Hairston clarified this foggy situation. "Is it your testimony," she asked in an arch tone, "that you didn't have a clue that Mr. Mungin was in the process of being asked to leave the firm or at least transfer to another office" at precisely the time of the Clemente snafu?

"I didn't know that," Walpole admitted.

In Walpole's experience, had Mungin previously gotten upset about receiving credit for his work?

No, Walpole said. But Mungin didn't mention in the midst of the Clemente affair that he was leaving Katten Muchin, the witness said.

"Wouldn't it have been irresponsible for Mr. Mungin to agree to take on a matter when he didn't know for sure whether or not he was still going to be with the firm?"

"No, not at all. This is a firm engagement, not a Mr. Mungin engagement."

But wasn't Mungin "presented to be the person in the office who was a bankruptcy specialist?"

"He was."

The jury didn't need to know much about big law firm procedures to sort this one out. The Washington office dangled

Mungin as an on-site bankruptcy expert, when the home office was in the process of pushing him out the door. Mungin added to the confusion by characteristically maintaining a polite public front, despite his obvious frustration. Rather than confront Walpole, Mungin insisted that the Washington office should have gone through his bosses in Chicago—who, presumably, would have mentioned that Mungin wasn't long for the Washington office. Adding to the irony, the Washington office was eager to advertise its bankruptcy capacity at a moment when headquarters was insisting that there was no demand for Mungin's bankruptcy expertise in D.C.

Walpole admitted that he never figured out what had happened and never explained to Mungin why the Washington partners were upset. Walpole testified that he did write a critical memo about the incident and sent it to Chicago, probably to be put in Mungin's personnel file. He didn't show the memo to Mungin, Walpole told the jury. But after all of this, he *apologized* to Mungin. "He seemed insulted about the way that he had been assigned to this case," Walpole said. "And I actually apologized to him . . . for anything that he suffered that he felt was unfair to him."

The eight jurors were kept away from the public during the workday, but each evening they left the courthouse by means of the public elevators. This was my only chance to eavesdrop on their conversation. Wednesday afternoon, the day before Walpole and Dombroff took the stand, the topic was getting home and rustling up dinner. One woman juror in the crowded elevator said she was "going to get together some chicken, potatoes, greens, and pie." Others registered approval. Another woman juror picked up on the phrase "get together," muttering softly: "I know a law firm, needs to get itself together." She obviously was referring to Katten Muchin. There was no audible reaction from the other jurors. Standing in the front, facing the closed elevator doors, I couldn't discreetly turn around to find out the speaker's identity. The doors opened, and the jurors walked out through the courthouse lobby into the cool dusk.

* * *

Katten Muchin's last witness on Thursday afternoon was Vincent Sergi. He seemed determined to prove that the firm was a jumbled, *un*managed place where Mungin lost his way through the fault of no one in particular. (As a member of the firm that was a party to the lawsuit, Sergi was permitted to testify, despite having been in the courtroom to hear other witnesses.)

Before getting to substance, Roberts asked Sergi to rehash his credentials. The witness said that he had needed scholarships to pay for college and law school. He "worked for meals, mopping floors and cleaning a hotel kitchen and floors and worked as a short-order cook in a fraternity." He interrupted law school to serve in the Peace Corps and helped defend accused drug pushers at the New York Legal Aid Society.

"Are you a bankruptcy attorney?" Roberts asked.

"No," Sergi sniffed. He was a "real estate finance lawyer," representing lenders in their deals with developers. He hadn't been in bankruptcy court for 15 years, "and I haven't done any bankruptcy work since."

Roberts asked about Mungin's being hired.

Sergi explained his worries about the need for another bankruptcy lawyer in Washington and about Mungin's changing law firms for a third time. Dombroff "checked it out, came back to me—or maybe it was in that same conversation," and persuaded Sergi to approve the move.

The process sounded as lackadaisical as it had in fact been. Sergi acknowledged that he failed to show up for Mungin's first visit to Chicago: "I don't know where I was. Otherwise, I would have met him. But I did set him up to meet" a number of other senior lawyers in the Finance and Reorganization Department. He said this blandly, seemingly unaware of how he had insulted the younger lawyer on what to Mungin was an important occasion. In the witness box, Sergi adjusted his aviator-style glasses frequently as he spoke, and touched his salt-and-pepper mustache.

Did Katten Muchin have a "mentor program" for associates? Roberts asked.

Yes, but by the time Mungin arrived, "the program [had] collapsed," said Sergi. "The assignments were forced. They weren't natural." Senior partners weren't interested in a formal program to bring along junior attorneys.

Did the Finance and Reorganization Department have regular meetings?

"No, we didn't."

"Excuse me, counsel." Robertson interrupted the soporific tour of Katten Muchin's non-structure. The judge called the lawyers to the sidebar and spoke sharply to Hairston: "Your client is sitting back there, rolling his eyes and making faces in [response to] this testimony," Robertson said. "It's very inappropriate. Please instruct him."

"Yes, it is," Hairston agreed. "And I will instruct him immediately." She spun around, marched to Mungin's chair and whispered to him, vehemently, making sure the judge could see. Mungin had been facing the witness box, his back to the spectators' section, but with his face visible in profile to the jurors. The judge had tolerated the plaintiff's earlier mugging, but now Mungin had crossed the line. Sergi stirred his anger. After hearing Hairston's lecture, he put his elbows on his thighs and hunkered down like someone anticipating a violent blow.

Roberts picked up where she left off: Did Sergi review Mungin's performance?

"No."

Did Sergi do written reviews for *any* associates?

"No."

Did Sergi try to integrate Mungin into the Chicago bankruptcy practice?

The witness described bringing Mungin to Chicago for the second time, in February 1993. "If we could find him work," Sergi said, "if we could build that practice on the East Coast, we wanted to do it." But it wasn't likely. Dombroff had no interest in Mungin's doing anything but the insurance-bankruptcy work. Sergi testified that Mungin was "solely hired to work . . . with the insurance group . . . We had no bankruptcy practice here in Washington and still don't." This was the partner who considered himself Mungin's *savior*.

Sergi testified that in early 1993, Mungin was in danger of being fired because the managing partners noticed that his billable hours had been "very low" for five months. Sergi said that to fix the situation, he brokered the deal with Gilmore: Mungin would get more basic insurance-bankruptcy work, for which his billing rate would be cut to $125 from $185. Gilmore wanted to slash the rate more, but Sergi resisted, he told the jury.

Sergi stressed that he sympathized with Mungin. "It was very difficult working for Ms. Gilmore," he said. "She was not supportive. She was not allowing him to have contact with her primary client, AIG, and maybe others. . . . It was a frustrating experience."

Still, when Mungin arrived in Chicago for his December 1993 showdown with Sergi, the senior lawyer told him that partnership was nowhere on the horizon. "He himself admitted that he was doing lower-level associate work. I told him the only way we would be able to change that situation would be if we could find a way to stimulate more work to come out of Chicago or somewhere, so that he would have the opportunity. Otherwise, there would be no way to recommend" Mungin for a promotion.

When Dombroff took his clients and left, Sergi said he advocated Mungin's moving to New York or Chicago. In a June 1994 phone conversation with Mungin, he recalled saying "that, perhaps, he could move to the other office." But Sergi's advocacy ended with that one phone call, his last contact with Mungin. Other partners in Chicago "were in charge of the whole transition" in Washington, he said. "And they finished it."

At the plaintiff's table, Mungin was now nearly doubled over. He looked like he was in physical pain. Hairston and Nelson ignored him, but members of the jury glanced furtively at the plaintiff and then back at Sergi.

* * *

Hairston began her cross-examination carefully. How much money did the former schoolboy janitor and short-order cook make these days? she asked.

"Five hundred fifty thousand a year."

Less than Dombroff, but more than minimum wage.

Hairston wanted to raise questions about Sergi's credibility. He and Dombroff were the bad guys in her version of the case. Communicating Mungin's character, ability, and desire had been her first priority. Now, she had to send the jury off to deliberate thinking that Katten Muchin hadn't given Mungin a fair chance.

Why did the firm wait until the breakup of the Washington office in mid-1994 to suggest that Mungin move to Chicago? Hairston asked. Why not invite him in early 1993, when questions arose about his low hours and billing rate?

Actually, we did invite him earlier, Sergi said. Managing partner Michael Zavis himself suggested the move sometime in the first half of 1993, in a face-to-face conversation with Mungin in Washington.

Hairston was floored. There was no reference to this alleged offer anywhere in the voluminous documents of the case. Mungin later told me the Zavis conversation never happened, that Sergi made it up on the stand. In court, Hairston assumed a look of disbelief and asked Sergi, "Mr. Zavis, *just out of the blue,* went to Mr. Mungin's office in D.C. and made this offer?"

Sergi backed off a half step. "I have no idea. I know he told me about the conversation. I don't know how he did it at all." Hit with one pointed question, the anecdote began to crumble.

Hairston asked who Mungin was supposed to report to after Jeff Sherman left the Washington office in February 1993.

"I don't know," Sergi said. "Technically, I was his department head, and so for many purposes, he would report to me." But then he acknowledged that he didn't supervise Mungin; Gilmore was Mungin's daily "contact." Sergi seemed bored by Hairston's slow-moving interrogation. He held his hands in front of him and, in clear view of the jury, twiddled his thumbs.

So, Mungin was at a disadvantage because he lacked a partner to provide complex assignments and look out for his interests? Hairston asked.

"Not necessarily correct," said Sergi. "Had Mr. Mungin come to us as a first- or second-year associate, I think you would be absolutely correct. But he came to us with a wide variety of experience and experience at one of the best firms in the nation, Weil Gotshal. . . . We've had associates in Chicago who are fifth- and sixth-year associates who start developing their own practice," *without* mentors. Mungin should have pulled up his socks, in other words.

But didn't reducing his billing rate hurt his chances of obtaining partnership? Hairston asked.

"I don't think so, no," Sergi said. The problem was the type of work Mungin did.

But didn't Gilmore cut the rate *because of* "the type of work he was performing?" Hairston asked. Her voice dripped dismay over Sergi's word games.

"Right," he said. "But all I'm saying to you is, it relates to the type of work that he was doing, not that his rate was lower."

Hairston thought the jury would know this was a distinction without a difference, she told me later. "I felt they would see the arrogance that I saw."

She turned to the issue of Mungin's hours, referring Sergi to a dense Katten Muchin computer printout labeled "Defendant's Exhibit K2." For the period of January through July 1993, did Sergi see an entry for a Washington lawyer named Thomas Gross?

"Yes, I do."

Gross's average monthly hours in that period were a meager 92. "Do you see that?"

"Yes, I do." Mungin wasn't the only Washington attorney failing to meet the 167 hours standard.

"And this individual had a base salary of one hundred thousand dollars, did he not?"

"Yes."

Did Sergi see John Enerson, class of 1986, same as Mungin? He averaged 96 hours. "Do you see that?"

"Yes, I do."

"His salary was one hundred four thousand, correct?"

"Correct."

And Lawrence Mungin was a few names down, with an average of 146 hours and a salary of $100,000, correct?

"Correct."

None of this necessarily meant that Mungin deserved a promotion or bigger raises. Gross and Enerson were in the Energy Department, which Katten Muchin soon jettisoned as unprofitable. But with her classic cross-examination—crisp, closed-end questions that have to be answered "yes" or "no"—Hairston was suggesting that Katten Muchin had exaggerated Mungin's status as a laggard.

Did Sergi ever recommend that Mungin attend a marketing seminar "to learn to better solicit business for the firm?"

"No, I never suggested that to anybody."

Did Mungin receive credit for the time he spent trying to collect Jeff Sherman's unpaid bills?

"I don't know."

"No other associate in the FAR Department had their hourly rate reduced; is that correct?"

"I don't know the answer to that. . . . The only one I'm aware of is Mr. Mungin."

And during the partners' meeting on associate raises in 1993, "Larry Mungin's name did not come up?"

"I don't recall it. I really don't recall."

It would seem unlikely, or at least surprising, that in anticipation of a high-stakes trial, a lawyer of 20 years' experience wouldn't have boned up on some of these basic factual questions.

Mungin wasn't even *considered* for partnership in 1993, correct? Hairston asked.

"It wasn't a partnership issue. It was how do we first survive in the firm, and then, if we can, try to move from there. It wasn't a partnership issue, even though he was in his seventh year, or whatever year it was."

"So you didn't discuss that issue of whether Larry should be nominated for partnership with anyone, correct?"

"I considered it, and I did not nominate him; that's correct." Mungin could have come to Chicago, Sergi said. "We were booming."

"Did you indicate to Mr. Mungin that he would receive complex work assignments" in Chicago? Hairston asked.

"I mean, he knew that we had—no, I didn't say it in those words. I relied on his knowledge of what we were doing in Chicago."

"Did you tell him which partner he would be assigned to work with?"

"No, I did not." Sergi explained associates weren't assigned to specific partners.

"Did you tell him that, if he moved to Chicago, you would consider him for partnership in 1994?"

"No. I didn't use those words, no."

Hairston had cast serious doubt on the enthusiasm behind the campaign to "save" Mungin in 1994.

Roberts, on redirect, took Sergi back to Defendant's Exhibit K2. She pointed out a Chicago real estate associate who had phenomenal hours in 1993 but, like Mungin, *wasn't* nominated for partnership. Sergi hastened to agree, although he added that the real estate attorney did make partner the next year.

With some ceremony, Roberts introduced a new statistics sheet, Exhibit K15, and asked Sergi to read from it Mungin's monthly billable hours, beginning in October 1992:

```
1992  October:     77
      November:  126.5
      December:  153.25
```

1993	January:	119.5
	February:	125.25
	March:	164.4
	April:	158.75
	May:	148.5
	June:	157.25
	July:	151.75
	August:	166.25
	September:	180.5

The requirement was 167. "It looks like, starting in March of 1993, the hours start to go up . . . after Patty and I adjusted the rate, and she moved the work back," Sergi said. Roberts asked no further questions about the hours.

Roberts, perversely, had shown that Mungin's hours *increased* after he received Sergi's warning. This was exactly what Hairston wanted the jury to see. Indeed, Hairston happily stayed with the billable-hours issue during her final crack at Sergi, on recross-examination. She asked him to read from a column entitled "Average Billable Hours Per Month." For 1992, Mungin's first, partial year with the firm, he averaged 142.5. In 1993, "he went up to 155.83 average hours per month, correct?" Hairston asked.

"Correct," Sergi answered.

And for 1994, 173 hours per month?

"Correct."

"So each year, Mr. Mungin's hours went up, correct?"

"Correct," Sergi conceded.

CHAPTER NINETEEN

"Teach the Firm a Lesson"

The evidence was in, and Judge Robertson admonished the jury one final time not to discuss the case. As the last juror left the courtroom Thursday afternoon, the judge turned to Roberts and Hairston and said, "You have either presented an unusually interesting case, or that's an unusually alert jury. That jury has been with you all every step of the way."

"Good jury," agreed Roberts.

"It's a good jury," Hairston added with a nod.

Mungin arrived at the courtroom before his attorneys Friday morning. He was in an expansive mood, even expressing sympathy for his adversary, Roberts. "She's working with what she has," he told me, "and it isn't much."

Hairston and Nelson appeared, lugging their boxy black litigation bags. Hairston had followed her usual trial routine each day that week: She reached her Silver Spring office by seven a.m. for ninety minutes of preparation; a full day in court; back to the office until ten p.m. She skipped eating dinner while on trial, sustained by nervous energy. She lost seven pounds in five days.

That Friday, Hairston wore an eye-catching dark green suit

with large gold-colored buttons. "Give me a hug," she said to her client. He did, carefully.

"The hard part's over," Mungin said, reversing the usual role of lawyer reassuring client.

"I don't know," said a worried Hairston.

Judge Robertson presided over a relaxed hearing during which the lawyers were allowed to request changes in the instructions he planned to give the jury. The jurors weren't yet in their seats. The judge teased the plaintiff's side over a requested change in punctuation in one instruction. "There's a subtlety of language there that escapes me," Robertson said, "but without objection from the—"

Roberts objected, admitting she felt "like a fool" because she couldn't figure out what her opponents were up to.

The judge chuckled and said he would take the suggested change under advisement. Despite the anger that drove the trial, Hairston, Roberts, and Robertson had maintained a friendly mutual respect. They were smiling that morning, until the jury was brought in, at which point the lawyers and judge put on their game faces.

Hairston rose for her closing argument. "Well," she told the jury, "this is my last chance to convince you that my client, Larry Mungin, is entitled to damages, because he is a victim of race discrimination." She reviewed the basic claims about pay, work assignments, and consideration for partnership.

Mungin was hired in 1992 at $92,000 a year. The four other members of the class of 1986 in Washington were making between $95,000 and $102,000. "At the very least, Larry should have been paid ninety-five thousand," Hairston said. "Was race a consideration at the time Larry was hired? You bet it was." Her evidence was the four words in the headhunter's note to Dombroff: ". . . and he is a minority."

"So race was a consideration when Larry was hired. And he was hired at minimum [for] three thousand dollars less. He had a Harvard-Harvard double degree. He had worked in one of the top-flight bankruptcy law firms in the country. But he couldn't be paid at the same rate as the lowest-paid associate in the class of '86, which was $95,000.

"Now, the defendant may say, Well, he never complained.

"How did he know? Wouldn't you logically assume when you start a job that you're being treated the same as people who are similarly situated to you? Why would you know to make a complaint at that point?"

Mungin did get an $8,000 raise in late 1992, "but he was still four thousand behind the next person in his class," Hairston said. "So the salary issue is pretty clear, we believe, that Larry was just behind every year. . . . And Larry, from the very beginning it was noted he was a minority."

Hairston's reasoning appeared to be that mere mention of Mungin's race, or the firm's wanting to hire him in part because he was black, was equivalent to race being the moving force behind his being treated differently. This reasoning seemed shaky. An employer's considering race in hiring a black person may be a good idea or a bad idea. But it doesn't *prove* that subsequent actions, like setting a salary, were motivated by race. Perhaps aware of how tenuous her first point was, Hairston moved on.

Once Jeff Sherman left the firm in early 1993, "Larry had . . . no one that was ensuring that he got quality work assignments. As a matter of fact, it was exactly the opposite. He had individuals coming from Chicago, working on a complex bankruptcy matter for a partner in the D.C. office. And that individual, Mr. Thomas, told you that all he did when he came to D.C. with Larry is walk by his office and said, Hello, and kept going.

"David Heller came in and said, 'When I started with the firm in 1993, Mr. Sergi told me that I needed to make sure I could find some work for Larry to do, because he was a minority and because the firm's philosophy was to advance minorities.' Was race an issue? Of course it was. Can't be debated here. Mr. Heller sat and told you that." Again, Hairston was equating mere mention of Mungin's skin color with evidence that race motivated action—or *in*action—that harmed him.

Mungin was isolated, Hairston told the jury. "No partner

ever took Larry anywhere to meet any clients," she said, outrage seeping into her tone. She rejected the notion that Katten Muchin had gone out of its way for Mungin. "Not one person sat there [in the witness box] and told you that Larry could not perform the work. They didn't say to you, 'We kept him because we felt sorry for him, because he really couldn't do the work, and so we decided we'd keep him and pay him because he was kind of pitiful.' They didn't do Larry any favors. Larry sat in the office. He did the work that was assigned to him. That was it. He had no control. What was he supposed to do? He told them, 'I don't have challenging work.' He told them, 'Give me more work. I need complex work.' They didn't give it to him. They could have. They chose not to. You figure out why. We say it's because of his race, and race was a consideration."

Judge Robertson's expression was stony, impossible to read. He sat straight in his black leather chair, his left hand cupping his chin. The jurors were following Hairston with their eyes as she moved from the lectern to a spot a few feet to her right, and back again. Mungin stared at the jury, motionless.

Hairston got a little snarled in her arithmetic when discussing the issue of Mungin's hours, but she reiterated clearly that overall, he was moving in the right direction by late 1993 and exceeding expectations in 1994. Sergi's claim that Mungin was low was "just wrong, not true," she said. "His hours were there."

On partnership, "Mr. Sergi said, 'I considered Mr. Mungin, and I chose not to nominate him.' Mr. Sergi did not have that veto power under the procedures of the law firm." Katten Muchin had a process that wasn't followed in Mungin's case, Hairston argued. "If you're in the class that's eligible for consideration, you discuss those individuals in a meeting with other partners within the department first, and a decision is made at that point. Mr. Sergi didn't testify that he talked to any other partners about Mr. Mungin. He didn't want to make Mr. Mungin a partner. Didn't have any notion of advancing Larry's career. . . . We're not saying that Larry necessarily would have been made a partner. . . . We've never said that.

All we said is he should have been considered, period. It was humiliating for Larry" to hear Sergi say, " 'I'm not even going to consider you. Your hours are low.'

"Wrong!" Hairston said sharply, as if she were reproving Sergi in person.

" 'You're not doing quality work,' " she said, echoing the Chicago lawyer.

" 'Well, is that my fault or yours?' " she asked, as if she were Mungin.

"And then we get to the point of why Larry left," Hairston said. " 'We gave him these wonderful offers to New York and to Chicago.' Well, I don't think I need to go into New York. You're reasonable people. No work. No information. How was it going to be any better than D.C.?

"Chicago? Again, you're reasonable people. Would you have gone to Chicago? You've been in the firm for two years. These people have ignored you for two years. They've sent you no work whatsoever. . . . They say, 'I saw Larry; I said, Hello.' Larry comes to Chicago: 'I saw Larry; I said, Hello. We went out to lunch one time. We talked about Patty Gilmore.' That's really helping him advance his career. You would have gone to work in Chicago with that kind of treatment . . . for two years? I don't think so. Larry was forced to quit. They wanted him to go at that point."

Where was the promised parade of unhappy white lawyers? Hairston demanded. "I didn't hear anybody come in and say, 'My . . . hourly rate was reduced. I had poor quality work. I had no partner assign me anything. I was excluded from meetings. My salary was lower than everybody else.' Never heard it."

That, of course, was true. Roberts hadn't delivered her heap of wailing white associates. Current and former Katten Muchin lawyers had noted the firm's loose structure and the difficulties between Washington and Chicago, but no one had complaints that in sum were anywhere near as powerful as Mungin's.

Reaching the bottom line, Hairston reminded the jury that her client's "dream of being a partner in a major law firm

[was] probably down the tubes." He had little hope as a lawyer of making $550,000 a year, like Sergi, let alone $950,000, like Dombroff. "He was humiliated. You saw that. He was in anguish. You saw that."

As Hairston saw it, Mungin deserved $1,000,000 for the actual harm he suffered. And then she asked for another $2,000,000—to "teach the firm a lesson and, also, to make sure they don't do it again."

Roberts had decided to use a prop to dramatize her closing argument. It was a Katten Muchin document outlining the at-will employment relationship. Shaking the pages of the document, she asked the jury, "Why didn't they just fire him?"

Roberts offered a toned-down version of the whole-heap-of-company pitch from her opening. "I told you that Mr. Mungin may have had reasons to be unhappy about his experience at Katten Muchin & Zavis. But I told you, and the evidence showed, that Mr. Mungin's complaints were not unique to him because of his race."

His opening salary? "He negotiated it. He asked for ninety-two thousand, and he got it." Experienced lawyers brought in from other firms frequently were "hired at a salary below the class . . . Where is the discrimination?"

No mentor? "Mr. Soberman, a white man, [was] asked: Mr. Soberman, who was your mentor? 'I didn't have a mentor.' Mr. Thomas, who was your mentor? 'I didn't have a mentor.' " Sergi testified that the mentor program had collapsed. "The attorneys either didn't have the time or make the time to make it work. . . . Black, white, gray, or brown, there was no mentor program. Where's the racism, ladies and gentlemen?"

Contact with Chicago? Neither of the other two Washington insurance-bankruptcy lawyers—Sherman and Soberman—had any contact. "Mr. Mungin had *more* contact in Chicago than the white men."

No serious review? "Nobody was reviewed . . . by the Chicago FAR Department if you weren't in Chicago. He was the same. It may not have been fun, and no one suggested that it was. But the point, ladies and gentlemen, is that he was treated just like everybody else."

When the complex insurance-bankruptcy work dried up in Washington, "Mr. Mungin could have been fired. And that mediocre nonsense bankruptcy work, they could have hired somebody at a lot less money to do that cleanup. Mr. Mungin was making one hundred eight thousand by then. The firm could have done that, but it didn't. It didn't. In fact, Mr. Sergi convinced Patricia Gilmore to work out a deal so that Mr. Mungin could stay busy and Mr. Mungin could stay employed. . . . Mr. Sergi told you why. You heard it from others: 'We were trying to help him.' "

She brandished the at-will employment document. "Ladies and gentlemen, the irony is that, to the extent Mr. Mungin was treated differently, they never cashed this check on him, did they? You learned through the course of this testimony that this check was cashed for a number of people, white people. They never cashed this check on Mr. Mungin. . . . The only attorney that did not go with Mark Dombroff and Patricia Gilmore who was offered the opportunity to move to Chicago or New York was Lawrence Mungin. They still didn't cash that check on him."

Roberts, switching metaphors, said that Mungin "speaks with forked tongue when he suggests to you, 'I was doing not very complicated work, and that's not the kind of work I should be doing if I want to be a partner and, at the same time, I should have been considered for a partnership. I should have been nominated for a partnership.' Ladies and gentlemen, it's inherently inconsistent.

"Punish the law firm? Punish Mr. Sergi for not firing Mr. Mungin because of his hours? Ladies and gentlemen, that doesn't make any sense. . . . Punish the law firm because it couldn't find bankruptcy business here in Washington, D.C.?"

Roberts paused to stare at the floor for an instant, then looked up at the jury, pointing to her document. "What happened to Larry Mungin," she said, "was that a law firm that could have cashed this check chose to try to help."

* * *

Hairston was on her feet before Roberts had returned to her seat. "This check, ladies and gentlemen, is void," Hairston said, pointing to the document that Roberts had left behind. "Why is it void? Because what Ms. Roberts didn't tell you is there is an exception for the employment at-will doctrine. . . . If you fire someone for a discriminatory reason, you are not shielded by the employment at-will doctrine. So, no good. Of no consequence here."

Her statement of the law was correct: If the jury found there was discrimination, Roberts's argument was irrelevant. It was a quick and punishing counterpunch.

"We're not saying that everyone in the law firm of Katten Muchin & Zavis are racists. Let me make that very clear," Hairston continued. "What we are saying is that race was one of the factors that . . . was considered in taking the actions or taking no actions with Larry. That race was considered. And because race was considered, that's why we're here. . . .

"Nobody likes to think that racism or discrimination or whatever you feel comfortable calling it can be so subtle and so pervasive that you can't even put your finger on it until it's too late. You don't want to even deal with it. But that's what the law is here for. And maybe someday we won't need a law like this. That's everyone's hope, I'm sure. But right now, it's unfortunately still necessary, because things like this happen."

Hairston succeeded in deflating Roberts's check-cashing gambit, but she had made another point, as well. An employer might well hesitate to fire a black, for fear of provoking a lawsuit, but still treat the employee differently, based on race. For example, the employer might retain the black worker but fail to provide him with support available to white co-workers. Hairston tried to persuade the jury not to accept Roberts's false dichotomy: that employees were either fired or treated equally. Bias in the real world, she said, is often implicit and hard to detect.

Judge Robertson took his time instructing the jury, reading slowly from a thick sheaf of papers. "It is your duty to accept the law as I state it to you," he said, glancing at the jurors over his silver glasses. But "you are the sole and exclusive judges of the facts. You alone determine the weight, the effect, and the value of the evidence, and the credibility of the witnesses." He spared no technical complexities, offering a lengthy explanation of the plaintiff's burden of proof. It wasn't the familiar "beyond a reasonable doubt" from criminal trials, Robertson said. Instead, Mungin had to meet the less-demanding standard known as "preponderance of the evidence," which means proving that "something is more likely *so* than *not so*."

"You are not being asked to judge whether the defendant's treatment of the plaintiff was fair or unfair apart from the question of race discrimination," the judge continued. "You are not to second-guess the business decisions of the defendant or otherwise substitute your judgment for that of the defendant. The only question you must decide is whether the plaintiff was treated differently because of his race." If they did find intentional discrimination, the jurors were permitted to go on to the question of "constructive discharge": Did Katten Muchin's bias make Mungin's job "so intolerable that a reasonable person would have felt forced to resign?"

Robertson sketched the extraordinarily loose parameters by which American juries are allowed to determine damages in discrimination cases. The jurors were allowed to award compensatory damages for "emotional pain, suffering, inconvenience, mental anguish, loss of enjoyment of life, and other nonpecuniary losses," the judge said, "if you find these were caused by the defendant's intentional act of discrimination."

As for limits on the money, he said only, "The damages that you award must be fair compensation, no more and no less. . . . You may not award damages based on sympathy or speculation or guesswork." To add punitive damages, the jury had to find that the defendant "was guilty of oppression or malice in the conduct on which you base your finding of liability. . . . The law provides no fixed standards as to the amount of such punitive damages but leaves the amount to the jury's sound discretion, exercised without passion or prejudice." Robertson instructed the jury to consider the *reprehensibility* of Katten Muchin's conduct, the potential for *deterrent effect* on the defendant in light of the firm's financial condition, and the need that any punitive damages bear a *reasonable relation* to the compensatory damages.

Robertson told the jurors that they had to seek a unanimous verdict in all aspects. "I've been telling you all week that you could not talk to each other," he said. "Now you must talk to each other and you must deliberate with one another and attempt to reach a verdict in this case." The jury left the courtroom at 12:15 p.m.

Mungin, Hairston, and Nelson took the elevator down to the basement cafeteria to wait. Hairston was so edgy she had trouble staying seated. She couldn't eat. She began unwinding the trial, identifying questions she should have asked, points she didn't bring across strongly enough. Nelson and Mungin tried to calm her. Mungin was confident the jury was on his side. "They will not let me walk away empty handed," he said. "Not after everything I've been through."

Back upstairs, a short while later, in the corridor outside the empty courtroom, he told me: "I felt it in my bones from the start; they understood the story we were telling. . . . We were so well prepared and Abbey executed so well, right according to plan." His equanimity was remarkable.

The conventional wisdom is that if you give a case to a jury at the end of the week, you'll get a verdict by the close of business Friday. Jurors want to be done with it and have the weekend to get back to a normal routine.

The jurors in the Mungin case sent Judge Robertson a note at 2:40 p.m., saying they had reached a verdict. They had been out only two hours and twenty-five minutes, and they had eaten lunch *before* starting to deliberate.

Reassembled in the courtroom, the opposing sides watched silently as the judge conducted the ritual questioning of Phyllis Allen, the foreperson. He then instructed his courtroom clerk, Joe Burgess, to read the verdict form, which Robertson had designed as a series of yes or no questions. Burgess read:

"Do you find that the plaintiff was treated differently because of his race from others similarly situated?

"With respect to his starting salary: *Yes.*

"With respect to his work assignments: *Yes.*

"With respect to his salary for 1994: *Yes.*

"With respect to consideration of partnership: *Yes.*"

There was no reaction in the courtroom. No one moved or uttered a sound.

Burgess continued: "Do you also find that plaintiff was constructively discharged on the basis of his race? Answer: *Yes.*

"What is the amount of your award to the plaintiff?

"For compensatory damages: *one million dollars.*"

Hairston, eyes wide, glanced back at her co-counsel, Adrian Nelson. She later said she had almost fallen out of her chair. Then came the capper:

"For punitive damages: *one million, five hundred thousand dollars.*"

Mungin had won $2.5 million in a race discrimination suit against a prominent law firm. It was unheard of.

"Is that your verdict?" Judge Robertson again asked the foreperson.

"Yes, it is, Your Honor," Allen answered firmly.

Roberts, betraying no emotion, asked that the jury be individually polled. All members said they agreed with the verdict.

"Very well," the judge said, releasing a large sigh. He thanked the jurors for their time and attention. "You have done the highest duty that you can as citizens, apart from voting."

Only after the jurors had filed out of the courtroom for the last time did Hairston turn to Mungin, who was now standing behind her. He thrust his hand toward her stiffly, smiling, and she shook it. Then Hairston threw both arms around Mungin in an awkward embrace. Beaming now, she looked far more excited than he did.

The judge ticked off a few housekeeping matters and departed for his chambers.

The defense lawyers quickly gathered their documents and

loose-leaf exhibit books and left, saying very little. Sergi maintained his outwardly placid appearance. He avoided looking at the plaintiff's table on his way out.

Hairston and Nelson lingered, luxuriating in the victory. "I have to say thank you, Larry, thank you. This is my biggest verdict ever," said Hairston.

"I didn't do anything for the past week," he answered. "You did it yourself."

"You brought us good facts, Larry," she responded. "They were good facts."

Nelson wore a huge smile. "You spoiled me," he said to Mungin. "This is my first case, and it's over two million. Now nothing will ever measure up."

"Can you get your comptroller to stop calling me?" Mungin asked Hairston. He was serious. Even as the trial got under way, the administrator in charge of billing at Hairston's law firm was calling Mungin at home, wanting money for expenses.

"There's money now," Hairston said, laughing.

Actually, she wasn't correct. Katten Muchin didn't have to hand over a dime until its appeals were exhausted. And the firm could be counted on to pursue those appeals zealously.

Leaving my seat in the spectators' gallery, I had joined the plaintiff's team in the well of the court. Mungin turned to me and asked whether "all those years ago" when we were roommates at Harvard Law, I would have guessed that "this is where we would end up?"

Of course this was not where I thought we would be. Still, I thought to myself that I was satisfied with my slightly unconventional law grad's career choice. Was Mungin happy with his? He had triumphed in court but effectively ended his chances of making it with any big firm. He had wanted to overcome race, yet now, in many people's eyes, he would always be entwined by race.

On the other hand, $2.5 million could buy a lot of consolation.

* * *

After the plaintiff team's muted celebration, Mungin and I left Hairston and Nelson in the courtroom. They seemed like they might be savoring victory for a while. I had been the only person in the spectators' section when the verdict came in. No one else was waiting to congratulate Mungin. He had discouraged his brother and sister in New York from attending the trial; he hadn't wanted the extra pressure of hosting out-of-town relatives.

The halls of the courthouse were empty, and our footsteps echoed off the marble. Mungin mused that if Katten Muchin had treated him respectfully near the end, and given him a sizable bonus to walk away, he never would have sued.

How much? I asked.

Maybe $10,000, he said, "if they had said they were sorry." He grinned. I couldn't tell whether he was being serious.

We were already across C Street, headed toward the subway station, when he realized he had left his raincoat in the courtroom. We doubled back. "I don't have the money yet," he joked. "I can't afford to forget about a raincoat." As we reentered the building, we were stopped by the African-American deputy U.S. marshal who guarded the courtroom during the trial. He wore an off-duty outfit of green and brown camouflage pants and a red flannel shirt. He broke into a big smile. "Congratulations, man, I was the marshal," he said, pumping Mungin's hand. "Congratulations! Great, great."

Mungin smiled and nodded, but he seemed flustered.

A few minutes later, at the Judiciary Square subway stop, Mungin stood among the prosecutors, criminal defense lawyers, social workers, clerks, and others who make their living in the courts. He looked like part of the crowd, and yet apart from it, too. His tan raincoat and gray suit blended easily. But to mark the trial finale, he had worn elegant black suede shoes, reminders of his days of fancy clothes shopping. The shoes stuck out. And rather than a standard briefcase, he carried his *Washington Post* in a giveaway canvas satchel stamped "Philip Morris"—evidence of his current tight budget.

What were his plans for the evening? I asked.

He said he would take a nap, call his brother and sister, and then ride his bike to the gym.

Ride his bike in the dark? I asked.

In the dark.

No champagne, no celebration?

No champagne, no celebration.

CHAPTER TWENTY

"We Were Pushing for Him"

Suspense did not hang in the jury room air. "Everyone was of one accord; that's what I could see," juror Robert Lucky said after the trial. The jurors admired Mungin and quickly came to agree that Katten Muchin had mistreated him.

"I thought it was unfair," said Lucky, the retired social club steward. The jurors "thought it was lopsided," he continued. "It's like if I step on your shoe and scuff it up, you have a right to come back at me. In other words, we felt like Mr. Mungin had a right to come back at the law firm." Before he retired, Lucky, 66, had served drinks and opened doors for wealthy white people. He'd brought his lunch to court each day in a brown paper bag because he couldn't afford to pay $4 or $5 for a meal in the cafeteria.

Elwood Vaughn also saw the case as clear-cut. "What happened here is they didn't treat this man fair," said Vaughn, the 74-year-old retired warehouse worker. "That's really all there was to it, and all there is to say."

"It was not really a hard decision to make," Lucky agreed. "We reviewed the options from both angles. The point was, Mr. Mungin was looking for his rights. We were pushing for him."

Most members of the jury weren't eager to discuss the details of how they reached their decision on liability or damages. "Mr. Mungin was misused" in connection with his pay and the work assignments he received, was about all Lucky would say when asked for specifics about his reasoning. Lucky thought that if Mungin were white, he might have gotten promoted to partner.

Vaughn politely refused to expand on his blanket statement about Katten Muchin's unfairness. He said he was very busy and didn't "want to go through all of that stuff again."

Sylvia Carroll, the 46-year-old federal employee, declined to say anything, other than that "the case hit too close to home" for her. She wouldn't explain what she meant.

Catherine Matthews told *The American Lawyer* shortly after the verdict that she accepted the contention that the firm had steered work away from Mungin and to white lawyers from Chicago: "They were sending it somewhere else, and he is right here in Washington and he couldn't do the work? They overlooked him."

The jury thought little of Katten Muchin's credibility or defense strategy. Matthews didn't believe Sergi's explanations. "When the defense said that he fell through the cracks, I looked at him," she explained. "Why do you say he fell through the cracks when he was walking up and down the halls?"

Lucky said that Dombroff "came across like he knew what he was doing, trying to convince the jurors, 'I'm in charge.' It was like he could do anything he wanted because he was at the head of the office."

One million dollars seemed like a good round estimate of the pocketbook harm to Mungin, several jurors said. It was also the amount that Hairston had requested. The $1.5 million punitive award—$500,000 less than Hairston's suggestion—was needed to deter Katten Muchin, a wealthy law firm, from treating any other black lawyer the same way, Lucky said.

In sum, the jury's reasoning appeared to break down into three parts:

- First, Mungin got a raw deal at Katten Muchin.
- Second, since he was black, his race probably had something to do with it.

- And third, the firm's defense that others suffered equally wasn't plausible; no other witness seemed to have been as thoroughly thwarted as Mungin.

The jury apparently equated this third conclusion with the legal requirement that Mungin demonstrate that he was treated differently from similarly situated white lawyers. Mungin was treated worse than others in the Washington office, the jury thought. And rather than demand proof that this different treatment was based on race, the jury relied instead on something like Mr. Lucky's intuitive assumption that if Mungin were white he probably would have gotten a fairer shake.

The jury imposed rough justice, then, on a defendant that failed to show respect to a black employee who had come a long way in life, followed the formal rules, and demanded his employer do the same.

Was the result preordained because almost all of the jurors were black? No, according to one juror who spoke on the condition of anonymity. "Black and white [as to the jurors] didn't come into it," this juror said. "There were people who had worked many years in many jobs and we knew what was happening" at Katten Muchin. "We had all seen that sort of thing at one time or another." Anna Marks, the lone white juror and a retired secretary who had been fired from two jobs during her working days, willingly joined the consensus backing Mungin, other jurors said. Still, some comments from black jurors—that the case "hit too close to home," that the jury was "pushing for" Mungin—indicate a sense of personal identification with the plaintiff. Part of this connection doubtless was based on race, but another part stemmed from a working-class jury's understanding the powerful frustration felt by a son of the projects whose professional dreams collapsed.

Mungin's victory made a big splash in the legal world. The *Wall Street Journal* and other major publications gave it prominent coverage. The verdict was the largest any expert could recall in a discrimination case involving a minority lawyer suing a law firm, my colleague Margaret Jacobs noted in her article in the *Journal*. Such cases were rare to begin with; a law firm, combative by instinct, isn't the sort of adversary you want to face in court. The *Washington Post*'s business law columnist, Saundra Torry, wrote that "major law firms, grappling for years with the issues of hiring and retaining minority lawyers, were jolted" by the Mungin case. Torry quoted Pauline Schneider, a former D.C. bar president and herself a black corporate lawyer, as saying that the Mungin case was all the more significant because it didn't involve egregious racist acts. "It certainly will send off warning bells at a lot of firms about how they need to behave or what they need to be concerned about, lest something they are doing is read in a way they may not intend," Schneider said.

White law firm partners, in Washington, New York, and elsewhere, told me in private conversation that the Mungin verdict would cause them to change their behavior, but in a perverse way that Schneider wasn't contemplating. Big firms, these partners insisted, would hire *fewer* blacks. Rather than reform their treatment of associates, firms would avoid the risk of being sued by simply limiting the number of potential race-bias plaintiffs who walked in the door. "Look, we're all concerned about [the dearth of blacks in the upper reaches of the profession] and worry about it, but the litigation risk will be seen as too great now," one big firm partner told me. "Since we're not going to guarantee that anyone is going to make partner, the irony is that this victory for one black will probably hurt other blacks."

Mungin's old friend from Houston, the white corporate lawyer Bruce Shortt, had followed the case from afar and celebrated the verdict. Shortt, who had himself quit big-firm life to practice on his own, doubted that race had much to do with Mungin's mistreatment. "There was no question that [Katten Muchin] had broken all kinds of promises," Shortt told me. "I've seen that sort of thing happen time and time and time again, regardless of race." But Shortt thought Mungin was justified in using any legal weapon at his disposal. "He was bent, spindled, and mutilated. The object was to vindicate himself. That's what I told him. In the final analysis, it doesn't really matter if there was a cabal of people sitting in a room saying, 'Let's get that nigger.' That never happens. It doesn't matter. The fact remains that he was brought in based on certain representations, and they didn't keep any promises. Even after it was pointed out to them, they didn't keep their promises. That is unfortunately very much the case with big law firms."

Deborah Mungin was glad her brother won, of course, but not surprised. "He deserved it," she told me in her matter-of-fact tone. She hoped that once he got his money, Larry would help underwrite her long-standing dream of moving her family out of Woodside Houses. Kenneth Mungin congratulated his brother and told him the money didn't matter. "I'm so happy for you," Kenneth said. "I don't care if you won ten dollars."

Katten Muchin, for its part, offered no apologies in defeat. "The reason we are upset is that this is not who we are," managing partner Michael Zavis said to the *Chicago Tribune*. "We have a very diverse group of people." Michele Roberts continued to use her own race as proof of the strength and authenticity of Katten Muchin's position. "When asked to defend this case, I needed to be satisfied that there was no 'there' there, and I was satisfied," she told *The American Lawyer*. "I am an African-American woman. Allegations of discrimination, sexual or racial, I take very seriously. [But] I would not have taken Mr. Mungin's case."

Katten Muchin moved swiftly to respond to questions from clients troubled by the discrimination verdict. Black executives, in particular, wanted explanations. The firm had an advantage in being able to point out that Roberts had closely examined Katten Muchin and found no racism. In the end, the firm didn't lose any substantial business. Katten Muchin vowed it would win on appeal.

For Hairston, the Mungin case was a huge boon. She became something of a celebrity in Washington legal circles. Flattering pictures of her accompanied articles about the trial in the local *Legal Times* and in the nationally distributed *American Lawyer*. She was quoted widely on law firms' obligation to follow through on their promises to minority associates. "If you're going to say that your philosophy is to hire and promote minorities in your firm, then your actions have to be consistent with your philosophy," she told me. The African-American magazine *Jet* portrayed "noted attorney" Abbey Hairston as a heroine. "Black folks should not allow themselves to be cheated out of moving up in the company where they work," she told *Jet*. "There is a way to deal with discrimination, and this case proves it."

New clients lined up at Alexander, Aponte & Marks, seeking Hairston's assistance. To her delight, in addition to several black professionals, she signed up four *white* women lawyers who claimed they had been victims of sex discrimination at Washington law firms. In a remarkable coincidence, the husbands of each of the women lawyers had read about Mungin's case and had suggested to their wives that they give Hairston a call. Having white lawyers come to the firm as clients gave morale at Alexander Aponte a big boost, Hairston added. By late 1996, she reported that she had settled all four of the sex-discrimination cases on confidential terms. "No one wants to go to trial," Hairston bragged. In recognition of her new prominence, Alexander promoted Hairston to name partner. The firm changed its name to Alexander, Bearden, Hairston & Marks.

The losing party in a civil trial may ask the trial judge to declare that "no reasonable juror" could have reached the verdict, and therefore the verdict must be thrown out. Katten Muchin filed such a "motion for judgment as a matter of law," which is a routine step, even though trial judges rarely second-guess juries in this fashion. The no-reasonable-juror standard is very difficult to meet; only verdicts patently based on prejudice or emotion are supposed to be negated on this ground.

"As a result of the verdict," Katten Muchin's brief stated, "the partners of KMZ now stand unjustly convicted of engaging in intentional racial bias. Such a result simply cannot be right on the record in this case. It is unfair and unjust. Juries are not infallible, and our judicial system recognizes the right and obligation of its trial judges to act when a jury goes awry. This is such a case."

The firm's arguments about what the evidence showed weren't much different from those at trial. But the brief's tone was harsher. The defense team apparently was less worried about offending Judge Robertson than it had been about irritating the jury.

"KMZ has no obligation to 'advance' any attorney's career," the brief said at one point. It then quoted at length from a 1992 ruling by the federal appeals court in Philadelphia in a sex discrimination case. Title VII of the 1964 Civil Rights Act "does not require employers to treat all employees fairly, closely monitor their progress and insure them every opportunity for advancement," the Philadelphia court said. "It is a sad fact of life in the working world that employees of ability are sometimes overlooked for promotion. Large law firms are not immune from unfairness in this imperfect world. The law limits its protection against that unfairness to cases of invidious discrimination."

On June 24, Judge Robertson issued a spare six-page ruling in response to Katten Muchin's brief. Mungin, the judge wrote, had demonstrated four key facts at trial:

- First, that his starting salary was less than the average salary of white associates with similar seniority.
- Second, that a white associate from Chicago got bankruptcy work for which Mungin was qualified.
- Third, that Mungin "fell between the cracks" when he was first eligible for partnership and wasn't considered.
- Fourth, that he was overlooked when it came time for his 1994 pay adjustment and didn't receive a base-pay raise until he complained.

Katten Muchin, in turn, introduced evidence of legitimate, non-discriminatory reasons for these facts:

- First, that Mungin's starting salary was set by the market-place.
- Second, that the Chicago associate had worked with the client before.
- Third, that Mungin's department head had considered and rejected nominating him for partnership.
- Fourth, that his 1994 salary was promptly adjusted after he complained.

"The jury evidently rejected the law firm's non-discriminatory reasons," the judge concluded. "That rejection permits a finding of racial discrimination. The jury's verdict was not irrational or unsupported by the record, and defendant's motion for judgment as a matter of law must be denied."

Robertson didn't reveal his own thoughts about the evidence. Implicit in his opinion was the possibility that were he deciding the case in the first instance, he might have ruled for the defendant. In his opinion, he could have—but didn't—describe Mungin's case as overwhelming in a legal sense. But under the jury system, a judge is obliged to refrain from substituting his judgment for that of the jurors, unless there is absolutely no evidence to support the result, or some sort of procedural mishap has occurred. Robertson saw neither problem in this case.

He had a further thought on the awarding of punitive damages. "Where, as here, the evidence supports a finding of racial discrimination, no additional evidence is required to support an award of punitive damages," he wrote. Race bias is egregious enough on its own that it may be punished with a penalty beyond compensatory damages. The $1.5 million punitive award in this case, he added, "cannot be said to be unrelated to the jury's compensatory award of $1 million and, on a record establishing that Mark Dombroff, the former partner who had hired plaintiff, earned $950,000 in his last year with the firm and that Vincent Sergi, the plaintiff's department head, earned $550,000 per year, it is not excessive and does not offend due process."

CHAPTER TWENTY-ONE

"God Has a Plan for Everybody"

AUGUST 1996

Several months after the trial, I accompanied Mungin on one of his regular trips to South Carolina. He had continued to make the long drive down I-95 after his father died. Now, he told me that when the Katten Muchin appeal was finished, he planned to move south permanently. He would live where his father had lived, and where his ancestors had lived for generations, back to slave times.

Did he think he would fit in? I asked.

He already felt comfortable among his relatives on Edisto and in Charleston and Beaufort, Mungin said. He would adjust. He would settle down. "Don't be surprised if you come down to see me, and I've got a wife and kids," he said.

I would be surprised, I said.

If he got to keep the $2.5 million the jury awarded him, he would buy some land from his relatives and build a house where friends from up north could drop by for visits. "If you don't know my phone number, just stop in [at a local business] and ask for Larry Mungin. They're all going to know. Even the white people are going to know," he said. "That's an amazing feeling."

Money from the trial would remove the pressure to work at

a conventional job. He talked about real estate development: Wouldn't wealthy, white Charleston businessmen welcome a well-educated black partner who knew his way around the islands? Maybe he would take the South Carolina bar and practice a little law on the side. He asked me to provide a character reference for the bar application, which I agreed to do.

But even if his award were reduced on appeal, or reversed altogether, Mungin believed he could make a new beginning in South Carolina. He wasn't spending any money yet. And his relatives didn't expect him to conquer worlds.

The local whites, while perhaps harboring some traditional prejudices, were on the whole more open and straightforward than their northern counterparts when dealing with blacks, Mungin found. There was less pretense in the South; people respected racial boundaries. Less burdened by frustrating interaction with whites, his relatives in South Carolina were more self-sufficient and self-assured than most of the people he grew up with in Queens, he said. Mungin imagined he might become a broker of sorts between black and white communities. He wasn't ruling out politics, he told me.

What about his dream of success in white society?

"I've worked hard. I'm tired," he said, suddenly sounding it. He would live among black people whom he didn't feel obliged to impress. Sure, there had been a minor fuss within his family in South Carolina over his winning the lawsuit. People knew about it; they were impressed by the article in *Jet*. But they didn't bring it up much in conversation with him. His relatives seemed more curious about and pleased by Mungin's desire to live among them than by the still-abstract idea that he was a millionaire.

Mungin himself didn't brag, exactly, but he did make glancing references to his good fortune. One evening, we sat in the cozy living room of his Aunt Florence Kentuck, talking with the elderly woman over the soft noise of a television sports broadcast.

"How about that, Aunt Florence, only thirty-eight, and I'm having a book written about me!"

"Hmmm," was the old woman's reply, as if this were truly ordinary news.

Mungin and I visited the Laurel Hill area on Edisto, where
almost everyone was related to him in one way or another.
Amelia Smalls, a matriarch and Mungin relative several generations back, had acquired much of Laurel Hill in a trade for
a place called Raccoon Island. We came upon a Mungin
cousin, Gerald Smalls, and his friend Leon Watson, who were
preparing for a "crab crack," or picnic, to be held on a small
landing that provided access to a wide marsh veined by placid
creeks. The air was heavy and scented by the spunky marsh
smells: fish, salt, and rot. Smalls and Watson were cutting two-
by-fours for the legs of tables and benches; they had already
strung light bulbs among the tree branches and run extension
cords back to a portable generator.

The local men were wary at first, until Mungin reminded
Smalls who he was. The cousin's confusion immediately
melted into a warm smile and big handshake. Watson was ec-
static. "Let me shake the hand of the son of Junior Mungin,"
he said in a thick Gullah accent. "Let me shake your hand
again, man. Your daddy was a very good friend of mine, very
good friend." Mungin's face lit up.

"Junior, he never around you unless he could do something
for you," Watson said. "He got me my disability" check, he
added with a wink and no details.

Mungin asked Watson about the old days. "Good times, good
times," said Watson, who wore a white T-shirt, tan slacks, and
Italian-style loafers that were getting muddy. "One day, Junior
made a hundred-dollar bet that driving his truck he could beat
some boy in a seventy-one Chevy from Steamboat Landing to
the bridge. It was raining, the road was wet, and I could feel that
truck just sliding across the road. I thought, Oh Lord, we gonna
crash. But damned if Junior didn't beat that boy and take his
hundred dollars!"

Another time, Watson and Junior were working together on
a shrimp boat that hit heavy water coming back from a run.
The boat was already listing when it was smacked by a huge
wave and nearly capsized. Junior fell, keeping himself from

going overboard by grabbing a piece of bolted-down equipment. Watson ended up in his lap. " 'Hold on, Junior!' " Watson recalled shouting. " 'You go over, I go too.' But Junior, he held on. He one tough boy."

The conversation turned to real estate. Smalls, who had come back to the coastal islands after working for many years in New York, laughed about the white developers who drove over from Charleston in their Land Rovers and Cherokees. "Now why would I want to sell?" he asked. "I got paradise here. This is where I want to be."

"That's right," Mungin said. "You do have paradise." Other relatives were gradually selling land, which bothered Mungin. He felt as if he had a personal stake in keeping the family's roots planted in the islands' spongy, fertile soil.

Sunday morning, Mungin was to give a talk at his family's church, New First Baptist. His cousin, Marie Bligen, had simply announced the assignment some weeks earlier. She had one piece of guidance: "Tie it to Scripture." This could be a problem, because even in the months of his becoming acquainted with the church-filled life of Edisto and environs, Mungin hadn't spent much time with the Bible. He hadn't attended church regularly since childhood.

Saturday night, we stayed with another cousin, Synthia Glover, the lawyer. She lived in a pleasant subdivision outside of Charleston and drove a Mercedes sedan. In her house, Mungin found a book by Robert Schuller, the television evangelist. Sitting at Synthia's dining room table, he leafed through it, looking for inspiration. Eventually, he found something he liked and scribbled a few notes. Then he went off to bed.

New First Baptist was built in 1818 by Hephzibah J. Townsend, a white woman who wanted slaves to have a place to worship. Townsend was buried in back of the church, along with generations of its black members. Junior Mungin lay in the same graveyard. Because of its age, New First Baptist bore a plaque from the National Register of Historic Places, a point of pride among members. The plain wood floors were covered by a rich red carpet, and the pews had recently been reupholstered in matching fabric. Palm trees were visible through the clear glass window behind the pulpit.

As the only white person in the place, I was naturally the object of some attention. Most parishioners who caught my eye smiled or nodded. Some people walked over to shake hands.

The service moved with an easy fluidity. Deacon Smith, an ancient-looking man in a loose-fitting blue suit, led the congregation in song, stamping from one foot to the other to keep time. "C'mon, church!" he urged. "C'mon, children!"

The children's choir, dressed in striking violet vestments, paraded to the pulpit, preceded by members of the Willing Workers, who wore the same white dresses, gloves, and shoes that Mungin's grandmother had worn decades earlier in her church in Harlem. New First Baptist's lone electric guitarist offered a thick gospel riff as the middle-aged Willing Workers stepped with syncopated grace, double-clapping children following behind.

One of the white-clad Willing Workers went to the lectern to officially recognize the visitors. "Greetings and welcome to worship," she said, looking at Mungin and me.

To my surprise, Mungin stepped forward from our seats in the front pew to respond. "Greetings to you," he said loudly. "I am Lawrence Mungin. Thank you for letting us worship with you and fellowship with you."

I had never heard him use "fellowship" as a verb before.

The service was devoted to the children of the congregation, a number of whom read selections or led hymns. The children's choir sang with strong, high-pitched voices, which shifted now and then into sneaky harmonies. One young man introduced the morning's special speaker with a run-down of Mungin's accomplishments, beginning with the fact that he was "the son of Lawrence Mungin."

"Good morning, everyone!" Mungin said when he stepped behind the lectern.

"Good morning!" the congregation answered.

He wore a light gray Armani suit and a good-humored smile. "As you all know, I'm a lawyer, not a preacher. . . .

Maybe we can pretend that you're my jury out there, and we can get a final verdict when this is all over. Hopefully it will be positive. I've had some pretty good success with juries. . . .

"My little talk is going to be about a plan, that God has a plan for you and God has a plan for me, and God has a plan for everybody."

"Amen!" some of his listeners answered.

He was speaking differently, cutting off some of his "y's," for example, so that "everybody" came out "ever'body," the way some of his relatives pronounced it. He didn't have notes, yet sounded as if he had given sermons his whole life.

"I have a little Scripture," he said, "which Cousin Marie said would be a good thing to do since I was going to come and fellowship with y'all." Mungin said he would recite from Jeremiah 29:11–13.

> *For I know, the thoughts that I think for you, saith the Lord, thoughts of peace, and not of evil, to give you an expected end.*
>
> *Then shall ye call upon me, and ye shall go and pray unto me, and I will harken unto you.*
>
> *And ye shall seek me, and find me, when ye shall search for me with all your heart.*

"When we're young and trying to figure out exactly what we're supposed to be doing," Mungin said, the Bible "teaches that the answers are found in Scripture. And they are found in good works that people do, that you do, and in all the beauty and all of God's gifts on this earth. That it can be used as instructions, as guideposts, as reminders of what your purpose is on this earth.

"If I can talk a little bit about myself, since I believe testimony is often the most effective instrument . . ."

"Yes! Yes!" his audience responded.

"I was born up in New York. My father, and my grandfather, and my great-grandfather are from these islands, going way back. . . . Over the past year, prior to his passing, I had spent a lot of time coming down and seeing my father who was very, very sick. I hadn't been close to my father in a very, very long time. I have his name. He had his father's name. We all have the same name. I always knew he was there, but I never got much time to come down and see him and talk to him and really get to know him as an adult. I had just a lot of childhood memories, because he came home a long time ago down to Edisto. So when he got sick, my Cousin Laird, Cousin Marie, they made sure that I was informed as to what was going on. And at some point it became necessary for me to come down and see my father and to get back in touch with the things that are really most important."

"Yes! Yes!"

"He suffered, but as I grew to know him and got to know the people who loved and cared about him down here, I found he really created a life for himself, a life I knew nothing about. I learned a lot. We talked a lot. And for me, the circle was complete.

"I've been very blessed and had a lot of people help me and have had a lot of success, worldly success. But I always knew there was something more. . . . I always kept the doors open. I never strayed too far. So when the call came to come back to the things that are most important in life, God had certain tools, God had certain ways of showing me where the path was, what his plan was for me. Sometimes you stray. Sometimes you don't know where you're supposed to be going. Sometimes you just want to make it through the day. But through my father, through the strength of his testimony, the testimony of his friends and cousins, and the life he left behind, good words people say about him, it just made it clear that I may not know exactly where I am going . . . but at least I know that I am following *God's* plan."

"Amen! Thank you, sir! Amen!"

"If you don't know where you're supposed to be going," Mungin preached, "keep your eyes on the *Lord*."

"Yes!"

"Keep your head to the skies."

"Uh-huh!"

"You'll find it. You might make some mistakes all along, but you have family, you have friends, you have the church. You have a lot of good people in this world who are going to try to keep you on track. . . . By participating in the community, you become part of the community. The community will help you in your time of need."

"Oh, yes!" People were applauding.

"Young people!" Mungin thundered. "Don't give up. Look to the good people who are around you and love you. Try to do the right thing. When all is lost, just know that God is watching over you. Thank you."

"Amens" rolled forward, over a wave of applause.

When the service ended a short time later, Mungin was enveloped by the congregation. Men clapped him on the back. Women crowded in to kiss him on the cheek, their oversized Sunday hats threatening to cause injury.

"Thank you," Mungin said. "Thank you."

CHAPTER TWENTY-TWO

"No Reasonable Juror . . ."

"People get held up!" declared Michael W. Zavis. He was addressing the subject of job discrimination lawsuits. "Small businesses that can't afford to defend themselves, nothing they can do but settle. Fortunately, we can afford to fight."

Zavis spoke as we waited on a late-April morning to hear the oral arguments in Katten Muchin's appeal of Mungin's trial victory. We sat in the reception area outside of the fifth-floor courtroom of the U.S. Court of Appeals for the District of Columbia, Zavis on a drooping couch, I on a faded high-backed chair. The furniture, arranged in a wide, sterile hallway, provided a fittingly artificial, movie-set feel for a stilted encounter.

When I arrived, he was sitting alone, reading a copy of *Offshore Investment* magazine. He fiddled with a wafer-thin cellular phone. Trim and smartly dressed, he wore a short beard and spoke with a broad Chicago accent.

"I've ridden the crest since sixty-one," Zavis told me. "I've been successful. But you've got to think there's something wrong when lawyers are draining off so many dollars. . . . When young lawyers—associates, income partners—are paid one hundred twenty or one hundred fifty thousand, and they think they're being screwed. Unbelievable. When employment cases are taking up fifty percent of the docket in federal district courts, there's something very wrong."

I suggested that his 50 percent figure was a bit high, but Zavis waved this off. I asked him for his thoughts on the Mungin case.

"It's over except for the argument," he said, sounding certain of vindication. "There's nothing to say. It's over."

The U.S. appeals court in Washington, known as the D.C. Circuit, had a long run from the 1950s through the mid-1980s as a bastion of liberalism. Its aggressive Democrat-appointed judges made new law on everything from the insanity defense to civil rights. In the 1980s, however, Presidents Ronald Reagan and George Bush filled vacancies on the court with equally spirited conservatives determined to steer sharply to the right. By the mid-1990s, even after a few Clinton appointments, the 11-member D.C. Circuit was split 6–5 between conservatives and liberals. Appeals are decided by three-judge panels, chosen at random. In politically charged cases, when judicial ideology affects the outcome, results often turn on which three judges are selected. Despite this unpredictability, Katten Muchin had reason to hope that it could get a panel far more sympathetic to a white out-of-town law firm than the trial jury had been. The firm wasn't at all disappointed with the three names produced by the D.C. Circuit's computer. Deeply divided in outlook, the panel was 2–1 conservative and 2–1 white versus black:

Judge A. Raymond Randolph shared a moderately conservative reputation with George Bush, the president who appointed him. One of the judge's mentors was arch-conservative icon Robert Bork, who'd failed famously in 1987 to be confirmed for the Supreme Court. Randolph worked for Bork in the Justice Department in the 1970s and then practiced privately.

Judge Stephen Williams, a Reagan appointee, was farther to the right than Randolph. A former professor specializing in oil-and-gas law at the University of Colorado, he was, like many Republicans in the Reagan-Bush era, deeply concerned about what he saw as the pernicious effects of liberal "political correctness," including racial-preference policies.

Harry Edwards, a black Carter appointee, was the imperious chief judge of the court. A labor-law expert and former professor at the prestigious University of Michigan Law School, he wrote opinions that typically reached liberal results but didn't attempt to revolutionize the law.

Zavis, the law firm's point man on the appeal, had decided that he wanted not just a fresh panel of judges to review the case, but also a new lawyer to argue it. He was angry with himself for not having paid closer attention to how the trial was handled. In particular, Zavis was irritated that the defense team at trial hadn't sought supportive testimony from a recently elevated African-American income partner in the Chicago office, and from the former managing partner of the Los Angeles office, Karen Randall, also an African-American, who'd left the firm amicably just before the trial. Michele Roberts had feared that the jury would interpret appearances by two purportedly contented black lawyers who had nothing to do with Mungin as irrelevant and possibly as patronizing. Worse, these witnesses might have opened the door for Hairston to explore the general experience of black lawyers at Katten Muchin, including Elaine Williams's suit and the firm's difficulty in retaining African-American recruits. Still, Zavis felt the trial defense hadn't been aggressive enough, and he was determined to retain the very best appellate lawyer he could find for the appeal.

The Seyfarth firm lacked anyone with superstar dazzle. Roberts wasn't known as an appellate attorney, and with an audience of judges rather than laymen, her race was no longer thought to be an advantage. The lawyer Zavis settled on was Andrew Frey, an appellate whiz known nationally for rescuing corporate defendants hit with big jury verdicts.

A burly Raymond Burr look-alike, Frey, 57, was delighted to receive the well-paid Katten Muchin assignment. Even a partial win—say, a reduction in the amount of damages—would enhance his considerable reputation. A loss wouldn't be embarrassing because, ordinarily, this kind of appeal didn't stand much of a chance. Judge Robertson had run a tight trial, without any obvious procedural flaws. Frey mainly would be arguing that the jury was simply "unreasonable," that it didn't act rationally. It was the same argument Seyfarth had made in its unsuccessful post-trial motion. Reversals on this theory were unusual, and for good reason. One of the fundamental principles of the American legal system is that expert judges determine questions of law, while lay juries, relying on common sense, assess the evidence and decide questions of fact.

Unlike his opposition, Mungin stuck with his law firm. Hairston was primarily a trial attorney, but Mungin thought that the newly renamed Alexander, Bearden, Hairston & Marks would rise to the occasion. The firm had a big incentive to defend the jury award: securing its prospective legal fee of $830,000, which would be paid only if Mungin prevailed. And there was also the matter of pride. Hairston and the firm had been hailed for vanquishing Katten Muchin and its outside lawyers. A reversal would wipe out that accomplishment. Mungin was pleased when managing partner Koteles Alexander, who had some appellate experience, promised that he personally would defend the trial verdict before the D.C. Circuit.

What Mungin didn't discover until about nine months after the trial was that Alexander wouldn't pay much attention to the appeal. The Alexander Bearden firm, it turned out, was staggering toward disaster.

Under Alexander's shaky leadership, the firm's costs had not been brought under control. Bills were not collected promptly from clients. Attorney turnover remained high, creating inefficiency. Unable to obtain sufficient bank credit, the firm borrowed from a commercial lending company whose high interest rates only compounded the financial problems. The law firm fell behind on its rent. Desperate, Alexander even called me in February 1997, asking for help in contacting New York financiers who might bail him out. I could offer only phone numbers, none of which led to relief. The firm stopped paying associates, paralegals, and secretaries. Resignations followed. To the end, Alexander believed that he had been undone by racial distrust on the part of white bankers and potential corporate clients.

But there was more. In early March, Koteles Alexander was arrested and charged with second-degree assault, based on a criminal complaint made out by his partner, Abbey Hairston. Hairston and Alexander had become romantically involved, and they had been living together at her Silver Spring home. The romance went sour, however, and on March 8, according to the complaint, Alexander threw Hairston to the ground as she attempted to move out of her residence. Alexander pleaded not guilty. Without formally convicting him, a Maryland judge ordered Alexander to serve six months probation, pay a $305 fine, and do 30 hours of community service. In Maryland, this sort of intermediate sanction is less severe than a standard finding of criminal guilt and can be expunged altogether after three years if the defendant stays out of trouble. Hairston resigned from the firm and rented office space near Baltimore. Alexander dropped out of sight, staying with relatives in Virginia. "I'm just trying to keep it together," he told me in a brief telephone conversation. Alexander Bearden eventually was forced to begin liquidating its assets under the supervision of a federal bankruptcy court.

The brief that Alexander filed in February with the D.C. Circuit was disjointed, to put it mildly, and wouldn't have been finished at all, were it not for the efforts of Adrian Nelson and another associate. Hairston reluctantly agreed to argue the Mungin appeal herself.

Mungin, who didn't closely monitor his law firm, was caught by surprise when it swiftly collapsed. He declared at the time, unconvincingly, that he wasn't troubled by the development. "I have very good judgment," he told me, sounding defensive. "I'm very proud that I went with them [Alexander and Hairston]. They did very well by me."

He thought a lot about the money, as anyone in his position would have. With $2.5 million, he could lend his brother enough to buy the small building in which he and his family lived. Then Kenneth could manage the place and forget about paying rent. Mungin also had discussed helping his sister and her family relocate to South Carolina. And he would spend some of the rest on a snug Sea Island house for himself.

Mungin expected to win on appeal. The D.C. Circuit would affirm at least some of the big jury award, he thought. But he believed that he had already accomplished something significant: He had received the jury's endorsement that he had been mistreated by Katten Muchin, and a white federal judge had let that determination stand. "Most people [who file discrimination suits] don't get that far," he said, and that was true.

The Katten Muchin appeal was the second case on the D.C. Circuit's docket on the morning of April 22. Judge Edwards had already warmed up on the preceding lawyers, whom he lacerated with disdainful questions. Respected for his sharp mind, the 56-year-old jurist also had a well-known nasty streak. He sharply interrupted Frey when the lawyer insisted it would be "irrational" to conclude that Katten Muchin may have treated race as a plus in hiring Mungin, but then harmed him because he was black.

"Lots of employers have hired because of race, because they felt they were made to but didn't prefer to," Edwards commented. "I just don't understand why you are raising the point. It didn't seem to me germane and certainly doesn't follow. It is intuitively not correct."

Frey wisely moved on. After hundreds of cases before the Supreme Court and lower appellate courts, he wasn't thrown by bluster from the bench. Appellate arguments before vigorous judges, such as the three he was now addressing, frequently resemble interrogation more than speech-making. Smart advocates absorb the verbal blows and try gently to steer the judges in their clients' direction. Frey was imparting this important lesson to a gaggle of more-junior lawyers from his firm who had come to watch the master at work.

One of Frey's main points was that Mungin had illegitimately asserted a right to *consideration* for partnership. It wasn't necessarily Mungin's fault that he hadn't been given a chance to prove himself, Frey told the judges, but failure to be considered for promotion wasn't "an adverse employment action" that amounted to discrimination.

This riled Judge Edwards. "Demeaning treatment based on race is not adverse action?" he demanded.

Careful not to concede that Katten Muchin had done anything based on race, Frey answered yes—that merely demeaning treatment didn't constitute discrimination. The maltreatment must actually hurt the victim in the performance of his job.

Mungin, who sat at the appellee's table with Hairston, stared straight ahead, seemingly ignoring Frey. He had developed a strong distaste for the stocky attorney during a couple of unsuccessful settlement negotiations ordered by the appeals court and held in front of two court-appointed mediators. "The great white hunter, sent in to slay me," was how Mungin referred to Frey. For his part, the appellate lawyer, a partner with the Chicago-based firm of Mayer, Brown & Platt, had no great admiration for Mungin. Frey believed the plaintiff had cleverly used "histrionics" during the trial to distract the jury and win a verdict he didn't deserve.

Judge Randolph had thrown a few questions into the mix but so far hadn't revealed his leanings. Randolph, 53, was jokingly called "Random Ray" by some of the court's young law clerks, because he wasn't as predictable in his rulings as some more conservative colleagues. But the issue of Mungin's credentials sparked Randolph's interest.

Frey scoffed at Mungin's trumpeting of his Harvard law degree as a reason that from the start, he should have received pay at least comparable to Katten Muchin veterans. "Six years out, you are looking at other things besides the identity of the law school where somebody went," Frey said.

"How did he do at Harvard?" Randolph asked.

"Excuse me?" a startled Frey responded.

"How did he *do* at Harvard?" Randolph repeated.

"As far as I know he did fine. I have no idea. I did not find anything in the record about that," said Frey, who adroitly eased away from the inquiry.

Randolph's question was jarring for what he left unsaid. His highly skeptical tone indicated that he was assuming that Mungin hadn't done well at Harvard. The judge appeared to be fishing for an indication that Mungin had done poorly—that his relying on his Harvard degree wasn't just irrelevant, as Frey had maintained, but possibly disingenuous.

In fact, Mungin had earned middling grades—mostly Bs—at Harvard. But since, as Frey noted, his academic record hadn't been disputed at trial—and neither his intellectual capacity nor competence as a lawyer had become an issue—Randolph's apparent suspicion was disconcerting.

The final point that Frey was able to squeeze in before his 20 minutes of argument time expired was a response to a central point in Mungin's brief. The jury had a right simply to disbelieve defense witnesses who contended that there were nondiscriminatory reasons for Mungin's treatment, the plaintiff's brief argued.

Not so, said Frey. There had to be "specific substantial evidence" that the defense witnesses were weaving a "pretext" for discrimination. The jury couldn't rely on some gut instinct about credibility. "The burden of proof remains at all times on the plaintiff in these cases," Frey told the three judges. "The plaintiff has to show discrimination."

Judge Randolph appeared to find the Frey argument too extreme. What if, under cross-examination, a key defense witness was "shown to be a liar?" Couldn't that be the basis of a finding of discrimination?

"When you say 'shown to be a liar,' " Frey responded, "I guess my question would be, how? If there is specific evidence—"

"Well," interrupted Judge Edwards, "it is for the *jury* to decide." He sounded as if he were instructing a first-year law student. "In this case they [the plaintiff's side] offer a set of facts with their gloss, and you offer a set, and the jury has to decide who is telling the truth."

In a sentence, Edwards had stated the plaintiff's strongest

theme on appeal: This was a case energetically argued to a jury under the supervision of an able trial judge. The jury deliberated and reached a verdict, apparently in good faith. A higher court shouldn't second-guess the jury's evaluation of witnesses whom the appellate judges didn't see or hear for themselves.

But Frey dug in. Sometimes, he insisted, a plaintiff offers such weak evidence of discrimination that the case should be taken away from the jury. As the chief judge spoke, Frey gripped the lectern and shook his head resolutely.

"How can you shake your head no?" Edwards said. "I haven't even decided which question I am going to ask."

The audience laughed, and, caught by surprise, even the grumpy judge allowed himself a quick smile.

Abbey Hairston wore a cherry-red business suit, in a self-conscious attempt to distinguish herself from the gray and blue crowd in the spacious hearing room. She did get attention, but not the sort that she thought.

Hairston tried to capitalize on Edwards's assertion that it was the jury's province to decide whether witnesses had credibility. Unfortunately for her, she chose a dubious illustration. She argued that the jurors could have concluded that Dombroff was lying when he insisted that firm policy dictated his hiring Mungin as an associate, rather than as a partner. She noted that there were documents entered as evidence that described Katten Muchin's hiring of a young, white lawyer as a partner in the Los Angeles office, even though he, like Mungin, didn't have any clients to bring with him.

"I don't know what all that means," Randolph said. In fact, the comparison didn't prove much of anything. It might have raised suspicions of an employer's inconsistent behavior, but many factors could have explained the hiring of this one white lawyer as a partner.

Randolph demanded to know where Mungin worked before Katten Muchin. When told, he asked peevishly, "And why did he leave? Was he fired?" As with his question about Mungin's grades, the judge used the exchange with Hairston seemingly to push for evidence that her client was a fraud of some sort.

No one, of course, had suggested Mungin was fired by his prior law firm. Why would Randolph jump to that conclusion, especially when the trial record was quite clear that Mungin left Powell Goldstein of his own choice? Had the Republican judge come to the oral argument assuming that the plaintiff was unqualified, a black lawyer carried along by affirmative action?

Randolph persisted in asking increasingly impatient questions about the basic evidence. This was precisely where Frey wanted the court to focus. On the topic of pay, Randolph growled, "What I don't understand is how the ninety-two-thousand-dollar starting salary figure was racially motivated disparate treatment. How does that possibly relate to anything like that?"

A moment later, Judge Williams added in a more courtly tone, "There were in fact negotiations, they made him an offer, and he said, 'I want more.' And they gave him more."

Hairston seemed not to have anticipated this kind of pointed questioning. She unwisely circled back to the lateral hiring of the young L.A. partner.

"Where in your brief do you talk about this L.A. partner?" Williams asked.

Hairston froze. She didn't know. The courtroom was silent as she searched the stack of papers she had brought to the lectern. Mungin remained impassive. It turned out that Hairston was making an argument based on trial evidence that hadn't been included in her appellate brief—a breach of basic appellate etiquette. The brief, cobbled together in the chaotic final months of the Alexander Bearden firm's existence, wasn't a model of organization or clarity. But whatever the extenuating circumstances, Hairston should have known its contents.

Edwards gave her a chance to recover by asking, "Suppose we assume the jury was right, that there was enough evidence for a jury to have found discrimination. Nonetheless, how do you get to a finding of constructive discharge when Mr.

Mungin had no reasonable expectation of continued employment in the Washington office?"

Edwards seemed to be floating a possible compromise: The appeals court could defer to the jury on its finding of discrimination, but reverse the verdict on Mungin's being forced out of his job. Mungin couldn't have been pushed out, Edwards suggested, if the job effectively disappeared in the bust-up of the Washington office.

Hairston appeared relieved to hear Edwards's proposal. But Williams and Randolph weren't through with her yet. They challenged her on the number of Washington office bankruptcy assignments that were routed to white lawyers from Chicago, rather than given to Mungin. In fact, the testimony at trial had been ambiguous on the volume of this disputed work.

Hairston referred to deposition testimony by Charlie Thomson, one of the Chicago lawyers. This testimony had been read into the record at trial. When she had asked Thomson how many bankruptcy "matters" he had worked on for Patricia Gilmore during Mungin's time in the Washington office, he answered, "More than I could put a number on." The jurors might have been impressed by this statement— imprecise though it was—especially since it came from a witness not particularly friendly to Mungin.

But Judge Williams dismissed it, observing testily that Hairston hadn't included in her brief the transcript page numbers referring to the Thomson testimony.

Hairston's 20 minutes seemed to have stretched to 120. When the red light on the lectern flashed to signal the end of her time, she wearily volunteered to sit down.

Afterward, Frey joined his client in the spectators' section. "It went well," Zavis said, smiling, as they shook hands. "It went very well."

In a nearby sitting room, Mungin tried in a restrained way to comfort a distraught Hairston. He put his hand lightly on her shoulder as they spoke. As had happened after the trial verdict, the litigator displayed far more emotion than her client. Mungin in this instance showed admirable charity, given that Hairston's poor performance might have helped jeopardize the jury verdict. Hairston couldn't stop the tears of frustration. She understandably had been distracted by her confrontation with Alexander and by her law firm's dissolution. She had never pretended that appellate argument was her strength. But these excuses didn't suffice.

Mungin and I walked from the courthouse toward Washington's tiny Chinatown. Over pork dumplings and Hunan chicken, he anxiously reviewed the morning's events, commenting on atmosphere as much as substance. He had noticed Frey's youthful minions tittering. "They were all laughing at me," he said, bitterness in his voice. "I heard them. Snickering. When did *I* become the bad guy? That's what I'd like to know."

I murmured something about snotty first-year associates.

"I thought I was a *sympathetic* character," Mungin continued, pouring on the sarcasm. "I thought I was *one of them*. Ha, ha, ha."

His simmering anger made me uneasy. I changed the subject: Had he heard from Koteles Alexander?

No. Mungin sounded more disappointed than angry about Alexander's collapse. "That's a tragedy," he said. The older attorney "threw it all away." Mungin recalled how Alexander was always late for meetings—even for the court-ordered mediation sessions. And why hadn't he ever gone to the trouble of getting a decent haircut? Mungin shook his head sadly.

The conversation turned back to the case. He wanted my opinion: "Do you think I'll get something?"

I was pretty sure he would. Perhaps there would be a compromise of the sort Edwards had suggested: affirmation of the basic discrimination finding but reversal of the constructive discharge part of the verdict.

Mungin mused that even if the damages were cut in half, there would be a lot left. Then he caught himself. "That's not the point," he said. He had brought the suit to make a statement, not get rich. He had learned to live on his temp-lawyer salary. He could move to South Carolina and start over there. It didn't matter exactly what his "career" would be. He was moving on to a new stage.

That evening, I found a message from Mungin on my home telephone answering machine. "My goal is to look back on a lot of this and laugh at it," he said. "I survived, right? I took them on and I survived. They didn't crush me."

"No reasonable juror could find . . ."
"Mungin presented no evidence . . ."
"No such evidence exists . . ."
"Mungin offered absolutely nothing that would have permitted a reasonable jury to conclude . . ."

On July 8, 1997, the D.C. Circuit panel, by a 2–1 vote, reversed Mungin's trial victory. He would receive not a penny of the $2.5 million award.

In an 18-page single-spaced majority opinion, Judge Randolph said he couldn't discern even a scintilla of evidence of bias. No *reasonable* juror could have found differently, he said. Therefore, the determination of the eight unreasonable people who sat for the better part of a week in the jury box had to be reversed.

Judge Williams joined Randolph's opinion in full. Chief Judge Edwards dissented from the reversal of the jury's main discrimination finding.

The Randolph opinion was notable for its economy and lack of flourish. It analyzed the facts of the Mungin case without broad statements of law. But it did everything that Katten Muchin asked for. On the issue of his starting $92,000 salary, "Mungin's mistake was comparing himself to homegrown associates, rather than to lateral entries like himself," Randolph wrote. Mungin had shown at trial that white sixth-year associates had received $95,000 to $105,000. But Randolph pointed to testimony from Katten Muchin witnesses that the firm paid lateral hires less than homegrown lawyers. Randolph assumed that this policy had been applied to Mungin.

Might the jury have been skeptical of the witnesses who

testified that there was a consistently applied policy to give lateral hires lower pay? Randolph didn't entertain the possibility.

As to Mungin's 1994 salary of $108,000, the plaintiff "introduced no evidence that he was underpaid relative to his peers," Randolph said. In defense of the jury verdict, Mungin had pointed to an average 1994 firm-wide salary for sixth-year associates of $116,000 (a figure that could be derived from the charts that Hairston introduced at trial). But that wasn't comparing apples to apples, Randolph said. The $116,000 figure included the better-paid Los Angeles and Chicago offices. "The mean salary in Washington, excluding Mungin's, was $108,800," Randolph maintained (although to reach that number, he had to quibble with the way Hairston calculated one Washington associate's pay).

The jury scanned the same salary charts as Randolph. Trial counsel for plaintiff and defendant examined and explained them. But Randolph was certain the jury had interpreted the numbers in a fashion that couldn't be squared with reason.

Randolph dismissed Mungin's complaint about being told that he had fallen through the cracks when it came to being evaluated. "Although it was the firm's formal 'policy' to provide substantive reviews semiannually," Randolph wrote, "Mungin presented no evidence that the firm ever consistently abided by its policy." Whereas the lateral-hiring salary policy was iron-clad, in Randolph's view, the semiannual review policy was a chimera. "No reasonable juror could find that the firm denied Mungin a review on the basis of his race," Randolph said. Mungin's objection that his name wasn't put through the ordinary pipeline for consideration for partnership met a similar fate. "It was well within Sergi's authority to decline to recommend Finance and Reorganization Department associates for partnership," the judge said.

On the question of work assignments being routed to white bankruptcy lawyers in Chicago, Mungin's side had undermined itself by failing to point clearly in its brief to evidence in the record. This embarrassing sloppiness allowed the judge to claim that "Mungin only introduced proof of one assignment rerouted from D.C. to Chicago. . . . This single instance is grossly insufficient to constitute a plausible discrimination claim."

But the record contained reference to more than a lone rerouted assignment. Charlie Thomson said under oath that from 1992 to 1994, he had worked on at least three bankruptcy matters for Patricia Gilmore. When asked for the total, he said, there had been "more than I could put a number on." The jury could not have reasonably relied on this testimony, Randolph apparently concluded.

Even if there had been more than one rerouted assignment, the judge observed, it probably wouldn't have mattered. "Perhaps in recognition of the judicial micromanagement of business practices that would result if we ruled otherwise," he explained, other appeals courts "have held that changes in assignments or work-related duties do not ordinarily constitute adverse employment decisions if unaccompanied by a decrease in salary or work-hour changes."

Finally, Randolph dispatched with the constructive discharge claim. "Circuit law is clear," he wrote, "that a finding of constructive discharge depends on whether the employer deliberately made working conditions intolerable and drove the employee out. . . . Having rejected all of Mungin's disparate treatment claims we are left without any discriminatory acts upon which Mungin could rest his constructive discharge claim."

Judge Edwards wrote a brief, bloodless dissent that proposed essentially the compromise he hinted at during the oral argument:

"I dissent from the majority's reversal of the jury finding of discrimination. Although a close question, there was sufficient evidence for a reasonable jury to have concluded that Katten Muchin intentionally discriminated against Mungin on the basis of race."

He agreed, however, that there was insufficient evidence to support a finding of constructive discharge. Most of Mungin's time at Katten Muchin was spent working for Dombroff's and Gilmore's clients. "Dombroff and Gilmore left Katten Muchin in July 1994 to form their own firm, and there was no record evidence to indicate that there was sufficient work in the D.C. office after their departure to support Mungin's continued employment," Edwards observed. "Mungin had no reasonable expectation of employment in the D.C. office after Dombroff's and Gilmore's departure." Edwards said he would have sent the case back to the trial court so that Robertson could reduce the amount of damages.

Mungin said he wasn't crushed. He had prepared himself for a reversal, he told me when we spoke by telephone the day of the D.C. Circuit ruling.

He had to feel angry, though, I said. He had to feel like something valuable had been snatched away.

"Yeah, something like two point five million," he said, with a brittle laugh.

He had received word from Hairston's secretary that the decision had been issued, but not what the result had been. Mungin walked to the court from his job at the SEC building. When he obtained his copy of the ruling, he quickly found the bottom line—"Reversed"—but couldn't bring himself to read either the majority or dissent.

At least he had gotten Edwards's vote, Mungin pointed out to me. "That says I'm not a total loser." And, in any event, he still had the jury's verdict, if not the money award.

But the jury verdict wouldn't build him a house on Edisto, or help his brother Kenneth buy his building.

"I've survived much worse than this," he answered. "I was prepared for this. I didn't spend the money. I have a job and a place to live. I can still go down to South Carolina, if I want to."

His protests sounded strained. "To be honest, I still see myself as a success. I'm a survivor." He imagined how his South Carolina relatives would react: "So, you lost. So what? Pass the chicken."

On the day of the ruling, we didn't discuss whether his law firm's breakdown played a significant role in the reversal. I feared upsetting him with the question. When I raised the issue later, Mungin was evasive. He interpreted the inquiry as an implied criticism of his having failed even to try to enlist an appellate specialist. While this failure was a mistake, because sometimes judges can be moved by the force of an argument, my view was that the D.C. Circuit panel probably would have reached the same result if Thurgood Marshall in his NAACP prime had made Mungin's case. The majority was unbending in its view that the trial record contained nothing having to do with race. A more deft appellate argument from Mungin's side might have forced the majority to grapple with the larger issue of superseding the jury. But Judge Edwards was fully capable of applying that pressure in the privacy of the judges' conference room; whatever he said there had no evident effect on the final result.

The Alexander firm's downfall nevertheless was troubling because in some people's eyes it would confirm the pernicious stereotype that African-American attorneys lack discipline and competence. Mungin himself had commented to me on Koteles Alexander's shortcomings long before the firm's survival came into doubt. But Alexander's undeniable foibles, Mungin and I had agreed, weren't determined by skin color or black professional culture, if there is such a thing, but by his relative inexperience and all-too-common weaknesses of personality. First-generation white law firms fold all the time, if rarely with quite so much sordid drama. That doesn't absolve Alexander of responsibility for his actions; on the contrary, it places the responsibility on the individual, not his race.

By a few days after the ruling, Mungin's anger had risen closer to the surface. He spoke of the D.C. Circuit panel majority not trusting the jury because it was black. Did the judges think the jurors were ignorant? Did the judges know what discrimination looked like? Or were they merely flexing their muscles, expressing disapproval of a black man who had taken on a white law firm? "Of course I'm angry. But I'm not going to cry about it. That's what they [Katten Muchin] would like: me slinking away, tail between my legs." He referred to discussing the reversal with colleagues at the SEC. "They think it's ridiculous; they don't understand it," he said. But as best I could tell, he didn't seek solace from family, or even take a break from his normal routine to absorb the blow.

Mungin recalled in conversation with me the controversy over "jury nullification," a term used in recent years to refer to the tendency of some black jurors to vote for the acquittal of black criminal defendants, regardless of the evidence, out of concern that too many young black men are being sent to prison. Some blacks have condoned jury nullification as an inevitable result of draconian and allegedly selective law enforcement. Mungin, however, disapproved of systematic flouting of the legal system. It only encouraged further racial division and, ultimately, anarchy. But he believed that the D.C. Circuit panel may have employed an equally deplorable *judicial* form of nullification in his case.

He sent me a copy of an opinion article on the topic he hoped to publish in the *Washington Post*. In the short essay, which the *Post* didn't run, Mungin defined "judicial nullification" as the reaction of white appellate judges to the verdict of a predominantly black jury that has found in favor of a black party. The danger of this happening is greater, he observed, "in cities like Washington, with a majority-black jury pool and an overwhelmingly white federal judiciary." Referring to his own case, Mungin wrote: "Taken at face value, the white judges disagreed not only with me, a black male, but also with the predominantly black jury, and with the chief judge, who was also black, providing a disturbing result in a race discrimination case." (The appellate judges also disagreed with the white trial judge.) "Was this an example of judicial nullification? Maybe yes, maybe no," Mungin continued. "But we can all agree that if strongly suspected, judicial nullification, like jury nullification, can easily undermine public confidence in the legal system."

CHAPTER TWENTY-THREE

Conclusion: Integration's Paradox

The D.C. Circuit was wrong. It should have left the jury's discrimination verdict undisturbed.

The jury could have reasonably discerned race discrimination in Mungin's unhappy encounter with Katten Muchin. That is not to say that there was only one reasonable interpretation of the facts in this lawsuit. As Judge Edwards said, the case presented a close question. A jury that looked more like the two-judge appellate majority, and shared its upper-middle-class experiences and conservative Republican outlook, could have reasonably doubted Mungin's interpretation of events and sided with the law firm. That hypothetical jury wouldn't be likely to materialize in majority-black, heavily liberal Washington. But if it did, and if its behavior showed no sign of prejudice or passion, its verdict in such a case—a case without easy answers—would deserve respect.

The inability of the real-world D.C. Circuit majority to conceive of how Mungin's problems could have had anything to do with his skin color was a reprise of Katten Muchin's insistence that race played absolutely no role in this story. The white judges, like the white law firm partners, didn't make a serious attempt to see events through the eyes of a black person, through Mungin's eyes. Most members of the jury couldn't help but see things that way.

The jury imagined being in the shoes of a talented black attorney who receives a raw deal, whose career is significantly damaged, and whose employers won't give him a straight answer when he asks about his future with the firm. Why was Mungin treated so unfairly? Based on his account, and on their own life experiences, the jurors suspected that race had to have been part of the explanation. Mungin was the only black attorney in a 50-lawyer office. Did the white lawyers receive similarly bad treatment?

Katten Muchin's main defense was that white lawyers did find themselves stymied in the same way. These white lawyers would be produced for the jury's inspection, defense attorney Michele Roberts had promised. But it didn't happen. No white lawyer testified, "Yes, across the board, I was treated like Mungin." In the jury's eyes, the law firm was dissembling. By contrast, Mungin gave the jury no reason to doubt his integrity. The jurors chose sides, based on their intuition and on fragmentary facts such as the salary discrepancies, rerouted assignments, and overlooked performance evaluations.

Finding it easy to pick the "good guy" in this fight, the jurors went a step too far by handing Mungin a victory on his claim that he was effectively fired. Abbey Hairston failed to muster any evidence that after the breakup of the Washington office, there would be a substantial amount of bankruptcy work for Mungin in that office. Katten Muchin may not have been very sincere in its offers to transfer Mungin to New York or Chicago, but the offers were made.

In any event, Mungin didn't really want to remain with the firm that he felt had wronged him so grievously. His real complaint was that he was marginalized and demeaned, not that he was effectively fired. Judge Edwards got it right in his dissent: The constructive discharge finding should have been reversed and the damages reduced accordingly, perhaps by one-third, to reflect the greater importance of the discrimination claim.

In reaching its verdict, the jury made inferences from

sketchy evidence of how Mungin was treated differently. But what was the proof that Mungin was treated differently *because of his race*?

The answer is that there wasn't any direct evidence. There almost never is in such cases. But Hairston could have said more on the subject of how race colored the law firm's view and supervision of Mungin.

Hairston asserted in her closing argument that race "was an issue" when Mungin was hired: Dombroff was happy to land a black with two Harvard degrees. Race was an issue again two years later, she added, when lawyers in Chicago paid lip service to "saving" Mungin.

But Hairston never explained how this tepid affirmative action talk amounted to *hurting* Mungin because of his race. The blacks on the jury may have understood, without needing any explanation, the danger of half-hearted affirmative action. Yet many whites probably would not, and might wonder how affirmative action could be considered injurious in this context.

Affirmative action—if no more ambitious than the desire to add a black face to a white office—can deteriorate into tokenism. It can turn a proud, capable professional into something akin to an ornament. That is one way to conceive of what happened to Mungin. There was talk of partner eligibility, but no thought actually given to integrating him into Katten Muchin. He wasn't part of the Washington insurance operation, and he certainly wasn't made to feel welcome by Sergi and the Chicago bankruptcy lawyers. Dombroff and Gilmore were pleased to have him do their scut work for a while, but when he made reasonable demands about the direction of his career, he received lectures about being grateful for having any position at all. "You have a job, a paycheck, no wife and kids," Pat Gilmore told him. "What's the problem?"

White employers who practice half-hearted affirmative action often feel they are doing black "beneficiaries" a favor merely by hiring them. That certainly became the attitude toward Mungin held by certain Katten Muchin partners. These partners also believed that they gave him special help when he ran into trouble. But their behavior strongly hinted that they didn't consider him as a potential peer. His status as an affirmative action hire made it much more likely he would be viewed as a convenient statistic, a decoration. As a lawyer, he was used until circumstances changed, and then was allowed to drift away.

Not fired, though. Katten Muchin saw itself as saving Mungin. But the rescue entailed giving him enough rope to hang himself, in career terms. The firm strung him along, diminishing the quality of his work and undercutting his professional stature. And when conflict sparked, the white partners displayed the most insidious aspect of phony affirmative action. They reassured each other that, on reflection, Mungin had actually been incompetent all along, that he wasn't willing to work hard. Other white lawyers who watched the case from afar, worrying about their own firms' race difficulties, generally assumed the same thing: Mungin must have been damaged goods. After all, hadn't he received a racial preference? A white lawyer in Mungin's place also might have been exploited. But *it is more likely than not*—the legal standard in civil cases—that Mungin's race played an important part in the particularly callous way he was handled.

Mungin's story warns of the danger of reckless, indifferent affirmative action, of allowing minority employees to wallow and stagnate. That said, it would be patronizing to view Mungin as a passive character, let alone a martyr. He walked into Katten Muchin as an experienced 34-year-old professional, and he stayed even after there were signs that the Washington office was in trouble. He made mistakes. He also chose to sue, knowing there would be a personal price to pay. He could have quietly left Katten Muchin and tried to reconstruct a law career, perhaps with a smaller firm or a corporation. He decided to fight instead. He wanted revenge. Mungin wasn't wholly innocent or heroic, but plaintiffs don't have to possess these qualities to deserve vindication in court.

What should we make, then, of the Mungin story? Does it reflect the hopelessness of trying to bridge the racial divide?

Is it a sign that at century's end, race relations are actually getting worse?

Mungin could easily have been a character in *Rage of a Privileged Class*, Ellis Cose's influential and pessimistic book on why so many middle-class blacks are alienated and angry. Cose acknowledged that few of his subjects were targets of old-fashioned, explicit racism. Rather, they felt barraged by what he called "soul-destroying slights," the sort of small-bore insults Mungin absorbed at Katten Muchin. Black fury over these incidents is amplified when slights in the workplace take place against a backdrop of indignities elsewhere. Mungin looked away from such irritants during his youth, choking back his anger over being called a nigger at Harvard and in the Navy, for example. But by the time he arrived at Katten Muchin, his soul was bruised. He had grown tired of white women clutching their purses in elevators and parking lots.

Yet Mungin doesn't see himself as just a casualty. Even as a temp-lawyer, doing work far below his rightful station, he stresses the distance he has traveled since childhood. Although he missed the height of the civil rights movement, Mungin in a lot of ways was still a pioneer. His parents' generation had little chance to mix with whites. Mungin had the opportunity and paid the costs that came with it. Pushed by his mother, he became a poster child for integration. He proved himself sturdy enough for that daunting task, at least to a point. But integration brings friction, whether on a factory floor or in a law firm conference room. One of the inevitable consequences of integration, sociologist Orlando Patterson has written, is that as blacks and whites "meet more and more, the possibility for conflict is bound to increase." And the acute awareness of race-related signals that allowed Mungin to decipher white society also made him hypersensitive to white disrespect. He could be criticized for being naive in expecting smooth enforcement of the bargain his mother made so much of: get your education, follow the rules, and the system will treat you right. But he felt the expectation earnestly. He expected to succeed in the white world and become a part of it. At Katten Muchin, he failed, and it was devastating.

The Mungin story, in the end, illustrates what Patterson has called "the paradox of integration." Progress in race relations made it possible for Mungin to rise from the ghetto to an enviable level of accomplishment. Only 15 years earlier, his presence in a corporate law firm would have been astounding. In the 1990s, it no longer was. But his success made possible the relationships with whites that led to frustration at Katten Muchin. The bitterness of his lawsuit, sadly, obscures his earlier achievements. Some blacks will see in Mungin's tale all the proof they need that white racism is increasing. Many whites will perceive in Mungin, and others like him in the black middle class, a tendency to embrace victimhood, a lack of gratitude for what they have. Each side's emotion fuels the other's resentment.

Mungin tried to transcend race and ultimately fell short. But even after the appeals court reversal, he couldn't completely abandon his mother's ideal. This became clear to me when listening to him talk about Tiger Woods. Like so many other people, Mungin reveled in the spectacular arrival in 1997 of the young African-Asian-American golf champion. Mungin saw Woods as accomplishing in racial terms what he had attempted on a more modest level. He tore out and mailed to me an insightful piece on Woods by *Washington Post* columnist William Raspberry. In a passage that Mungin highlighted in purple ink, Raspberry asserted that Woods had joined an elect group of African-Americans who transcended race. Colin Powell, Bryant Gumbel, and the late Arthur Ashe were leading members of this club. "It may be that some people simply are that way—that some combination of self-confidence and self-evident success leads them to see themselves not as unblack but as not merely, not primarily, black," Raspberry wrote. "And maybe these same qualities lead whites to see them in the same way."

This is what Mungin sought: to be seen not as unblack but not merely, not primarily, black. The particular paradox of his story is that by suing his employer, Mungin, who in some ways personified progress and integration, ensured that almost everyone would see him primarily in terms of race. This seems a tragedy, because if the establishment cannot find room for a Mungin at the higher altitudes of professional accomplishment, the Colin Powells and Arthur Ashes of American society will remain the very rare exceptions.

Epilogue

1998

Mark Dombroff and Patricia Gilmore are thriving in their insurance-defense practice. As profit margins continue to shrink in this cutthroat specialty, the small Dombroff & Gilmore firm has reduced amenities and eliminated the partnership track, according to *The National Law Journal*. Junior lawyers now joining the firm typically remain on salary, without expectation of promotion. Dombroff has enticed some clients with a "frequent litigant club," in which repeat customers receive discounts.

Katten Muchin & Zavis, after a modest dip in 1995, bounced back in 1996 and 1997, with average per-partner profits nearing $500,000, *The American Lawyer* reports. Katten Muchin has rebuilt its Washington office, this time choosing real estate, rather than insurance, as an anchor practice. The firm remains among the 10 largest in Chicago but no longer is seen as a candidate to become a truly national institution. Management authority continues to shift from co-founder Michael Zavis to Vincent Sergi, who has introduced a more democratic style of leadership.

A 1998 book, *Presumed Equal: What America's Top Women Lawyers Really Think about Their Firms*, states that Katten Muchin received mixed marks on "diversity" issues. "A few" of the 19 women lawyers from Katten Muchin who answered a detailed survey praised the firm's commitment to promoting women and minorities. But others said, in the words of one partner, "The firm has spent a lot of money on diversity training, but it is for the public image." Another partner said that in requiring attendance at seminars on diversity and tolerance, "the firm is motivated more out of . . . fear of legal repercussions [i.e. lawsuits] for a failure to honor people's right to be different than any underlying belief that it is, in fact, the proper approach." Katten Muchin has roughly 400 lawyers, with seven African-American attorneys working in the Chicago office, according to *Chicago Lawyer*. The firm itself refused to tell me how many black attorneys it employs overall.

Elaine Williams, the black Katten Muchin income partner in Chicago, saw her lawsuit diverted from the federal courts to private arbitration, as required by the firm's partnership agreement. The arbitration panel found in May 1996 that the firm retaliated against Williams by eliminating her medical benefits after she filed suit. She was awarded $112,000 in damages. The arbitrators didn't find any underlying discrimination by the law firm, however. She is practicing law in Chicago.

Abbey Hairston's career didn't suffer from the reversal of the Mungin trial verdict. In late 1997, she became a partner with Epstein Becker & Green, a big New York–based firm with a well-known management-defense practice. Hairston says she isn't so much switching sides as returning to the management side; as general counsel to the Palm Beach County school system, she defended against many employee lawsuits. Hairston praises Epstein Becker for being open about its desire to add black partners to its Washington office. Some corporate clients, she notes, request specifically that minority lawyers be included on trial teams. As a result of publicity from the Mungin case, Hairston regularly receives phone calls from distressed black attorneys seeking advice on whether to sue their employers. She tells them she can't help in her current position and refers the callers to other lawyers.

Koteles Alexander, Hairston's former boss and lover, has dropped out of Washington-area law practice. He is thought to be staying with relatives in Virginia, but has been incommunicado for long stretches of time. That has made it more difficult for Hairston to sort out the creditor lawsuits lingering from the bankruptcy of the Alexander Bearden firm.

Michele Roberts, the Katten Muchin defense attorney, "is becoming known as one of the outstanding legal talents in Washington," according to *Washingtonian* magazine. The Mungin trial loss apparently forgotten, Roberts was ranked number 24 on the magazine's 1997 top-50 list of legal "Heavy Hitters" in the capital. (Hairston weighed in at number 49.) In a concession to age, Roberts has given up martial arts, but her law practice is flourishing. She has received other civil assignments from business clients, in addition to her staple of defending accused criminals. She continues to insist to anyone who asks that Katten Muchin didn't discriminate against Mungin.

Lawrence Mungin still plans to move to the Sea Islands and live on family land there. He believes that in South Carolina, he won't have to explain himself: why he went to Harvard but doesn't have a fancy job; why his trial verdict was reversed. Going south feels like circling home, even though he grew up in Queens. He will inherit a modest amount of family land once some probate tangles are straightened out, and hopes one day to buy more from older relatives. Mungin hasn't decided what he will do for a living over the long term. He hasn't ruled out starting a law practice in Charleston. His huge family in the area would offer a ready clientele, although drafting their modest wills, contracts, and real estate documents wouldn't make him a rich man.

The D.C. Circuit reversal and legal difficulties in South Carolina concerning his father's unpaid hospital bills caused him to postpone the move, however. After maintaining a brave front in the days after the ruling, he slipped into what he calls "two months of the worst depression of my life." He received some consolation from his sister and brother, but mostly he just waited out the dark mood. He has moved on now, he says, and insists the whole experience "will make me stronger."

Money remains tight. Mungin still works as a temp-lawyer, recently at a Washington law firm specializing in antitrust cases. Colleagues there teasingly refer to him as "the Energizer" because he puts in so much overtime. He lives alone in the same small suburban apartment and works out every evening. He is writing a family history, tracing the Mungins back to their arrival as slaves in the 17th century.

Afterword

"So, how is Larry Mungin doing now?" That has been the most common question I have heard from readers since the hardcover version of *The Good Black* appeared in 1999. Most ask with a tone of concern and hope. They want to hear a reassuring final chapter to Mungin's troubling tale, an encouraging life lesson to dilute the bitterness.

Mungin has heard the same question. People leave messages on his answering machine, stop him in the street. "Hey, you're the guy in the book. . . ." He understands the desire for a happy ending. But, without exactly complaining, he resists putting on a falsely cheerful face. His days of being the good black are over.

"Nothing much has changed in fundamental ways," he tells me. "After my father's death, I figured I'd move to South Carolina, and I still plan to. That's the goal I'm working toward." He has been doing legal work for his relatives on the Sea Islands and visiting there regularly. He continues research for a family history. But he remains in the Washington, D.C., area, pursuing his solitary, ascetic routine of work and weight lifting. The simple fact is that moving to Edisto seemed a lot more attractive with $2.5 million in hand.

Mungin recently quit contract lawyering to become a legal

headhunter. He helps law firms recruit footloose attorneys from rival firms, in exchange for a fee. I see his new activity as a subtle form of revenge on the business that treated him so poorly; headhunters have accelerated the destabilization of the old order among law firms, making clear that these institutions are in fact engaged in commerce, not some lofty profession. Mungin views headhunting merely as a better job. He has a business card again and more independence. He isn't supervised by law firm associates ten years his junior, and he will have the chance to earn more money.

Working long hours to establish himself in the highly competitive headhunting game, he says he doesn't have much time to worry about the larger lessons his story might teach. He seems impatient when I press him on this question. Both blacks and whites are capable of intolerance and moral corruption, he says. "There are just more white people out there."

Reactions to the book, like the real-time reactions to the case itself, have ranged from curt dismissal—"It *couldn't* have been race"—to impassioned identification. Scores of black lawyers have contacted me to say that aspects of Mungin's story resemble their own. And the response hasn't been limited to lawyers. "You could scratch out Larry Mungin's name and put mine in its place," a veteran black colleague at *The Wall Street Journal* told me, choking back emotion. A black securities-firm executive, one of the dozens of financial-industry employees who have called or written, said that she had settled down calmly to read the book "over a double latté" but within hours was "shedding tears of frustration." Many white readers and reviewers, even if skeptical of Mungin's legal claims, have tended to soften criticism of him with expressions of respect. Or they at least acknowledge that they can't imagine what it is like to be the sole black in an all-white office rife with uncertainty and betrayal. Some black readers and reviewers, however, haven't been as charitable toward Mungin.

A substantial number of blacks—including many of those who have praised the book—have lashed out at Mungin as a person. "At the risk of appearing that I'm blaming the victim, I must say that Mungin was simply too old to be that stupid!" said one African-American participant in an Internet discussion group that debated *The Good Black*. "Because he didn't associate with blacks or seek any relationships with any black lawyer associations or even other black lawyers, he didn't know what a tightrope he was on. . . . Let Mungin serve as a model of what *not* to do." Others were even harsher. The mantra that Mungin's mother repeated about being a human being first, an American second, and a black third has attracted angry scorn from those who believe that race is always the first thing on white minds.

Learning from Mungin's mistakes is, of course, one reasonable use to make of the book (and one that needn't be limited to blacks, for some of his frustrations could befall anyone in corporate America). But the idea that Mungin's punishment fit the alleged crime of abandoning his people strikes me as pernicious.

Members of racial minority groups employ various strategies to deal with the disadvantages of being nonwhite in America. Some rely on solidarity and the comforts of the common cause to give them strength in the face of real or imagined hostility. Others, including Mungin, identify themselves as individuals trying to "get past" race, or make it irrelevant to their professional and personal lives. They steer away from group labels, even when they know at some level that the labels can't be entirely erased. The latter course arguably is both riskier and more naive. The wholehearted assimilationist may sacrifice the security of a minority community that shares aspects of his experience and gain in return only a grudging toleration, or less, from the predominant white community. Beyond his family, who knew little about his professional world, Mungin never cultivated a base of black friends and backers. Yet his efforts to fit in among whites as an inoffensive African American produced little real support from those whites. Being the good black wasn't enough.

Still, castigating him for the choices he made distracts from something more important: that he was forced to make the choices in the first place. The more appropriate target for anger is the lingering bigotry that creates the perceived need for blacks to choose between race-based solidarity and racial neutrality. What's more, we should not casually abandon the ideal of complete integration that Mungin, taught by his mother, sought to achieve. If blacks or members of other minority groups attempt to transcend race in hopes of being judged solely on their character and ability, that aspiration should be respected, even if fully realizing the goal in our race-conscious society remains difficult.

Mungin was not helpless. He selected his employer, pursued material goals in the American tradition, and decided to live his life in a solitary manner. Some of his decisions, in hindsight, did not serve him well. His prickly personality doubtless helped determine his fate. He wasn't a pristine victim and didn't expect to be viewed that way. But the distortions that race imposed on his life and career for the most part weren't of his making. His proud, awkward struggle deserves if not approval, then understanding and compassion.

And what of Katten Muchin & Zavis? What did the law firm think of *The Good Black*? "No comment," a Katten Muchin spokeswoman told me when I called the home office in Chicago. The firm did issue a short statement to other journalists. "We are deeply offended by the false characterizations in Mr. Barrett's book of the firm, its people, and the entrepreneurial environment in which they work," Katten Muchin said. The firm added that, by its calculation, it hires and retains more minority lawyers than the average large law firm.

—Paul M. Barrett
June 1999

INDEX